Spices, Condiments, and Seasonings

Spices, Condiments, and Seasonings

KENNETH T. FARRELL

Daytona Beach, Florida

The AVI Publishing Company, Inc. Westport, Connecticut

Library of Congress Cataloging in Publication Data

Farrell, Kenneth T.
  Spices, condiments, and seasonings.

  Bibliography: p.
  Includes index.
  1. Spices. 2. Condiments. 3. Herbs. I. Title.
TX406.F37 1985   664'.53   85-22808
ISBN 0–87055–464–6

Printed in the United States of America
ABCDE   4321098765

To the memory of Dr. Carl R. Fellers, Professor of Food
Science and Technology; head of the department at the
University of Massachusetts; one of the founding fathers
of the Institute of Food Technology; an inspiring
teacher, a dedicated leader and father; a student's
friend, and the gentleman who guided my early
professional career in food science and technology.

To the memory of Dr. Donald K. Tressler, former
professor of chemistry and chairman of the chemistry
department at Cornell University State Agricultural
Experiment Station, also a co-founder of the Institute of
Food Technology, founder of AVI Publishing Company,
a valued co-worker and friend, and one who inspired
me to compile this manuscript.

Contents

Contents

Preface

Spices, Condiments, and Seasonings has been written for use as a text in food technology and as a general reference book for anyone associated with the food industry who has a desire to know more about these fabled, fragrant, pungent plant substances and how they are utilized in the formulation of condiments and seasonings. Dietitians concerned with low sodium diets will find the spice substitute information and nutritional data on spices useful.

Part One introduces the reader to the significance of spices throughout history in a concise, chronological sequence of events.

Part Two defines spice and describes fifty of the more prominent spices, culinary herbs, and spice blends. The description of each spice includes the following: common name, botannical name, family, historical/legendary backgrounds, indigenous and cultivated sources of supply, physical and sensory characteristics, extractives obtained therefrom with their chemical and sensory attributes, federal specifications, approximate composition and nutritional data, household and commercial uses. Photographs of each spice and sketches of each spice plant are included. Recipes for home cooking with spices and herbs have been omitted purposely as there are many good spice cookbooks available. Suggested spice substitutes for salt in sodium-restricted diets are listed together with the natural antioxidant activity of each spice. The microbiological aspects of spices are covered and the means for sterilizing them described.

Part Three includes a discussion of spice extractives and soluble spice, how they are made, used, and substituted for freshly ground spices. Current federal specifications and proposed specifications for those not listed under federal guidelines are presented. Analytical methods for the determination of residual solvents in spice extractives, volatile oils, piperine; color values for capsicum, cumin and paprika; Scoville heat units for capsicum; storage conditions and labeling requirements are included. The advantages and disadvantages of varous spice forms are outlined.

Condiments and sauces are discussed in Part Four. A new definition for condiments is advanced. Formulas for the three simple condiments—celery, garlic, and onion salts and several compound condiments—prepared mustards, tomato catsup, chili sauce, meat sauces, Worcestershire sauce, and soy sauces—are clearly demonstrated. Over 100 sauces are listed with their predominant flavoring ingredients. A few original formulas for instant sauces are also presented.

In Part Five a new definition for seasonings is proposed. Formulas for seasoning prepared meats, bouillons, instant soups, instant sauces, instant gravies, and miscellaneous products are given. The technology of seasoning is discussed from a practical point of view and means for duplicating a soluble pork sausage seasoning, without the use of sophisticated laboratory equipment are outlined.

A complete bibliography is included after each of the five sections.

Acknowledgments

The author acknowledges with sincere appreciation the invaluable assistance of the following individuals, companies, and publishers for granting permission to quote or use parts of their outstanding contributions to the historical and scientific literature on spices.

Armenino Farms, Inc. of California, William Mennuti, Vice-President, most of the data on freeze-dried chives incorporated in Part Two.

AVI Publishing Co., Inc. of Westport, CT, for permission to use data from H.B. Heath, *Flavor Technology* and J. Merory *Food Flavorings* in Part Two.

Chemical Publishing Co., Inc., New York, for the use of excerpts from J.W. Parry, *Spices,* Volumes 1 and 2, which appear in Part Two.

Fritzsche, Dodge and Olcott Co., Inc., New York, Dr. Robert G. Eiserle, Vice-President, for most of the data on oleoresins and analytical procedures which appear in Part Three.

Houghton Mifflin Co., Boston, for some of the historical data on spices which appeared in *An Encyclopedia of World History* by William L. Langer, Copyright 1940, 1948.

Basic Vegetable Products Co. of Vacaville, California, William J. Hume, President, for analytical and specification data on dehydrated garlic and onions used in Part Two.

The Pepper Marketing Board of Malaysia, C. Mahendra, General Manager, Tanah Putih, Kiching, Sarawak, for reproduction of its brochure on Malaysian pepper which appears in the Appendix.

USDA Agricultural Handbook No. 8-2, Revised Jan. 1977 for the data on the composition of spices in Part Two.

David White Inc., Port Washington, New York, Publishers of *The Spice Cookbook* by Avanelle Day and Lillie Stuckey for the use of a limited number of historical references and household uses for spices.

The Cunningham Spice Company, Mel Darack, President, for the spices used in the photographs of spices in Part Two.

Dr. Vilem Silar of Czechoslovakia and Octopus Books Limited, London W1 for permission to reproduce their engravings of spice and herb plants which appear in *Kitchen Herbs and Spices.*

PART ONE

The History of Spices

A Short Look at the History of Spice

The story of spices and the spice trade is a long and romantic one replete with battles, power struggles, conquests, intrigue—all the elements of a first-rate swash-buckling tale. Spices were a valuable commodity and as a result the spice trade was much fought over.

Undoubtedly, prehistoric man learned to discriminate between edible and inedible plants either by trial and error or by watching the birds and animals try something because it looked or smelled good and discard that which was objectionable.

Herbs and spices were not only used for meat (food) but in medicines for healing the sick. It is believed that the practice of utilizing herbs as medicines began more than 5000 years ago by Fo Hi, a Chinese Emperor. The first Chinese herbal contained over a thousand remedies attributed to herbs. The Egyptian Papyrus, written around 3000 BC, is the oldest known, recorded manuscript dealing with the healing of the sick. Records exist from 400 years later of the Babylonians prescribing herbal medicines based on earlier data found in the Papyrus.

Herbs and spices were also used as entrapments for making love, for the acquisition of wealth, for embalming and burying the dead. King Solomon, the richest and wisest of all kings, acquired much of his wealth from spices.

And when the Queen of Sheba (now called Yemen) came to Jerusalem with a very great train, with camels that bare spices, and very much gold and precious stones: and when she was come to Solomon, she communed with him of all that was in her heart. . . . she gave the king an hundred and twenty talents of gold, and of spices very great store, and precious stones there came no more such abundance of spices as these which the Queen of Sheba gave to King Solomon. I. Kings 10:2 and 10.

Ancient Egyptians preserved the revered bodies of their kings by mummifying them with spices and herbs. Anise, sweet marjoram, and cumin were used at first to be followed by cinnamon, cassia, cloves, and others as they became available from the Far East. This practice of using spices is mentioned in two familiar verses from the New Testament, St. Luke 24:1 and St. John 19:40:

> Now upon the first day of the week, very early in the morning, they came unto the sepulchre, bringing the spices which they had prepared (to annoint him); then took they the body of Jesus and wound it in linen clothes with the spices, as the manner of Jews is to bury.

The first reference to the spice trade we find in the Bible appears in Genesis 37:25–36. Some historians have calculated the year to be 1729 BC.

> And they sat down to eat bread: and they lifted up their eyes and looked, and, behold, a company of Ishmealites came from Gilead with their camels bearing spiceary and balm and myrrh, going to carry it down to Egypt.

The Ishmealites were Arab merchants who dealt in the transport of spices thousands of miles from the east, by camel caravan and ship, from India, Burma, the Malay Peninsula and the Persian Gulf area to the trading centers of Alexandria and Carthage in the west. Their journeys took as long as four or five years.

There are over sixty other references in the Old Testament relating to the high esteem in which spices were held in ancient times. There are numerous historical records written by such renowned historians as Herodotus (484–424 BC), Hippocrates (477–360 BC), the father of modern medicine, Theophrastus (372–287 BC), considered by many to be the father of botany, Pliny the Elder (62–110 AD), the greatest writer of Vespasian's reign, whose zeal for scientific truth and research caused his death in the destruction of Pompeii by the erupting Vesuvius, and Publius Cornelius Tacitus, an important historian of Rome (55–117 AD), which document the trading practices of the Arab spice merchants between the Orient and the western world up to the Christian Era. Each contributes much to the intriguing, if not always true, story of spices. It is not the purpose of this chapter to document the complete fascinating history of spices, but rather to provide sufficient information on the significant contributions to history that events have provided in order to give the reader a fuller appreciation of the value of spices.

Since the sixth century BC the Arabian spice traders controlled the shipment of spices from China, Indonesia, Ceylon, India, the Malay Peninsula, and other eastern spice growing nations to Egypt, Greece, Italy, and the west, whether they were shipped by boat, camel caravan or river raft.

In the seventh century, followers of Mohammed, a camel driver from Mecca, who married the wealthy widow of an Arabian spice trader, spread the new religion of Islam to all of the Red Sea areas, to Syria, Egypt, Babylonia, Persia, India, and westward to Greece, Turkey, Spain, Tripoli, and Morocco. Their mission was not entirely of a religious nature; they were told to bring spices from each of the lands they visited, to provide funds for subsequent crusades and the extension of the Islamic religion. Mohammed was aggressive; the demand for spices continued to increase; opposition to his teachings began to surface but he was quick to quell any further opposition by raising an army to intimidate the Arabs and thereby convert them. The prophet died at the age of 62 but the merchants of Venice were quick to capitalize on the opportunity of filling the demand for the growing spice market. They immediately sent ships across the Mediterranean to Alexandria for the far eastern spices and by the ninth century these Venetian ships were sailing south and north across the great sea as fast as their sails would carry them, with their holds filled with spices of every description.

Spain was invaded in the eighth century by Mohammed followers, bringing with them abundant supplies of saffron. Saffron has been an essential component of Spanish cuisine ever since.

Early in the ninth century a pound of mace was worth three sheep, an ounce of cardamom was worth a poor man's yearly wages, a slave could be purchased for a cupful of peppercorns. The Europeans still had no concept of the source of the spices. Even the Venetian merchants did not know their origin. The Arab merchants would never reveal their sources to anyone. New travellers and spice seekers would be given the most unbelievable stories of monsters in the wilderness, of robbers at every mountain pass, treacherous weather conditions at sea and in the desert; they would be given wrong directions in which to travel; anything to frustrate the newcomer or inquisitive merchant to prevent him from learning the secrets of the lucrative market in spices. This deception was carried on until late in the fifteenth century when Marco Polo's mysteries of the far eastern spice trade were first revealed in a German Translation of his various experiences.

Part of Venice's great wealth came from trading in the spices of

India, Ceylon, the East Indies, and Cathay, obtained in Alexandria and sold to northern and western European buyer/distributors at exhorbitant prices. It is not clear as to the exact time or route traveled by the teen-aged Marco Polo, his father Nicolo, and his uncle Maffeo on their three to four year journey from Venice to China. It is believed to have begun sometime in the year 1271. The journey took them from Venice by ship to Acre, overland to Mosul, a city in Iraq, down along the Tigris River to Baghdad in Iraq, the capital of the Moslem world. From Baghdad it is believed they travelled to Kerman in Iran, to Shibarghan in Afghanistan across the Chinese border to Cashegar, then across the great Gobi Desert in Mongolia to Sou-tcheou and then to Tai-yuen-fou, a short distance from Peking, the domain of the great Kublai Khan. The young Polo made an indelible impression on the khan and he and his relatives were immediately taken into the service of the emperor, for whom they worked diligently for about fifteen years. Marco was a very intelligent man; he took advantage of this unique opportunity to observe the local customs in each country he visited; he kept a detailed diary on everything he witnessed along with his own personal impressions. He recorded distances between countries and cities, the number of kingdoms in each country, the peculiarities of the inhabitants, the means for marketing the merchandise within the cities and the shipment of goods in and out of the ports—where they came from and their destination. He even included in his diary the approximate consumption of spices within the larger cities. He was most meticulous with his data because everything he witnessed was so new to him. He left the employ of the khan in 1292 on a ship awarded to him for his faithful service and travelled westward by way of Java and Sumatra, Ceylon, India, Persia, Armenia, and Turkey, then by camel caravan overland to Egypt and again by ship back to Genoa. Observations were recorded of the sea conditions, the winds, the traffic in ships, and the transport of goods, the loading and unloading of precious cargoes at each port, and the nationalities of all the merchants. Upon his return to Genoa, he was imprisoned during one of the many battles between the Genoans and Venetians. It was while he was in prison in 1298 that a cell mate, Rustigialo of Pisa, a scribe, recorded the conversations he had with the Venetian adventurer. The original treatise, which later became known as *The Travels of Marco Polo* was received with a great deal of skepticism; the minds of the Europeans were not accustomed to such commercialism and such outlandish fabrications. It was not until 1477 when

Fig. 1.1
Marco Polo dictating his memoirs from a prison cell in Genoa, 1298. Accounts of
the spices and riches of the Orient stimulated the great age of exploration.

the treatise was translated into German, with a Venetian version in
1496, followed by a Portugese translation in 1502 and a Spanish one
a year later that the world began to recognize the importance of
Marco's experiences two hundred years earlier. His was the first
complete description of China and its customs, Japan and the Arctic
Ocean, the wonders of Madagascar and Zanzibar, the marvels and
potentials of the Indian Archipelago, and the tropical luxuries of
Sumatra and Java. Concerning Java, he wrote: "The territory is
very rich, yielding pepper, nutmegs, galanga, cubebs, cloves, and all
the richest of spices. Many merchants from Zai-tun and Manji come
and carry on a great and profitable traffic. Its treasure is so immen-
se that it can scarcely be estimated. On account of the long and
difficult navigation, the Great Khan never could acquire dominion
over it." Ships from the west would visit the islands and trade their
western goods for the abundant spices. These spices would be transported to ports on the coast of India where merchants would receive

them, unload their vessels and reship them along with Indian spices, pepper, ginger, cubeb and native nuts, to Aden, on the southwest coast of Arabia. Again, the merchandise would be unloaded and distributed on to smaller craft for navigating the Red Sea Gulf to an unloading site for overland hauling by camel caravan to the Nile River, a thirty day journey, where the spices were again transferred to smaller vessels for the trip down the Nile to Cairo and Alexandria. Duties were imposed at each stop, ransoms were extracted by the rulers of each kingdom and in some instances the ships were subject to piracy off the Malabar coast. Each transaction increased the eventual cost of the spice to the Venetian merchants and the ultimate consumer.

Marco Polo died in 1324 but his extraordinary experiences, lasting nearly twenty years, were so accurately described that his revelations led to an intellectual revolution in Europe of greater magnitude than the discoveries of Columbus and the ultimate fall of Venice as a trading center for spices.

The desire to discover the shortest route to the Indies and thus reduce the price of spice was probably one of the reasons for Columbus' voyages to the west. He persuaded Queen Isabella of Spain in 1492 to finance his proposed western route to the Indies. According to some accounts, he carried with him letters of introduction to the Great Khan. Gradually, European powers became involved in the spice trade, attracted by the possibility of making huge profits. The Portuguese were among the first Europeans to participate. They made several voyages, but the decisive expedition was Vasco da Gama's (1497–98). He discovered a new route to India by sailing around Africa.

Ferdinand Magellan left Spain in 1519 with a fleet of five vessels to visit the Spice Islands by following the western route. Survivors of the expedition eventually managed to reach the Spice Islands, but only one ship returned home to San Lucar three years later. Its holds were literally bursting with spices, enough to pay the cost of the entire expedition.

As it was in the thirteenth century, so it was throughout history. The country that controlled the spice trade, became the richest and most powerful in the world.

The beginning of the sixteenth century witnessed the Dutch initiate its conquest of the Far East spice trade by taking over Malacca, the Malay Peninsula and the northern half of Sumatra. By midcentury, Ceylon's cinnamon trade and the wealthy pepper port of

Fig. 1.2
Sixteenth century European cargo boats transporting spices and other produce.

Malabar came under its domination. By the end of the century, the spice exports of Java and the Celebes were added to its dynasty.

At the turn of the next century, England's trade with the Indies had reached such proportions that it had to form the East Indian Company to handle the spice business. The Dutch, meanwhile, were beginning to feel England's encroachment, and fearing this new competition from its neighbor across the channel, formed its own trading company. For two centuries the competition continued between the two countries for the domination of the lucrative spice trade.

By the eighteenth century, the demand for spices in the fledgling new world began to grow. The ship building industry of New England began building sea-going clipper ships capable of sailing to the East Indies. A small seaport town of Salem, Massachusetts, became the center of spice imports for the colonies. The import duties collected there were of such magnitude that they were able to cover over five percent of the entire Government's expenses. Trade was becoming so great that some of the pepper arriving in Salem had to be reshipped to European ports as it was too much for Americans to consume and its price plummeted to three cents a pound.

Fig. 1.3
Cinnamon quills being readied for shipment. Courtesy of the American Spice Trade
Assoc.

Toward the end of the nineteenth century and the beginning of
the twentieth, Europeans began entering America in droves, seeking their freedom in the new world. Each group of immigrants had
its own culture, ethnic dishes, and eating habits. To satisfy these
demands, they brought with them spices and herbs from the old
country, many of which were unfamiliar to the local inhabitants.
However, as each group was absorbed into the population of the
area, so were their customs. The demand for spices grew as rapidly
as the population, and it was not long before the ancient spice
trade's dominance shifted to the United States. The center of the
spice trade today is focused in the Wall Street area of New York City
with a substantial volume of spices entering west coast ports of San
Francisco and Los Angeles.

Spices are shipped into the United States usually in the whole form. Spice extracts, the oils and oleoresins, are also imported in large quantities. Imported spices are inspected for wholesomeness and cleanliness by the United States Food and Drug Administration inspectors on the docks and temporarily warehoused by the importer until sold to spice companies scattered throughout the country. The spice companies further process the product by cleaning, grinding, extracting, compounding, blending or repacking into smaller containers for retail distribution.

Most of the tropical spices still come from the eastern hemisphere, as they have for centuries, but Central and South America, as well as the West Indies are contributing significant quantities of high quality spices to the world market. The United States now produces great quantities of herbs and spices, adaptable to the temperate cli-

Fig. 1.4
Inspection of black pepper. Courtesy of Joseph Adams Corp.

mate, as we shall see under each of the individual headings for these aromatics. If we include dehydrated onions, shallots, chives, and garlic products as spices, and who, even in government circles, could dispute such an inclusion, at least from a practical point of view, we find that our increasing domestic production now approximates 35% of our spice needs. According to a March 1980 article, "Dehydrated Ingredients" which appeared in *Processed Prepared Foods* magazine, "California alone produces 1.5 to 2.0 million pounds of dried parsley flakes, 250,000 pounds of freeze-dried chives, 25,000,000 pounds of dehydrated garlic and one company alone is said to produce 250 million pounds of dehydrated onion and garlic products. In addition, 750,000 pounds of dried dill, basil and tarragon are produced annually in the United States along with millions of pounds of mustard seed."

Supermarket availability of aromatic spices from all over the world, conveniently and attractively packaged for the daring culinary achievers, at a cost that anyone can afford, have caused us to accept their presence as routinely as we do sugar, flour, tea, or coffee. Let us not forget the exploits of such daring men as Marco Polo, Columbus, Magellan and others who made all of this possible.

Bibliography Part I

Anderson, F. J. 1977. An Illustrated History of the Herbals. Columbia University Press, New York.

Arber, A. 1970. Herbals, Their Origin and Evolution; A Chapter in the History of Botany, 1470–1670, 2nd Ed. Hafner Press, New York.

Budge, Sir E. A. T. A. 1971. The Divine Origin of the Craft of the Herbalist. London Society of Herbalists, 1928. Gale Research Co., Detroit, Michigan.

Burland, C. A. 1970. The Travels of Marco Polo. McGraw Hill Book Co., New York.

Central Food Technological Institute of Research, 1974. Select Bibliography on Spices. Mysore, India.

Hart, H. H. 1967. Marco Polo, Venetian Adventurer 1254–1323. University of Oklahoma Press, Norman, Oklahoma.

Howe, S. 1946. In Quest of Spices. Gale Research Co., Detroit, Michigan.

Knox, T. W. 1885. The Travels of Marco Polo. G. P. Putnam's Sons, New York.

Langer, W. 1972. An Encyclopedia of World History 5th Edition. Houghton Mifflin Co., Boston, Massachusetts.

Liebman, M. W. 1977. From Caravan to Casserole: Herbs and Spices in Legend History and Recipes. E. A. Seeman Publishing Co., Miami, Florida.

Lowenfeld, C., and Back, P. 1980. The Complete Book of Herbs and Spices. David and Charles, North Pomfret, Vermont.

Miller, J. I. 1898. The Spice Trade of the Roman Empire—29 B.C. to 641 A.D. Clarendon Press, Oxford.

Mitchell, J. I. 1942. The Lives and Achievements of the Great Explorers. The New Home Library, New York.

Morrison, S. E. 1942. Admiral of the Ocean Sea—A Life of Christopher Columbus. Little Brown and Co., Boston, Massachusetts.

Mottram, R. H. 1939. Traders' Dream—The Romance of the East India Company. Appleton-Century-Crofts, Norwalk, Connecticut.

Murray, H. 1845. The Travels of Marco Polo. Harper & Row, New York.

Parry, J. W. 1969. Spices, Vol I. The Story of Spices; Spices Described. Chemical Publishing Co., Cleveland, Ohio.

Rawlinson, G. 1859. The History of Herodotus, 4 vols. English translation. D. Appleton & Co., New York.

Tacitus, P. C. 1952. The Annals and the Histories. Encyclopedia Britannica Inc. Chicago, Illinois.

The Holy Bible, Authorized King James Version, Cambridge University Press, Cambridge, England.

Wilson, Lt. Col. Sir A. T. 1930. The Persian Gulf. Clarendon Press, Oxford, England.

Wright, C. D. 1909. The New Century Book of Facts. The King-Richardson Co. Springfield, Massachusetts.

PART TWO

Spices, Culinary Herbs, and Spice Blends

2

What Are Spices and Herbs?

There is a wide discrepancy among experts over the definition of the simple word, herb. What is an herb? Funk and Wagnalls Dictionary defines an herb as "a plant without woody tissue, that withers and dies after flowering." Von Nostrand Chemist's Dictionary defines an herb as "a plant or portion of a plant, used in medicine, in cookery, for the extraction of certain essential oils." Collier's National Encyclopedia considers an herb "to be a plant with little or no woody tissue, no winter buds above ground and consequently one that dies down to the ground at the end of the growing season. Most herbs, however, persist for many years because they have underground buds, borne on such stem structures as bulbs, rootstocks or tubers. Such perennials far out number the biennial herbs which complete their life cycle in two years, or the annuals, which live only a single season. Herbs apparently originated, and are most common, in the north temperate zone, but in the tropics they are largely replaced by woody plants." When Charlemagne was asked to define an herb, he replied: "An herb is a friend of physicians and the praise of cooks." Heath (1981) defines herbs as "soft stemmed plants whose main stem dies down to the root and regrows each year. Culinary herbs include annual and biennial plants as well as the leaves of some bushes or even trees. Herbs may or may not be strongly aromatic in character but those of value in food flavoring have a quite distinctive character." Heath further classifies herbs into the following five groups, according to their sensory attributes (i.e., those having as their prime constituent a specific essential oil).

GROUP I.   Those herbs containing cineole
               Sweet Bay Laurel
               Rosemary
               Spanish Sage

GROUP II.   Those herbs containing thymol and/or carvacol
            Thyme
            Wild Thyme
            Origanum
            Wild Marjoram
            Sweet Savory
            Mexican Sage
GROUP III. Those herbs containing sweet alcohols
            Sweet Basil
            Sweet Marjoram
            Tarragon
GROUP IV.   Those herbs containing thujone
            Dalmatian Sage
            Greek Sage
            English Sage
GROUP V.   Those herbs containing menthol
            Peppermint
            Spearmint
            Garden Mint
            Corn Mint

Another recent author defined an herb simply as "any plant useful to man that grows in a temperate climate."

Some, if not all herbs, have been grown and used since biblical times for one purpose or another. About 400 BC, Hippocrates, the acknowledged father of modern medicine, was the first person to separate medicine from mythology when he classified over 400 herbs into various useful categories in his *Materia Medica*. The classification included such groups as insect repellants, seasoning agents, dyes, fragrances and plants with many uses. Of the 400 plants classified over 2400 years ago, 200 are still officially listed. Of these, however, only 20 to 30 may be considered commercially useful culinary herbs or spices.

The United States Food and Drug Administration does not differentiate between culinary herbs and spices. They group them all together as spices, for which there is much justification. Some of us would even include dehydrated onions, shallots, chives, and garlic as spices. The agency classifies these bulbous flavoring agents as vegetables. It also classifies the spices—saffron, paprika, and turmeric as colors and they must be so labeled, when used specifically for the coloring of foods.

The term spice was derived originally from the Latin "species aromatacea" meaning fruits of the earth. It was subsequently shortened to "species" meaning a commodity of special value or distinction. Classical authors in ancient times classified spices into four different categories, such as 1. Species Aromata—those used for perfumes, like cassia, cardamom, sweet marjoram and cinnamon; 2. Species Thumiamata—those used for incense, such as thyme, cinnamon, cassia, and rosemary; 3. Species Condimenta—spices used for embalming or preservation, like cassia, cumin, cinnamon, anise, cloves, and sweet marjoram; 4. Species Theriaca—those spices used for neutralizing poisons, such as anise, coriander, garlic, and oregano. Obviously, such a classification would be without much foundation today. Most of the herbs and spices used today, for whatever purpose, were known to the ancient Greeks and Romans. Their athletes used the oils for relieving muscle tension; ladies used them to perfume their baths, and the clergy used them in funeral rites for distinguished townspeople.

Funk and Wagnalls defines spice as "an aromatic, pungent vegetable substance as cinnamon, cloves, etc. used to flavor food and beverages. That which gives zest or adds interest. An aromatic odor." Colliers National Encyclopedia simply states that "the flavor and pungency of most spices is due to their volatile oils, for example, oil of cloves, oil of cinnamon, oil of mustard, etcetera, and sometimes to other substances as well, such as the alkaloids piperine in black and white pepper, capsicine in cayenne pepper."

As we see, there are many contradictions, limitations, generalities and even some fallacies in the foregoing definitions.

Perhaps one of the better definitions is that of Parry (1969), who defines spices as "dried plant products which add flavor, relish or piquancy to foods. Most are fragrant, aromatic and pungent. They consist of rhizomes, bark, leaves, fruit, seeds and other parts of plants."

The Food and Drug Administration, in the Code of Federal Regulations on food labeling: spices, flavorings, colorings, and chemical preservatives, defines spices as:

The term "spice" means any aromatic vegetable substance in the whole, broken or ground form, except for those substances which have been traditionally regarded as foods, such as onions, garlic and celery; whose significant function in food is seasoning rather than nutritional; that is true to name; and from which no portion of any volatile oil or other flavoring principle has been removed. Spices include the following:

Allspice	Cloves	Marjoram	Rosemary
Anise	Coriander	Mustard flour	Saffron
Basil	Cumin seed	Nutmeg	Sage
Bay leaves	Dill seed	Oregano	Savory
Caraway seed	Fennel seed	Paprika	Star anise seed
Cardamom	Fenugreek	Parsley	Tarragon
Celery seed	Ginger	Pepper, black	Thyme
Chervil	Horseradish	Pepper, white	Turmeric
Cinnamon	Mace	Pepper, red	

Paprika, turmeric and saffron are also colors which, under 1.10(c) shall be declared as "spice and coloring" unless declared by their common or usual name.

From a technical and practical point of view, this author proposes a combination of Parry's definition with that of the Food and Drug Administration, plus a few added clauses for specificity. It is a reasonable compromise and one that should satisfy the scientific community as well as the government. The definition proposes that dehydrated onions, shallots, chives, and garlic be included in the spice category and that all major culinary herbs that are used commercially in foods, beverages, and seasonings, be classified as spices.

This author proposes that the term "spice" shall mean, or be applied to *any dried, fragrant, aromatic or pungent, edible vegetable or plant substance, in the whole, broken or ground form which contributes flavor; whose primary function in food is seasoning rather than nutrition, and which may contribute relish or piquancy to foods or beverages, that is true to name, and from which, no portion of any volatile oil or other flavoring principle has been purposely removed, or to which no additive or spent spice has been added. Spices may be either the dried arilla, bark, buds, bulbs, flowers, fruit, leaves, rhizomes, roots, seeds, stigmas and styles or the entire plant tops.*

The above definition is offered in the sanguine expectation that the U.S. Food and Drug Administration will reconsider and modify its more limited definition because of the following reasons: 1. dehydrated vegetables like onions, shallots, chives, and garlic, are used extensively in condiments and seasonings primarily for their flavor-enhancing qualities and not for their nutritional contributions. 2. Some fruits, or portions of them, are recognized as spices, such as mace, nutmeg, allspice, capsicum, chilli peppers, and cumin. Why single out the aromatic, pungent vegetables for separate label declaration? 3. A news release of July 1980 by the American Spice Trade Association stated: "All the products typically found on the spice shelf today are properly called spices. This includes herbs and the items historically called spices as well as spicy seeds, blends and dehydrated vegetable seasonings." 4. Colliers National Encyclopedia includes in its definition of herbs "bulbs, rootstocks or tubers." Without knowing the intended use of saffron, paprika, or turmeric, the possibility exists that the wrong interpretation might be made by government inspectors as to whether they are being used as colorants or as spices. Unless either one is being used to conceal inferior merchandise, how it is used is academic. Saffron is so expensive that it is seldom used commercially in food products. If it should be used, the manufacturer would be sure to label it to advise the public that such an expensive ingredient really does exist in his product. Good quality paprika is also quite expensive, but it is not as prohibitive as saffron. The food manufacturer usually will not use any more paprika than is required to give the desired quality to the finished product. Paprika is a mild capsicum, and capsicum need not be declared on the label. Manufacturers may circumvent the regulations by considering paprika as a mild capsicum, which it actually is, and therefore do not declare it on the label. High quality paprika has an unusually pleasant taste and is used for flavoring as well as for color enhancing attributes.

As for turmeric, this spice is seldom used strictly as a spice though it does have a characteristic, peppery, spicy flavor and a bitter, pungent taste. It is usually used for its coloring properties in pickle products, chow-chow, yellow mustard and in most commercial curry powder preparations. The general public expects yellow mustard to be yellow, with or without turmeric; some pickle products as well as curry powder blends are expected to have a yellowish caste. Why legislate, or single out one particular spice for labeling purposes as long as it is a natural, harmless ingredient? The government can discourage flagrant violations of the pure food laws, but the laws should be meaningful, not picky.

With reference to the following format on individual spices, it may be noted that some of the Federal specifications for spices appear to be less definitive or less rigid than many of the other analyses given for the particular spice. The reason given by government authorities is that the products purchased under the specifications are used by many different agencies of local, state and Federal government where optimum quality is not necessarily required. Those individuals responsible for writing spice specifications should remember this.

The term "indigenous" refers to the country where the spices presumably originated or where they grow naturally, whereas the term "cultivated" implies that the spices have been adapted to the climatic and growing conditions of a specified area under more or less controlled cultivation practices. Under such cultivation, the plant may modify somewhat, and if the cultivation should cease, the plant may revert back to its native condition thereby quickly losing many of its desirable, acquired attributes. Some plants that have been economically important for centuries, and are still growing wild rather profusely, have been supplanted by other cultivars better suited to the industrial trade and producing higher yields per acre.

An example of good breeding and cultivation practices can be seen in California-grown onions. These onions have been grown, bred, and cultivated in such a manner, specifically for dehydration purposes, that they are now specially adapted to the soils and climate of that area. These onions contain up to 20% total solids, whereas their ancestors of only 50 years ago had less than 10%.

Finally, in the pages that follow, in which household and commercial uses for spices are given, it should be noted that spices are seldom used singularly as flavoring agents. A spice is usually blended with other complementary spices to give a fuller, more pleasing aroma and flavor to the finished product. It should also be realized, particularly for commercial uses, that a specific spice, like allspice, in flavoring bologna, is not always used in every bologna seasoning; it may be replaced with clove, nutmeg, and pepper, with other combinations of spices, or it may not be used at all. It should also be emphasized, that most spices, and particularly their extractives, are very potent. Only small quantities, measured in grams, are sufficient for one hundred pounds of seasoned meat. This will be described in greater detail under seasonings in Part V. Many of the pictures of spices which follow, particularly those where the leaf portion of the plant is the prime flavoring contributor, may appear to be indistinguishable, particularly in black and white photographs and when ground to a uniform, particle size. Color photographs would not be much better as they would each appear in some shade of green, depending on the freshness of the spice, the method employed in drying the spice and the conditions under which the spice were stored. Thus, the beginning technologist cannot always depend on the physical characteristics of a spice, he must become familiar with the sensory properties of each spice both before and after rehydration. An attempt has been made to give sufficient information on the physical and sensory attributes of each spice so that with some practise a technologist can become proficient in spice identification and usage.

Dried spices appear different than their fresh counterparts; they smell and taste differently because drying alters the chemical composition, particularly if a large percent of the volatile oil is lost or oxidized in dehydration. Accompanying such possible loss is an apparent concentration of the nonvolatile components, resulting in the domination of bitter elements. But as most technologists or companies will not have fresh herbs or spices available to them, we have assumed the use of dried materials.

3

Spices and Culinary Herbs

This chapter is a compendium of 45 spices. For each spice, there will be a short history, source, physical description, federal specifications, composition, and uses. In addition, there will be photographs of the spice itself and the entire plant from which it comes.

Fig. 3.1
Allspice. Fruit bearing portion of allspice tree.

Allspice[1]

Pimenta dioica L. Merril
Family Myrtaceae

Historical/Legendary Background _____

Spanish explorers discovered allspice in the West Indies shortly after Columbus discovered the islands. Though the dried berries were 20 to 30% larger, they resembled black peppercorns in shape and color and the explorers called them pepper. The botannical

[1]Also known as Pimento, Jamaica Pimento, Jamaica Pepper or Clove Pepper.

name Pimenta was given to the spice. Allspice was used by the Aztecs to sweeten and flavor their daily chocolate drink. During the seventeenth century, the pirates used it to smoke and barbecue their meat prior to their rampaging voyages throughout the West Indian waters; they called the meat *boucan,* from the French verb *boucaner* for cured or barbecued, and the pirates became known as buccaneers. Allspice was first exported to Europe in 1601 as a substitute for cardamom.

Source

Whole allspice is indigenous to Central America, Mexico and the West Indies. Most of the world's production comes from Jamaica. Upwards of 700 metric tons are grown and exported annually from this small island. Hondurus, Guatamala, the Leeward Islands and Mexico also produce commercial quantities of allspice, but the quality is inferior to that from Jamaica.

Physical Description and Sensory Characteristics

Whole allspice is the dried, unripened, but mature berries from a 12 m (40 ft) tall, evergreen tree. The hard berries are dark, reddish brown in color, 4–5 mm in diameter with a globular shape. The aroma is very fragrant, similar to clove, and the pungent aromatic flavor suggests a blend of cinnamon, clove, nutmeg and pepper; hence, its name allspice. The oblong, lanceolate, 6 in. long (15 cm) leaves of the allspice tree are equally aromatic and are used in the preparation of essential oil of pimenta leaf. The berries are used both for essential oil and oleoresin production.

Mexican allspice is a littler larger than Jamaican, being five to six mm in diameter but is far inferior in flavor. The name allspice is applied also to many other trees and shrubs like the Carolina Allspice, Japanese Allspice, Wild Allspice, and Spice Bush, but these are seldom used for commercial purposes as spice.

Fig. 3.2
Allspice berries.

Extractives

Jamaica allspice contains up to 4.5% volatile oil, consisting of up to 80% eugenol and nearly 30 other chemical components like eugenol, methyl ether, cineol, phellandrene, caryophyllene, resins, tannin, fixed oils, and gum. Allspice from elsewhere yields only half as much essential oil and is of a poorer quality. Pimenta leaf oil is less spicy, thinner and more woody in aroma than that made exclusively from the berries. The latter is more rounded, warmer, more spicy, fuller bodied, slightly pungent, and peppery, with a fruity, cinnamon-clovelike flavor and astringent aftertaste.

The essential oil is obviously strong: (1.13 kg) (2½ lb) of the essential oil will normally replace 45.45 kg (100 lb) of freshly ground allspice in seasonings.

The oleoresin of allspice is prepared by solvent extraction of Jamaican berries. It is brownish-green in color and contains 40–50 ml of volatile oil per 100 g. For a good quality oleoresin, 2.27 kg (5 lb) is equivalent to 45.45 kg (100 lb) of freshly ground allspice in odor and flavor characteristics.

Federal Specifications _____

The Federal specifications for whole and ground allspice require
that the spice be the dried, nearly ripe fruit of *Pimenta officinalis* L.
The whole berries, globular in form, must be of a dark, reddish-
brown color, with an aromatic, clovelike odor and a strong aromatic
taste. The product shall contain not less than 5% total ash, 0.3% acid
insoluble ash, 10% moisture and not less than 3 ml of volatile oil in
100 g. 95% of the ground spice shall pass through a U.S. Standard
No. 25 sieve.

Approximate Composition of Allspice (100 g, Edible Portion) _____

Water	8.5g	Phosphorus	113 mg
Food energy	263 kcal	Potassium	1044 mg
Protein	6.1g	Sodium	77 mg
Fat	8.7 g	Zinc	1 mg
Total carbohydrate	72.1 g	Ascorbic acid	39.2 mg
Fiber	21.6 g	Thiamin	0.1 mg
Ash	4.7g	Riboflavin	0.1 mg
Calcium	661 mg	Niacin	2.9 mg
Iron	7 mg	Vitamin A	540 IU
Magnesium	135 mg		

Household Uses _____

Whole or ground allspice, usually the latter, is used to flavor
vegetables like beets, carrots, parsnips, sweet potatoes, turnips,
winter squash, and spinach; such appetizers as cranberry juice and
tomato juice; chicken, tomato, turtle, vegetable, and vegetable beef
soups; fruit compote, apple pie, mincemeat, and pumpkin pies, tomato, meat and chili sauces, plum and rice puddings, gingerbread,
cookies, coffee and spice cakes, sweet rolls, fish dishes, pickles, rel-

ishes, preserves, gravies, poultry dressings, hamburgers, meat balls, lamb roast and stew, veal roast and stew, beef roast and stew, meat marinades, pot roasts and curries.

Allspice should be used carefully; it is very potent in flavor; only 0.62 ml (⅛ tsp) of ground allspice is sufficient to flavor 1.89 l (2 qt) of soup, stew, stock or marinade.

Commercial Uses

Ground allspice or soluble allspice, made by dispersing the oil of pimenta leaf or the oleoresin made from allspice berries on an inert, edible base (see Part III), is used as a component of prepared mince-meat, baked pies, curry powder blends, relishes, pickles, mixed pickling spices, tomato catsup, chili sauce, gravy mixes, soups, seasoning mixes for bologna, German bologna, boiled ham, ham glazes, salami, blood sausage, chicken loaf, head cheese, pepperoni, pressed sausage, frankfurters, knockwurst, pork sausage, fish marinades, smoked meats, canned meats, fried chicken, pickled pig's feet, and pickled tongue. The quantity to use depends on the other spice components in the formula, the quality of meat being used and the regional preferences of the customer. In general, 9.5 g (⅓ oz) of ground allspice or 0.25 g of oil of pimenta leaf or 0.5 g of the oleoresin is sufficient, along with other spices, salt, etc. for seasoning 45.45 kg (100 lb) of meat.

Pimenta leaf oil is also used commercially in ice creams, ices, confections, pickles, baked goods, puddings, chewing gums, gelatins, liqueurs, nonalcoholic beverages, perfumery, and medicines. The oleoresin of allspice is also used in baked goods and condiments.

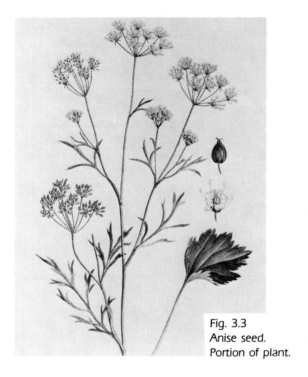

Fig. 3.3
Anise seed.
Portion of plant.

Anise Seed
Pimpinella anisum L.
Family Umbelliferae

Historical/Legendary Background

It has been claimed that anise seed was found in Egypt as early as 1500 BC. Pliny the Elder claimed that if it were tucked under the pillow at night, the inhalation of the aroma would prevent disagreeable dreams. Anise seed was one of the herbs considered to be an aphrodisiac as "it maketh abundence of milk and stirreth up bodily lust." In the sixth century, Pythagorus believed that the herb would prevent belching and stomach disorders, that it was useful for scorpion bites while others taught it would provoke the flow of urine, would sweeten the breath and prevent the shortness of breath in sufferers of that malady. The oil of anise was said to destroy lice while the seed was an excellent bait for mice and other rodents. It was not until the Middle Ages that the Romans began to flavor their foods with anise seed. Anise seed was blended with honey and vinegar and a little hyssop, and then boiled together to make a tonic for use as a gargle to soothe a sore and swollen throat, known as Quincie. During the reign of King Edward I, which began in 1305, anise seed was one of the drugs that was taxed as it crossed over the London Bridge. By the time of Edward IV it was used to perfume royal garments. In 1619, the Virginia Assembly decreed that each household should plant at least six anise seeds in that year and repeat the plantings the following year from the seeds thus produced.

Source

Anise seed is indigenous to Egypt, Greece, Lebanon, and Turkey. It is now cultivated in Argentina, Bulgaria, Chile, China, Cyprus, Egypt, France, Germany, Greece, Japan, Malagasy Republic, Mexico, India, Pakistan, Russia, Syria and, the United States.

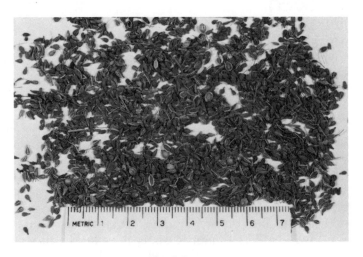

Fig. 3.4
Anise seed.

Physical Description and Sensory Characteristics ___

The anise plant grows to about 45–75 cm (18–30 in.) in height, on an erect, cylindrical stalk, with a deep, penetrating root. The plant has two distinctive, bright green, leaf patterns, long stalked basal leaves, and shorter stalked stem leaves. The small, ovoid seeds are 3 to 5 mm long and 1 to 2 mm wide with pedicles attached; they are grayish-green-brown in color, ribbed with surface down or hairs that tend to give them a rough feeling. The aroma and flavor of freshly ground anise seed is powerfully sweet, aromatic, licoricelike, warm, fruity, camphoraceous, and cooling with little perceptible aftertaste. The feathery leaves are also flavorful, resembling the seeds.

Extractives ___

Anise seed contains from 8 to 11% fixed oil and 1½ to 4% essential oil. The latter consists primarily of 80 to 90% anethole and 10 to 15% chavicol. The essential oil of anise is delicately smooth, highly aromatic and superior to the synthetic oil of anise seed made from methyl chavicol, isolated from fractions of pine oil or to the corresponding oil distilled from China Star Anise. Usually, 1.13 kg (2½ lb) of the essential oil is used to replace 45.45 kg (100 lb) of freshly ground anise seed in seasoning mixes.

The oleoresin of anise seed is a yellowish-green to orange colored liquid of unusually good aroma and flavor. The volatile oil content ranges from 15 to 18 ml per 100 g. Usually, 3.75 kg (8¼ lb) of oleoresin is equivalent to 45.45 kg (100 lb) of freshly ground anise seed in organoleptic quality.

Federal Specifications ___

No specifications exist for this item at the present time as the Federal government does not purchase whole or ground anise seed.

Approximate Composition of Anise Seed (100 g, Edible Portion)

Water	9.5 g	Iron	37 mg
Food energy	337 kcal	Magnesium	170 mg
Protein	17.6 g	Phosphorous	440 mg
Fat	15.9 g	Potassium	1441 mg
Total carbohydrate	50.0 g	Sodium	16 mg
Fiber	14.6 g	Zinc	5 mg
Ash	7.0 g	Vitamins	data not available
Calcium	646 mg		

Household Uses

Portuguese and Neapolitans relish anise and use it in several of their dishes. German and Italian style cookies, coffee cakes, and sweet rolls are flavored with it; Scandanavians use it in their rye bread and the French in their pancakes. It is also used in confections, with fruit and fruit dishes, soups, sauces, pies, cheese and shellfish canapes, cottage and other mild cheeses, cole slaw, wine, relishes, beef stew, French and Italian salad dressings, pickles, salads, poultry dressings, and in pineapple juice, it is particularly refreshing. Anise seed, like most herbs and spices, should be used with discretion; a very little goes a long way. Generally, 0.62 ml (⅛ tsp) of the spice is sufficient to season 454 g (1 lb) of canned green beans, for example. The leaves may be used as a garnish or in salads and for flavoring soups, stews, and other meat dishes.

Commercial Uses

Anise seed, one of its various extracts, or the soluble form of spice is used in seasonings for bologna, frankfurters, knockwurst, dry sausage, mortadella, pepperoni, spiced luncheon loaf, Italian sweet sausage, Italian hot sausage, and other Italian-style prepared meats. Approximately 7 g (¼ oz) is used with other spices for 45.45 kg (100 lb) of meat. The oil of anise seed is also used to flavor liqueurs like Absinthe and Anisette, Rosolio de Torino, and Usquebough, dentifrices, perfumes, confections, and medicines designed for increasing lactation and for use as a carminative.

Fig. 3.5
Anise, China star. Small stem of plant.

Anise, China Star
Illicium verum Hooker f.
Family Magnoliaceae

Source

This substitute for anise seed comes from an evergreen tree which reaches a height of 18 m (60 ft). It is indigenous to the southern and southwestern provinces of China and North Vietnam. It is a member of the magnoliaceae family, totally unrelated to the anise seed.

Physical Description and Sensory Attributes _____

The fruit is star shaped, made up of eight, canoe-shaped, carpels radiating from a central axis. Each carpel contains one seed which is dark brown after drying. The seeds are small, smooth and shiny ovoids. Only a small portion of the crop is exported, as most of it is converted to oil by steam distillation in Vietnam and the province of Kwangsi for export. The aroma and flavor of the extract is very similar to that of the true anise seed, except it is considered by experts to be harsher and lacking in the fine bouquet. The carpels of star anise have a pleasant, aniselike aroma and an agreeable, aromatic, sweet, aniselike taste. The seeds do not have the fullness of aroma and flavor of the carpels.

Fig. 3.6
Anise, China Star

Household and Commercial Uses _____

Because of its similarity to anise seed in aroma and flavor, the ground spice and the essential oil of China star anise may be used as direct replacements on a one to one basis. See Anise Seed for the many uses for this spice.

Fig. 3.7
Sweet basil. Portion of branched stem.

Basil, Sweet
Ocimum basilicum L.
Family Labiatae

Historical/Legendary Background _____

Dioscorides (40–90 AD) warned against eating too much basil "as it dulleth the eyesight, breedeth wind, provoketh urine, drieth up milk and is difficult to digest." He prescribed it for nervous headaches. Pliny considered it an aphrodisiac; it was given to horses and asses during the mating season. Early physicians claimed that the smell of basil was good for the heart and head, that it took away sorrow caused by melancholy and made a man merry and glad.

Italian women wore a sprig of basil to engender sympathy. Basil symbolized love in Italy—a pot of basil in a lady's window was a signal to her lover that she was expecting him. In Romania, a young man was considered to be engaged if he accepted a sprig of basil from a young lady. Basil was considered to be a sacred herb among the Hindus and other religious sects of India. Early Africans claimed that only those who had eaten basil were immune to pain from the bites of scorpions. Boccacio's Decameron describes the story of Isabella watering the pot of basil with her tears because within the pot was also the head of her lost lover. It is an interesting note that the Greeks considered basil a symbol of hatred.

The juice of basil mixed with fine barley meal, oil of roses and vinegar was supposed to be a good remedy for all inflammations of the body. Basil was advertised as early as 1775 in the *Virginia Gazette*.

Source

Sweet basil is indigenous to India, Iran and Africa. It is claimed that over 50 species are native to India. The Mediterranean type has a linalool odor and is cultivated in Belgium and France, as well as Bulgaria, Hungary, India, Italy, Poland, Spain and the United States. The reunion type of exotic basil, with a pronounced camphoraceous odor, is cultivated in the Comoro Islands, the Malagasy Republic and the Seychelles. The Bulgarian type of basil is characterized by a methyl-cinnamate odor and grows in the East Indies, Indonesia and West Africa. Java type basil, typified by a eugenol odor, grows in Java and the South Pacific Islands.

Physical Description and Sensory Characteristics

Sweet basil is a fragrant, low growing, annual herb of the mint family, boasting purple flowers and foliage. Basil is considered one of the most delicate and fragrant herbs. When fresh, it has a fragrant, minty note with a hint of sweet clove. It has a pleasantly sweet, spicy flavor, warm, slightly pungent, anise-like back note and a slightly bitter aftertaste. The plant grows to a height of 0.6 m

Fig. 3.8
Sweet basil, crushed, dried leaves.

(24 in.) bearing oval, bright green leaves which measure up to 4.0 cm (1½ in.) in length. When dried, the leaves turn grayish-brown and are usually ground to one of three sizes: fine medium or coarse. The flowers of the plant are small and bluish-white.

Extractives

The essential oil of sweet basil contains about 40% d-linalool, 25% methyl chavicol and the balance is principally eugenol, cineole and geraniol. Its odor is sweet, aniselike, cooling and floral, whereas its nearest competitor, the exotic basil is harsh, penetrating, camphoraceous, phenolic, warm, hearty, spicy with a lingering aftertaste. The latter consists of about 85% methyl chavicol, less than 1% l-linalool and the balance primarily camphor, borneol, eugenol and cineole.

The oleoresin of basil is prepared primarily from varieties having a high methyl chavicol content. The extract is very dark green, very viscous, almost solid, with a minimum volatile oil content of 40 ml per 100 g. The equivalency of the oleoresin to freshly ground basil in flavor and odor characteristics is 0.34 kg (0.75 lb) to 45.45 kg (100 lb).

Federal Specifications _____

Current specifications for spices do not include requirements for basil, whole or ground.

Approximate Composition of Sweet Basil (100 g, Edible Portion) _____

Water	6.4 g	Phosphorous	490 mg
Food energy	251 kcal	Potassium	3433 mg
Protein	14.4 g	Sodium	34 mg
Fat	4.0 g	Zinc	6 mg
Total carbohydrate	61.0 g	Ascorbic acid	61.2 mg
Fiber	17.8 g	Thiamin	0.1 mg
Ash	14.3 g	Riboflavin	0.3 mg
Calcium	2113 mg	Niacin	6.9 mg
Iron	42 mg	Vitamin A	9375 IU
Magnesium	422 mg		

Household Uses _____

Sweet basil is a natural accompaniment to tomatoes and tomato products but it is also desirable with artichokes, broccoli, green beans, carrots, cabbage, peas, potatoes, spinach, squash, and zucchini. The green leaves may be used in salads and on pizzas in addition to, or in lieu of, oregano. Sweet basil is good for flavoring beef stew, pork, meat loaf, omelets, tomato, turtle and oxtail soups, cheese, noodle and rice dishes, shish kabobs, and seafood dishes. Sweet basil can give canned beef stew a homemade flavor. Basil flavored vinegar is delightful.

The French use sweet basil for flavoring omelets and some soups while the Italians use it with beans and in many of their tomato dishes.

Commercial Uses _____

Sweet basil is used in seasonings for canned spaghetti sauces, meat balls and salad croutons. It is not used extensively in processed meat products. Sweet basil or one of its extracts, is used in combination with other spices, in flavoring confections, baked goods, puddings, condiments, vinegars, ice creams, nonalcoholic beverages, liqueurs, and perfumes.

Fig. 3.9
Bay (laurel) leaf.

Bay (Laurel) Leaves
Laurus nobilis L.
Family Lauraceae

Historical/Legendary Background _____

According to legend bay leaf is supposed to mean "I change but in death." The emperors of Rome were crowned with laurel leaves; the winners of chariot races received laurel wreaths—symbols of victory. Distinguished scholars and young physicians were given laurel berries (*Baca lauri*) and were called bacculaureates. At fashionable dinners during the Middle Ages, the spice would be boiled with orange peel and used in finger bowls.

Dioscorides claimed the leaves were useful in treating diseases of the bladder, wasp and bee stings, and general inflammation. Bay laurel berries crushed with saffron and scammorie, vinegar, and oil of roses, makes an ointment useful in reducing migraine pain when rubbed on the temples and forehead.

Source

The laurel plant is an evergreen cultivated in many parts of the world, particularly in or near countries on the Mediterranean: France, Greece, Morocco, Israel, Portugal, Spain, Turkey, Yugoslavia. It is also cultivated in Guatamala, Mexico, and Russia. The dried leaves of the laurel plant are called bay leaves and are not to be confused with the West Indian bay (*Pimenta racemosa* Miller) or with the California bay (*Umbelleleria California* Nutt) or with the Chinese variety whose leaves have a marked phenolic odor similar to the West Indian bay.

Physical Description and Sensory Attributes

The genuine bay leaf from the Mediterranean area is about 6.5 cm (2½ in.) long by 2.5 cm (⅞ in.) wide, with a grayish-green color. The aroma of the crushed leaf is fragrantly sweet with a delicate lemon clovelike perception. The taste is mildly aromatic at first, intensifying within a few minutes. The provocative aroma and flavor of bay leaf is characteristic of the traditional *bouquet garni* seen on French menus. One leaf is sufficient to flavor six servings of stew or soup. The leaves are used in the manufacture of essential oil and oleoresins.

Extractives

Bay leaves yield 30% volatile oil which consists of 45 to 50% cineole and other components like *l*-linalool, eugenol, methyl eu-

Fig. 3.10
Bay (laurel) leaves.

genol, geraniol, geranyl and eugenyl esters, l-α-terpineol, α-pinene
and β-phellandrene. The oil has a warm, fresh, penetrating, cam-
phorlike odor resembling eucalyptus; it has a distinctly sweet,
soothing, medicinal, spicy, peppery flavor with good persistence and
a somewhat bitter aftertaste.

The oleoresin is a dark green, extremely viscous extract, with a
volatile oil content of 25 to 30 ml per 100 g. Bay leaves are very
potent: 2.27 kg (5.0 lb) of the oleoresin is equivalent to 45.45 kg (100
lb) of freshly ground bay leaves in odor and overall flavor
characteristics.

Federal Specifications

Federal specifications for imported, whole bay leaves specify the
dried leaves of *Laurus nobilis* L. The pale green to green and occasionally brown, hued leaves should be stiff and brittle, with a
smooth and slightly shiny surface; the under part of the leaf should

have a dull finish. When crushed, the leaf has a delicate, aromatic odor and an aromatic, bitter taste. A maximum of 3.0% stems, by weight, excluding petioles is acceptable. 95% by weight, of the ground bay leaves must pass through a U.S. Standard No. 30 sieve.

Bay leaves shall contain not more than 4.5% total ash, 0.5% acid insoluble ash, 7.0% moisture and 3.0% stems, by weight. Bay leaves shall contain not less than 1.0 ml of volatile oil per 100 g.

Approximate Composition of Bay Leaves, 100 g, Edible Portion

Water	5.4 g	Magnesium	120 mg
Food energy	313 kcal	Phosphorous	113 mg
Protein	7.6 g	Potassium	529 mg
Fat	8.4 g	Sodium	23 mg
Total carbohydrate	75.0 g	Zinc	4 mg
Fiber	26.3 g	Niacin	2 mg
Ash	3.6 g	Vitamin A	6185 IU
Calcium	834 mg	Other vitamins	Insignificant
Iron	43 mg		

Household Uses

Bay leaf is traditionally used in French cuisine. Bay leaf lends a unique aroma to calves liver, lamb, meat loaf, fish, poultry, soup stocks and all stews. A leaf or two on the skewer for barbecuing meats adds a delicious flavor. A few grains of the ground spice added to tomato soup or tomato aspic, eggs creole or spaghetti sauce perks up the flavor and aroma of the dish. Liver paté is improved tremendously with a touch of ground bay leaves. The ground spice may also be added to marinades, pot roasts, stews, ragouts, game dishes, fish sauces, home made pickles, cream sauces, onions and squash.

Commercial Uses _____

Bay leaf is essential in mixed pickling spices. The ground spice, or one of its extractives, is used in seasonings for delicatessen-style meats like corned beef, chicken loaf, mortadella, pressed sausage, special luncheon loaf; as well as in barbecue sauces, preserves, pastries, and some condiments. The oil of bay leaf is used to scent soaps, candles, and nonalcoholic beverages. The berries are cold-pressed in the manufacture of laurel oil for use in medicines.

Fig. 3.11
Caper. Flowering stalk of the caper shrub with fruit.

Capers
Capparis spinosa L.
Family Capparidaceae

Historical/Legendary Background _____

Dioscorides reported that "capers stirred the appetite to meat, that they were good for a moist stomach, stayed the watering thereof, cleanseth away the phlegm and opened the stoppings of the liver."

Source _____

The caper plant is usually found growing wild in rocky soil areas, creeping over old stone walls or ruins of buildings, in the warmer and temperate areas of Europe. It is cultivated in France, Italy, and Sicily, in Spain, and other southern parts of Europe and northern Africa. It is grown on a limited scale in Florida and California.

Physical Description and Sensory Characteristics ___

The caper plant is a wild, prickly, low lying shrub, sometimes known as the caper bush. It grows in a creeping manner similar to other common brambles and may reach a height of 1.5 m (5 ft). It bears simple, alternate, ovate 5 cm (2 in.) leaves and four petaled flowers with very colorful stamens that protrude beyond the petals before maturing into many seeded, ovoid or round berries. The plant has woody, cylindrical, branched, gray-white roots with many stems. The flower buds are harvested before opening and are pickled

Fig. 3.12
Capers, pickled.

in salt and vinegar to become capers. The younger, more tender buds are preferable to the more mature open buds which have a sour, astringent flavor.

Household Uses

Because of the salty, acidic taste of capers, they tend to whet one's appetite. They are desirable in salads, with tomatoes, and with meat, fish, and poultry.

Commercial Uses

Capers are used commercially for flavoring relishes, sauces and pickles. Derivatives of the bark are used in pharmaceutical preparations.

Fig. 3.13.
Cayenne pepper. Fruit bearing branch of the plant.

Capsicum (Cayenne or Red Pepper)
Capsicum annum L.
Family Solanaceae

Historical/Legendary Background _____

Cayenne pepper was first discovered in a small town in French Guiana on the northeast coast of South America. It is one of many capsicum varieties, including paprika, red pepper, tabasco, chili, pimiento, crushed red pepper and sweet pepper. In its early days it was referred to as Ginnie Pepper. According to Gerard's *Herbal,* "it hath a malicious quality whereby it is an enemy of the liver and the entrails." When mixed with honey and lentils it was used for removing facial spots. The West Indian natives used it to season their meats in much the same manner as pepper was used by others. In early colonial times in Jamaica, the juice of red pepper was dropped into the eyes of slaves as a punishment for misdemeanors. Capsicum was considered by some to be a stimulant for sluggish digestive systems, effective in curing sore throats, malaria, colic, and alcoholism.

Source

Cayenne pepper is indigenous to French Guiana, but similar, small fruited, pungent and hot varieties are to be found and culti-vated in Brazil, the Congo, India, Japan, Honduras, Guatamala, Mexico, Mombassa, Uganda, Zanzibar, and the United States. Usu-ally the smaller the capsicum, the hotter and more pungent it is to the taste.

Physical Description and Sensory Characteristics

The drooping pods are borne on smooth, erect stems, with oblong leaves. The pods vary in length from a few millimeters up to 15 cm; they are usually conical in shape. The most pungent varieties are cultivated in Uganda. These contain up to 1% capsaicin whereas most commercial varieties of cayenne pepper contain less than 0.5%. These smaller varieties of peppers are referred to as chillies. Their color is dark to bright red with numerous yellow seeds. The aroma at first is pleasant, warm and peppery, becoming acrid and irritat-ing if inhaled for too long a time.

The flavor is intensely pungent, biting hot, sharp and cumulative to the point of being overwhelming, with a long, lingering effect, deep in the throat but not too perceptible in the front of the mouth. The caretenoid pigments capsanthin, cryptoxanthin, carotene, and zeaxanthin contribute most of the color to red pepper. Red pepper (cayenne pepper or capsicum) contains appreciable volatile oil, but its pungency allows it to be used as a partial replacement for black pepper in commercial seasonings where color may not be important. The bite of black pepper is noticed on the lips and front portion of the

Fig. 3.14
Cayenne pepper pods.

tongue and mouth. This distinguishes it from cayenne or red pepper when the two peppers are mixed in a seasoning.

Extractives

As capsicums contain minimal quantities, if any, of essential oils, the soluble spice of red pepper (cayenne) is dependent solely on the oleoresin. The oleoresin of red pepper, as manufactured, contains 6.38% capsaicin, equivalent to one million Scoville units. The product is then diluted and standardized at lower levels of 500,000, 250,000 and 100,000 Scoville units. The color is also standardized and available at 25,000 color units down to a completely bleached product. These products are extremely hazardous to handle and proper precautions must be taken when weighing and handling them—severe burns are possible on the skin or eyes. It is possible to blend capsicums with oleoresin of paprika to vary color and pungency.

The oleoresin is usually made from related varieties of capsicum.

Six lb (2.73 kg) is equivalent to 100 lb (45.45 kg) of freshly ground cayenne pepper in color, odor, flavor, and heat value.

Federal Specifications

Ground cayenne pepper is the dried, ripe fruit of any brownish-red to red species of capsicum. Three out of five taste testers must be able to note a perceptible sensation of pungency when tested by the Scoville method. It must be uniformly ground to allow for a minimum of 95% by weight to pass through a U.S. Standard No. 20 sieve. The product must not contain more than 8.0% total ash, 1.0% acid insoluble ash, 10.0% moisture, 55,000 Scoville heat units, and not less than 30,000 Scoville heat units.

Approximate Composition of Red or Cayenne Pepper, 100 g, Edible Portion

Water	8.1 g	Phosphorous	293 mg
Food energy	318 kcal	Potassium	2014 mg
Protein	12.0 g	Sodium	30 mg
Fat	17.3 g	Zinc	2 mg
Total carbohydrate	56.6 g	Ascorbic acid	76 mg
Fiber	24.9 g	Riboflavin	1 mg
Ash	6.0 g	Niacin	9 mg
Calcium	148 mg	Vitamin A	41,610 IU
Iron	8 mg	Other vitamins	insignificant
Magnesium	152 mg		

Household Uses

Cayenne pepper is used in many Mexican, Italian, and Indian dishes that call for a pungent taste, like hot sauces, chili con carne, soups, spaghetti, pizza, chicken, fish, vegetable dishes, pickles, a few egg dishes, meats and curries. It is used frequently in the southern part of the United States.

Commercial Uses

Cayenne pepper is used in chili powder blends, pickling spices and in many meat seasonings where it replaces part or adds to the black pepper bite, especially in sweet and hot Italian sausage seasonings. It is also used in seasonings for bologna, frankfurters, smoked country sausage, Mexican sausage, mortadella, pepperoni, cappicola, pizza loaf, pork sausage, pork patties, German bologna, chicken loaf, liverwurst, and Braunschweiger liverwurst.

Cayenne or red pepper is also used in condiments, pickles, soups, baked goods, confections, and nonalcoholic beverages. It is used medicinally as a counterirritant and as a carminative.

Fig. 3.15
Caraway. Flowering portion of caraway plant.

Caraway Seed
Carum carvi L.
Family Umbelliferae

Historical/Legendary Background

It has been noted that caraway seeds were among the 5000 year old debris left by primitive lake inhabitants of Switzerland. The word caraway originated in a former province of Asia Minor called Caria. In ancient times the seeds were used to mask the breath, today, some people still use them to mask alcoholic breath. Dioscorides prescribed caraway seeds for stomach problems. Banckes's *Herbal* indicated that the seeds "were good for the frenzy and the biting of venomous beasts." Its other virtues were "to destroy wicked winds and other evils in a man's stomach." Dioscorides recommended it for pale faced girls. Julius Caesar ate a form of bread called Chara which was made from milk and caraway seeds. In Shakespeare's "Henry the Fourth," the character Squire Shallot invites Falstaff "for a pippin of my own graffin and a dish of caraways."

Source

The principal commercial source of caraway seed is the Netherlands. The seed is also cultivated in Bulgaria, Canada, Great Britain, Morocco, India, Newfoundland, Poland, Romania, Russia, Syria and the United States. Over seven million pounds or about 3500 metric tons are imported annually into the United States.

Physical Description and Sensory Characteristics

Caraway seed is the dried fruit of *Carum carvi* L., the white flowered annual or biennial of the parsley family. The plant grows to about 62 cm (24 in.) in height, bearing finely divided leaves and strongly ribbed fruit. The fruit must be harvested early in the morning before the sun reaches it, as the heads shatter and scatter the seeds rather explosively when they are dry. The color of the crescent shaped, hard seeds is grayish tan. The seeds average 6 mm (¼ in.) in length. The aroma from the seeds is very aromatic, sweet, spicy, fresh, characteristic, agreeable, slightly minty, with a penetrating medicinal effect resembling anise. The flavor characteristics are similar except for a bitter aftertaste accompanied by astringency and a slight soapiness.

Fig. 3.16
Caraway seeds

Extractives

The ground seed yields up to 7.5% volatile oil, consisting primarily of 60% *d*-carvone and 15% fixed oil, of which, oleic, linoleic, petroselinic and palmitic are the major fatty acids. Seed grown in the northern latitudes yield higher quantities of volatile oil than those cultivated in the warmer climates.

The oleoresin of caraway seed is a greenish-yellow liquid, with a minimum volatile oil content of 60 ml per 100 g. Five pounds (2.27 kg) of the oleoresin is equivalent to 100 lb (45.45 kg) of freshly ground caraway seed in overall flavor and odor characteristics.

Federal Specifications

Caraway seeds are the clean, sound, dried fruit of *Carum carvi* L. The hard seeds have a characteristic agreeable odor, and an aromatic, pleasant, warm, sharp taste. The ground product is uniform, allowing a miminum of 95% by weight to pass through a U.S. Standard No. 30 sieve.

Caraway seed contains not more than 8.0% total ash, 1.0% acid insoluble ash, 9.0% moisture, and not less than 2 ml of volatile oil per 100 g.

Approximate Composition of Caraway Seed, 100 g, Edible Portion

Water	9.9 g	Magnesium	258 mg
Food energy	333 kcal	Phosphorous	568 mg
Protein	19.8 g	Potassium	1351 mg
Fat	14.6 g	Sodium	17 mg
Total carbohydrate	49.9 g	Zinc	6 mg
Fiber	12.7 g	Niacin	4 mg
Ash	5.9 g	Vitamin A	363 IU
Calcium	689 mg	Other vitamins	insignificant
Iron	16 mg		

Household Uses

The Germans use caraway seed in many of their baked goods—breads, pie crusts, sauces and their famous sauerbraten. Austrians like it in stews, while Italians boil hot chestnuts with caraway seed before roasting them. Generally, it may be said, that caraway lightens the flavor of heavy foods like spareribs, roast goose, pork, mutton, oxtail stew, other hearty meat dishes, and adds an interesting sweetness to apples, pound cake, and cheeses. Caraway seed may be used in canapes, onion bread, cheese spreads, omelets, cole slaw, cooked pastas, rye bread, soups, salad dressings, sauces, rice, boiled seafoods, cabbage and potato soups, sauerkraut, cucumber salad, poultry dressings, stews, home made sausage, and with any of the following vegetables: beets, carrots, cabbage, cucumbers, onions, turnip, green beans, potatoes, cauliflower, and zucchini.

Commercial Uses _____

Caraway seed contributes much of the distinctive flavor of kummel liqueur. Extracts of cumin and anise are other spice flavorings used in this popular liqueur. Caraway or one of its soluble forms is used in perfumes, nonalcoholic beverages, condiments, baked goods, Dutch cheeses, ice cream flavorings, marinades, German style sauerkraut, and pharmaceutical preparations. Caraway is used in blended seasonings for head cheese, chicken loaf, and a few other delicatessen style prepared meats.

Fig. 3.17
Cardamom. Flower bearing stalks of the plant.

Cardamom
Elettaria cardamomum L. Maton
Family Zingiberaceae

Historical/Legendary Background _____

The Greeks and Romans used cardamom over 2000 years ago in food, medicines and perfumes. The Vikings purchased it from traders in Constantinople more than a thousand years ago, and it is still a special ingredient in Danish pastry to this day. The Orientals used it over 2000 years ago to sweeten their breath when appearing before their rulers.

Source _____

Cardamom is indigenous to China, Sumatra, India, and Sri Lanka (Ceylon). It is cultivated in Costa Rica, El Salvador, Guatamala, Laos, Mangalore, Misore and the Malabar regions of India. It thrives in most tropical climates. Cardamom grows wild in the rain forests of Sri Lanka. It is one of the world's costliest spices, second only to saffron.

Physical Description and Sensory Characteristics ___

Cardamom is a bushy perennial herb of the ginger family which bears fruits in pods. Each fruit, about the size of a cranberry, is straw colored, oval to oblong in shape, three sided, and varying in length from 7 mm to 11 mm ($\frac{5}{16}$ to $\frac{9}{16}$ in.). Each fruit holds 15 to 20 reddish brown, three sided seeds, somewhat angular, 3 mm long by 2 mm wide. The seeds are unusually and exotically aromatic, pungent and spicy with a flavor that is sweet and somewhat cam-

Fig. 3.18
Cardamom, ripe fruit capsules with seeds.

phoraceous. The seeds must be shipped in the shell, because once removed, the volatile oil dissipates rapidly, as much as 50% in a week's time and practically all within three months. The fruit is harvested just before it turns yellow. The fruit is cut, sun dried, and the pedicels and calyxes are removed. The seeds are sorted and graded for export. The world's total crop is approximately 3000 metric tons.

Extractives

The essential oil content of cardamom seeds varies in strength and quality depending on the source and growing conditions. The yield varies from two to ten percent. Only very high quality seeds will yield ten percent essential oil. Although the oil is extremely volatile, it will withstand baking temperatures when used as an emulsion. The major organic flavoring substances of cardamom oil are cineole, methyl heptanone, β-terpineol, borneol, neryl acetate, geraniol, nerol, nerolidol, α-pinene, sabinene, myrcene, limonene and p-cymene. Cineole amounts to 25–40% and α-terpinyl acetate about 28–34% of the essential oil's composition. The oil is very penetrating, irritating, cineolic, camphoraceous, warm, sweet, spicy, aromatic, pleasing, citruslike, with a marked musty note after airing. The oil has no residual odor after 24 hours of exposure. The fixed oil content averages 1–2% and consists of glycerides of oleic, stearic, linoleic, palmitic, caprylic, and caproic acids.

The oleoresin prepared from ground cardamom seeds is a dark green liquid with a minimum volatile oil content of 70 ml per 100 g. It is pungent, cool, spicy and has a burning flavor. Approximately 1.81 kg (4 lb) of the oleoresin is equivalent to 45.45 kg (100 lb) of freshly ground cardamom seeds in flavoring value.

Federal Specifications

Cardamom seed, decorticated, is the dried, ripe fruit of *Elletaria cardamomum* L. Maton. The hard, wrinkled, light reddish-brown to dark reddish-brown seed has a pleasant aromatic odor and a characteristic warm, slightly pungent taste. The ground product must be uniformly ground to allow for a minimum of 95% by weight, to pass through a U.S. Standard No. 40 sieve. Whole or ground cardamom must contain not more than 7.0% total ash, 3.0% acid insoluble ash, and 11.0% moisture. It may not contain less than 3 ml of volatile oil per 100 g.

Approximate Composition of Cardamom, 100 g, Edible Portion

Water	8.3 g	Iron	14 mg
Food energy	311 kcal	Magnesium	229 mg
Protein	10.8 g	Phosphorous	178 mg
Fat	6.7 g	Potassium	1119 mg
Total carbohydrate	68.5 g	Sodium	18 mg
Fiber	11.3 g	Zinc	7 mg
Ash	5.8 g	Niacin	1 mg
Calcium	383 mg	Other vitamins	negligible

Household Uses

Scandinavians use cardamom seed liberally in Danish pastries. Indians use it in their after-dinner coffee, snacks, curries, and cakes. The tantalizing flavor of Swedish meatballs is partly due to the judicious use of cardamom. One cardamom seed is sufficient to flavor one cup of coffee. Cardamom is also appealing when it is used to flavor such items as grape jellies, sweet potatoes, pumpkin, winter squash, carrots, apple and pumpkin pies, hard sauces, citrus fruit sauces, fruit soups, cookies, coffee cakes, liver patés, beef, lamb, pork, chicken, and veal dishes. One half teaspoon of ground cardamom added to and mixed with 227 g (8 oz) of sugar may be used the same way as cinnamon sugar on toast for breakfast.

Commercial Uses

Cardamom seed is used in blended seasonings for the following meat items: bologna, German bologna, frankfurters, liver sausage, head cheese, pressed ham, pizza loaf, knockwurst, pork sausage, Braunschweiger liverwurst, as well as in mixed pickling spice blends and curry powder blends.

Cardamom is also used commercially in ice cream flavorings, confections, baked goods, liqueurs, and in some nonalcoholic beverages. The oil of cardamom is used in pickles, chewing gums, alcoholic beverages, pharmaceutical syrups, and in many of the items listed for the spice.

Because of the exotic nature of the aroma of cardamom seed, it is used in the perfume industry to give an unusual scent.

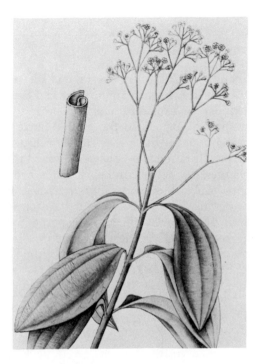

Fig. 3.19
Cassia. Portion of cassia bark tree.

Cassia
Cinnamomum cassia Blume
Family Lauraceae

Historical/Legendary Background _____

Ancient religious believers in China regarded the cassia tree as the Tree of Life, having flourished from the beginning of time in Paradise, an exquisite garden at the headquarters of the Yellow River. Whoever entered Paradise, it was believed, and ate the fruit of this tree, would win immortality and everlasting bliss.

Source _____

Cassia is indigenous to China, Indonesia, and Vietnam. It is cultivated in Laos, Cambodia, French Indochina, and Sumatra. Cassia
bark is known under several different names in the spice trade,
depending on its port of export. In the United States, it is usually
referred to as cinnamon, to which it is closely related.

Chinese cassia, or cinnamon, is cultivated and obtained from the
provinces of Kwangsi, Kweichow, and Kwantung. French Indochina
cassia is the bark of *Cinnamomum loureirii* Nees. In addition to
French Indochina, this type of cassia is cultivated in Laos, Cambodia and Vietnam but exported through the port of Saigon. Batavia
cassia, now referred to as Korintje cinnamon, is the bark of *Cinnamomum burmannii* Blume. It is cultivated in the lowlands along
the west coast of Sumatra and exported through the port of Padang.
The dried unripe fruit of these cassia trees are known as Cassia
buds.

Physical Description and Sensory Characteristics ___

Cassia is the dried bark of evergreen trees of the Cinnamomum
group. The young shoots of the cassia tree are cut and the bark
peeled twice a year. New shoots then grow from the stump. The thin
bark is slightly rough and shows longitudinal ridges. The bark is
rolled into quills to minimize breakage. Broken quills are sold as
chips.

Chinese cassia quills average 25–38 cm (10 to 15 in.) long and 2–6
mm thick. They are light reddish brown with patches of gray. The
aroma is faintly aromatic and the taste is sweet, aromatic, pungent,
and slightly astringent.

Cassia quills from Saigon average 30 cm long (12 in.) and 0.6 mm
thick. The outer surface is light grayish-brown to dark reddish-
brown. The aroma and flavor characteristics are similar to Chinese
cassia.

Batavia cassia quills are smoother and more regular and have
about the same dimensions as those from Saigon. They are light

reddish-brown in color, have an agreeable odor and a sweet, pungent taste.

Cassia buds are usually obtained from Saigon. They have a slight cinnamonlike odor and a sweet, warm, pungent taste like that of the bark, which makes them useful for flavoring pickles and pickled products. They are grayish-brown in color. The cassia bud consists of a brown seed which is quite smooth and only partially visible. The chief constituent of the oil is cinnamic aldehyde but the buds also contain a fixed oil, proteins, cellulose, starch, pentosans and minerals.

Inasmuch as cassia bark and cinnamon bark are used interchangeably throughout the United States and elsewhere, see notes under Cinnamon for the Federal specifications, extractives, approximate composition, and uses for this spice.

Fig. 3.20
Celery. The entire celery plant.

Celery Seed
Apium graveolens L.
Family Umbelliferae

Historical/Legendary Background _____

Celery seed has been known for over 3000 years. It was mentioned in Homer's *Odyssey*, written about the seventh century BC, as an excellent medicament. The earliest recorded use of celery seed as a seasoning for food was not until 1623 in France.

Source _____

Celery seed is native to the Near East, the southern Mediterranean countries of Europe and the northern countries of Africa. It is cultivated in France, Great Britain, Hungary, Japan, India, the Netherlands, and the United States. The world production is in excess of 2000 metric tons, most of which, is diverted to the essential oil and oleoresin industries.

Physical Description and Sensory Characteristics ___

Celery seed is the dried fruit (seed) of a wild variety of celery called smallage which grows to a height of about 45 cm (18 in.). It is not derived from the vegetable of the same name. The minute, globular, light brown seeds, have paler ridges, a characteristic,

Fig. 3.21
Celery seed.

harsh celery aroma and warm, bitter, celery taste. The seeds seldom exceed 1 mm in diameter.

Extractives

The volatile oil content of celery seeds averages three percent. It consists primarily of 60% *d*-limonene, 10–20% selinene, sedanolid and sedanonic anhydride. The aroma is warm, spicy, slightly fatty, fruity, penetrating and very persistent. Its flavor is similar in character but has a burning sensation and very bitter. The fixed oil content is 16%.

The oleoresin of celery seed is of two types: French and Indian. The French type is sweet, herbal and tenacious with only a slight, citrus undertone, whereas the Indian type is more herbal with a slight lemonlike aroma and tenacious herbal undertones. The flavors are slightly different, with the French product being more pleasing. Each is quite bitter. The oleoresin is a green liquid, having a volatile oil content of 9 ml per 100 g. Approximately 2.16 kg (4.75 lb) is equivalent to 45.45 kg (100 lb) of freshly ground celery seed in aroma and flavor.

Federal Specifications

Celery seed shall be the dried fruit of *Apium graveolens* L. The light brown to brown seeds have a characteristic aroma and warm, bitter taste. The spice contains not more than 12.0% total ash, 1.5% acid insoluble ash and 10.0% moisture. It shall contain not less than 2.0 ml of volatile oil per 100 g and not less than 12.0% non-volatile ether extract. At least 95% of the ground spice shall pass through a U.S. Standard No. 55 sieve.

Approximate Composition of Celery Seed, 100 g, Edible Portion _____

Water	6.0 g	Magnesium	440 mg
Food energy	392 kcal	Phosphorous	547 mg
Protein	18.1 g	Potassium	1400 mg
Fat	25.3 g	Sodium	160 mg
Total carbohydrate	41.4 g	Zinc	7 mg
Fiber	11.9 g	Ascorbic acid	17 mg
Ash	9.3 g	Vitamin A	52 IU
Calcium	1767 mg	Other vitamins	Data not available
Iron	45 mg		

Household Uses _____

Although celery seed has little similarity with the edible stalks of the vegetable celery with which we are all familiar the spice may be used for seasoning practically any dish that calls for the flavor of celery. It is particularly useful in dishes where fresh celery stalks would be impractical. Celery seed may be used in tomato and other vegetable juices, bouillons, pea soup, chicken and turkey soups, cole slaw, pickles, scrambled eggs and omelets, chicken and tuna casseroles, salads and salad dressings, seafood chowders, sandwich spreads, and on cucumbers, cabbage, beets, and cole slaw. Celery seed is used in many Balkan, French, English, and American recipes.

Commercial Uses _____

Celery seed or one of its extractives in soluble form is used extensively in many meat seasonings, such as bologna, German bologna, frankfurters, knockwurst, salami, Dutch loaf, chicken loaf, baked liver loaf, Braunschweiger liverwurst, pressed sausage, liverwurst, pork sausage, pizza loaf, jellied corned beef, hot and sweet Italian sausages, and roast beef rubs. It is also used in seasonings for chicken, pea and tomato soups, fish chowder, chicken, mushroom and beef gravies, in celery salt, pickling spice mixtures, and on salad croutons. The literature indicates that the extracts are used in the flavoring of nonalcoholic beverages, confections, chewing gums, ice creams, and baked goods.

Fig. 3.22
Chervil. Plant in blossom.

Chervil
Anthriscus cerefolium L. Hoffm.
Family Umbelliferae

Historical/Legendary Background ⸻

Legend has it that chervil makes one merry, sharpens a dull wit, prods the memory and gives the aged the dash of youth. Chervil is supposed to symbolize sincerity.

Source

Chervil is native to southwestern temperate Russia and western Asia from where it reached the northern shores of the Mediterranean about 300 BC. It is now cultivated in France, Italy, Russia, Spain, and the United States.

Physical Description and Sensory Characteristics

Chervil is a small, fine leafed, annual herb of the carrot family. It grows to a height of about 30 to 62 cm (12 to 24 in.) bearing delicately curly, feathery leaves, with small white flowers. It is widely known in Europe but scarcely recognized in the United States. Its flavor is similar to that of mild parsley with a hint of anise seed, caraway, and/or tarragon. Whatever the analogy, it is aromatic, spicy and somewhat pharmaceutical in taste.

Fig. 3.23
Chervil, crushed leaves.

Household Uses

Chervil, tarragon, parsley, and chives make up the *fines herbes* combination so frequently used in French cuisine. The herb is chopped fine and sprinkled over fish, chicken, egg dishes, soups and salads. It is a handsome garnish for meat platters and adds a delightful touch to canned peas. It goes well with cheese dips, goulash, stuffings, and Liptauer cheese.

Approximate Composition of Chervil, 100 g, Edible Portion

Water	7.2 g	Iron	32 mg
Food energy	237 kcal	Magnesium	130 mg
Protein	23.2 g	Phosphorous	450 mg
Fat	3.9 g	Potassium	4740 mg
Total carbohydrate	49.1 g	Sodium	83 mg
Fiber	11.3 g	Zinc	9 mg
Ash	16.6 g	Vitamin data	not available
Calcium	1346 mg		

Federal Specifications

None

Commercial Uses

Chervil has been used to flavor instant soups, baked goods, condiments, ice creams, and nonalcoholic beverages.

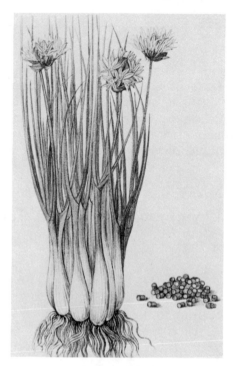

Fig. 3.24
Chives.

Chives
Allium schoenoprasum L.
Family Amaryllidaceae

Historical/Legendary Background _____

   Though chives have been known for at least 5000 years, very little was recorded prior to the nineteenth century when, it was claimed, chives rose to great popularity in Europe, particularly in the French haute cuisine. Chives became so popular that Dutch farmers are supposed to have fed them to their cows to produce a chive flavored milk.

Source ─────────────────────────

Chives have been found growing wild in most all temperate regions of the globe. They are cultivated in France, Germany, Great Britain, the Netherlands, and the United States. G. Armanimo & Sons, Inc. of San Francisco, pioneered the development of freeze-dried chives on their extensive farms south of San Francisco on the peninsula. The freeze-drying method has proved to be the best method for preserving the delicate flavor and aroma of chives, which, heretofore, had to be consumed fresh or not at all.

Physical Description and Sensory Attributes ─────────

Chives are a perennial plant belonging to the onion family. They are aromatic, hardy and grow in clumps of slender, onionlike tubular leaves with lavender flowers in the spring. They are dormant in the winter. They have small, densely clustered, white, elongated

Fig. 3.25
Chives, freeze-dried cuts.

bulbs with intertangling fibrous roots. The tender, young, green, elongated leaves are used for seasoning foods and are, perhaps, the most delicately flavored of the onion family.

After the chives have been cleaned, sorted and trimmed, they are transversely cut into uniform 3 mm (⅛ in.) pieces; the chives are flash frozen and then freeze dried to assure a finished product, which when reconstituted is virtually indistinguishable from the fresh chive. Reconstitution in water is not necessary as the moisture contained in the host product is sufficient to reconstitute the freeze dried chives in less than a minute.

The product is packed in special nitrogen-flushed, poly-lined containers to retain its natural, bright green color and delicate aroma and flavor. Cool, dry storage at 70°F or below is recommended.

Specifications—Commercial

The moisture content must not be more than 3.0% or less than 1%; one pound is equivalent to about 12 lb of fresh chives; the standard plate count shall not exceed 20,000 per g; the coliform count not more than 20 per gram and all pathogens must be completely absent from the product. The product must be bright green, free from scorched or yellow pieces, uniformly sized to 3 mm (⅛ in.) pieces, approximately one million pieces to the pound.

Household Uses

With the introduction of freeze dried chives in the late 1950s, the spice became available to everyone the year round, to add an epicurean flavor and appearance to everday foods such as prepared egg dishes, cottage and cream cheese dishes, cocktail dips, dried soups, rice, noodles, salads and salad dressings, sour cream, almost any cooked vegetable, sauces, and on baked potatoes.

Commercial Uses _____

Freeze dried chives may be used in prepared soup mixes, salad dressings, cocktail dips, sour cream, and cottage cheese products.

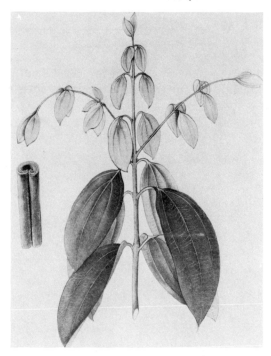

Fig. 3.26
Cinnamon. A young shoot of the cinnamon tree with a bark scroll to the side.

Cinnamon, Ceylon
Cinnamomum zeylanicum Blume
Family Lauraceae

Historical/Legendary Background _____

Cinnamon is perhaps the oldest spice. In Exodus 30:22–26, the Lord spoke to Moses saying

> Take thou also unto thee principle spices, of pure myrrh 500 shekels, and of sweet cinnamon half so much, even 250 shekels, and of sweet calamus 250 shekels. And of cassia five hundred shekels, after the shekel of the sanctuary, and of olive oil an hin: And thou shalt make it

an oil of holy ointment, an ointment compound after the art of the apothecary; it shall be an holy annointing oil.

From the days before Moses, cinnamon has been one of the spices burned in incense at religious ceremonies. At one time it was more valuable than gold. Because of its preservation qualities, along with cloves, it was sought for embalming by the Egyptians over 3000 years ago and was the more profitable commodity later in the Dutch East India spice trade. Dioscorides wrote in his journal that

> cinnamon provoked urine, it cleared the eyes and made the breath sweet. An extract of cinnamon would bring down the menses and would counteract the stings and bites of venomous beasts, reduce the inflammation of the intestines and kidneys, comfort the stomach, break wind, would aid in digestion and when mixed with honey would remove spots from the face that was annointed there-with.

Source

Cinnamon is indigenous to the hot, moist climate of Sri Lanka, which still maintains 70% or more of the world market, southern India, Sumatra, and Borneo. Siagon cinnamon (*C. loureieii* Nees), once considered to be the finest of all cinnamons, is believed to have originated in Cochin, China. It is now cultivated widely in Java, Sumatra, and South America. Cinnamon is also widely cultivated in Africa, Egypt, Malagasy Republic, the Seychelles, and Mexico. Brazil began cultivating cinnamon but subsequently reduced its acreage in favor of additional coffee plantations.

Physical Description and Sensory Attributes

The wild cinnamon tree grows to a height of 9–15 m (30 to 50 feet) at elevations up to 1525 m (5000 ft). It bears very stiff, oblong leaves up to 17 cm (6.5 in.) long, yellowish-white flowers in silky clusters and a dry, pointed, berrylike fruit. Under cultivation, the tree is cut back to no more than 2.4 m (8 ft) to encourage the growth of numer-

Fig. 3.27
Cinnamon bark.

ous shoots. The bark, slit longitudinally, once on either side of a shoot, is removed in two similar sized strips. The outer side of one piece is laid against the inner side of the other; they are closely bound together and allowed to ferment for at least 24 hours. Then the outer bark is removed with a curved knife. The bark pieces are placed within the other and allowed to dry. As the bark dries, it contracts, curls inward and forms a "quill." The bark is graded for color and texture before quilling. The quills may be as long as one meter, one centimeter in diameter and 0.5 mm thick. The cinnamon quills of commerce are known as cinnamon sticks. The broken quills of various grades are called quillings. They vary in length from 5–20 cm (2–8 in.). Quillings lack the full flavor and aroma of the quills. Short shavings and small pieces of bark called featherings have a flavor and aroma similar to quillings. Mature bark that is difficult to peel is chopped into chips. The chips are grayish-brown and are deficient in aroma and taste.

Freshly ground cinnamon bark of good quality contains 0.9 to 2.3% essential oil, depending on the variety. The spice is reddish-brown and has a warm, spicy, aromatic, woody aroma with similar flavor characteristics. It also has a pungent, burning, slightly bitter persistence.

Extractives

The fine oil of cinnamon from Ceylon has a strong, immediate impact in its aroma; it is sweet, pleasantly aromatic, warm, spicy, pungent, slightly woody and clovelike. The oil airs off very slowly and when dried out has a terpeney, piny and slight floral back note. The flavor may be described as spicy, warm, pungent, clovelike, and slightly bitter with an aftertaste that is warm, spicy, and very pleasing.

Cinnamic aldehyde makes up 65 to 75% of the oil's components. The remainder being *l*-linalool, furfural, methyl amyl ketone, nonyl aldehyde, benzaldehyde, hydrocinnamic aldehyde, cumin aldehyde, caryophyllene, *l*-phellandrene, *p*-cymene and *l*-α-pinene.

The terpenes present in the bark, leaves, and roots are also in the oil, but in different proportions. Oil from the leaves and stems is rich in eugenol, the principal flavoring ingredient in oil of cloves. Cinnamon leaf oil is often designated, improperly, as clove oil.

The Korintji bark is particularly well suited for oleoresin production although various types of cinnamon species may be used in its preparation. The end product is a dark brown liquid with a minimum volatile oil content of 65 ml per 100 g. Two pounds (0.91 kg), of oleoresin of cinnamon is equivalent to 100 lb (45.45 kg) of freshly ground cinnamon in flavor and odor characteristics.

Federal Specifications

Federal specifications divide cinnamon into three types: 1. Batavia cassia shall be the dried bark of cultivated varieties of *Cinnamomum burmanni* Nees Blume. It shall have not more than 5.0% total ash, 2.0% acid insoluble ash, 11% moisture, and not less than 1.25 ml of volatile oil per 100 g. 2. Saigon cassia shall be the dried bark of cultivated varieties of *Cinnamonum loureirii* Nees. It shall have not more than 6.0% total ash, 2.0% acid insoluble ash, 10.0% moisture, and not less than 3.0 ml of volatile oil per 100 g. 3. Korintji cassia shall meet the requirements of Batavia cassia except that the minimum volatile oil content per 100 g shall be 1.5 ml. Each type must be uniformly ground to allow for a minimum of 95%

to pass through a U.S. Standard No. 60 sieve. The color must be uniformly reddish-brown.

The specifications also refer to stick cinnamon which must be cut to specified length from Batavia cassia not exceeding 15 mm in diameter.

The specifications also allow for a fortified ground cinnamon which shall be made from a natural cassia or cinnamon base with the addition of an encapsulated essential oil of cinnamon or cassia or a combination thereof. The minimum volatile oil content of the fortified ground cinnamon or cassia shall be 2.0 ml per 100 g.

Approximate Composition of Cinnamon, 100 g, Edible Portion

Water	9.5 g	Magnesium	56 mg
Food energy	355 kcal	Phosphorous	61 mg
Protein	3.9 g	Potassium	500 mg
Fat	3.2 g	Sodium	26 mg
Total carbohydrate	79.9 g	Zinc	2 mg
Fiber	24.4 g	Ascorbic acid	28 mg
Ash	3.6 g	Niacin	1 mg
Calcium	1228 mg	Vitamin A	260 IU
Iron	38 mg	Other vitamins	negligible

Household Uses

The Pennsylvania Dutch sprinkle cinnamon sugar on ripe tomatoes; other Americans sprinkle it on toast for breakfast. The Greeks use a stick of cinnamon in their beef stews; Indians use it in their curries and Mexicans use it in their chocolate. Cinnamon may be used in tomato and cranberry juice cocktails, raisin, chocolate, lemon, orange and other fruit sauces, on meats, especially lamb, pork, tongue, lamb and beef stews, sausage, corned beef, chicken, and any meat cooked with fruit. Cinnamon enhances the flavor of carrots, squash, eggplant, tomatoes, beets, sweet potatoes, and onions. A touch of cinnamon goes well with chocolate, hot apple cider, espresso, and Irish coffee. It is frequently used to flavor cakes and pastries.

Commercial Uses

Ground cinnamon bark, cinnamon oil and/or the oleoresin of cinnamon is used commercially in the manufacture of perfumes, confections, ice creams, beverages, chewing gums, cakes, cookies, pies and other baked goods, pickles, relishes, spiced goods, preserves, apple butter, mincemeat, sauces, icings, curries, condiments, soup bases, and in seasonings for bologna, blood sausage, mortadella, pressed sausage, boiled ham, spiced luncheon loaf, Braunschweiger liverwurst, and many others.

Extracts of cinnamon are also used in the pharmaceutical trade as a carminative, an antidiarrhetic, and as a flavor enhancer in syrups.

Fig. 3.28
Clove. Branch of the tree with unopened buds.

Cloves
Eugenia caryophyllata Thunb.
Family Myrtaceae

Historical/Legendary Background _____

   Centuries before Christ, courtiers in the presence of their emperors sucked cloves to perfume their breath. This custom began in the early days of the Han dynasty in China and was carried on for centuries. Portugese women in the East Indies used to distill a liquor from the green cloves for its effectiveness in consoling the heart and for its fragrant aroma. Early physicians prescribed cloves as an aid to digestion believing that clove strengthened the stomach, liver, and heart. In the early seventeenth century, the Dutch directed the removal of all clove trees from all islands except Amboina and Ternate in order to create a shorter supply and raise the price.

Source

The clove tree is indigenous to the five small islands of Ternate, Tidore, Mutir, Machian, and Bachian, which are adjacent to the west coast of Gilolo island. These six islands make up the Moluccas Islands. The Banda group of islands to the south of the Moluccas, constitute the Spice Islands sought by the early spice explorers of the fifteenth century. They are situated near the equator in eastern Indonesia.

Cloves are now cultivated in many parts of the tropics, particularly Zanzibar, Pembra (now called Tanzania), Malagasy Republic off the east coast of Africa (formerly Madagascar), Malaysia, Amboina (in the Banda group of islands), India, and Sri Lanka. In the western hemisphere cloves are grown in Jamaica and French Guiana. It is claimed that over five million trees are under cultivation on the east coast of Africa and the Malagasy Republic, making this area the world's largest supplier of cloves to the world. About 80% of the world's supply is exported from Tanzania and the balance from the Malagasy Republic, Sri Lanka, India, Indonesia, Amboina, and the Molucca Islands.

The United States imports nearly three million pounds of clove and clove stems annually, or about 6.0% of the available spice.

Physical Description and Sensory Attributes

The term clove is derived from the French and Spanish words meaning nail, which explains why cloves have often been referred to as "round headed nails."

Fig. 3.29
Cloves.

Cloves are dried, unopened flower buds, of an evergreen tree, borne in clusters of 10 to 15. The buds are picked when they begin to turn red at the base. Their color darkens to reddish-brown after drying in the sun. The buds are picked by hand before flowering and are separated from the short stems prior to drying. The evergreen trees grow to a height of nearly 15 m (50 ft) at full maturity and yield up to 34 kg (75 lb) of dried cloves each year. The flower stalks are the clove stems of commerce.

Clove is considered to be the most fragrant of all aromatic spices. Gustatory experts have described it "to be exquisitely scented, exhaling a perfume both rare and delicious." The aroma of ground cloves has been characterized as being spicy, peppery, sweet, fruity, phenolic, woody, and musty. The flavor has been similarly characterized as warm, spicy, fruity, astringent, slightly bitter with a warm numbing effect.

Extractives

The essential oil of clove is primarily extracted from clove buds, but some is also obtained from the stems and leaves. The aroma and flavor of the oil, expressed exclusively from the clove buds, are far superior with a richer bouquet than that prepared from the stems and leaves as the following analysis would indicate:

Clove buds: average yield of essential oil, 17%, (93% eugenol)

Clove stems: average yield of essential oil, 6% (83% eugenol)

Clove leaves: average yield of essential oil, 2% (80% eugenol)

In addition to the eugenol, the oil contains caryophyllin, tannin, gum and resin. Although the oil from the stems and leaves is inferior, it is of tremendous commercial value and has a wide market.

Eugenol, 2 methoxy-4-allyl phenol gives the pleasant odor to cloves and contributes to the sharp, burning flavor. It is used for making vanillin synthetically. Eugenol is also found in cinnamon leaf, allspice and West Indian Bay.

The oleoresin of cloves, prepared from clove buds, is standardized to contain 70 ml of essential oil in 100 g. It is brownish-green in color and is viscous. 2.72 kg (6 lb) of oleoresin is equivalent to 45.45 kg (100 lb) of freshly ground cloves in flavor and aroma attributes. Similarly, 1.7 g is equivalent to 1 oz of spice.

A water dispersible extract of cloves, called Aquaresin [R], is also prepared from clove buds but is standardized to contain 20–30 ml of essential oil in 100 g. It is also dispersible in oil. It is reported that 4.1 kg (9 lb) is equivalent to 45.45 kg (100 lb) of freshly ground cloves. Aquaresin is a registered trademark of Kalsec Inc. of Kalamazoo, Michigan. In addition to the natural extractives of cloves, it contains mono-, di-, and triglycerides, lecithin, and lactic acid derived from natural sources.

Federal Specifications

The specifications require that the whole or ground cloves shall be the dried, unopened flower buds of *Caryophyllus aromaticus* L. The dried bulbs resemble a round headed nail, are dark reddish-brown in color, have a strong, aromatic odor and a hot pungent taste. The product contains not more than 5%, by weight, of clove stems, and not less than 15 ml of volatile oil per 100 g. The product must contain no more than 6.0% total ash, 0.5% acid insoluble ash, and 8.0% moisture. Ninety five percent of the ground product shall pass through a U.S. Standard No. 30 sieve.

Approximate Composition of Cloves, 100 g, Edible Portion

Water	6.9 g	Magnesium	264 mg
Food energy	323 kcal	Phosphorous	105 mg
Protein	6.0 g	Potassium	1102 mg
Fat	20.1 g	Sodium	243 mg
Total carbohydrate	61.2 g	Zinc	1 mg
Fiber	9.6 g	Ascorbic acid	81 mg
Ash	5.9 g	Niacin	1 mg
Calcium	646 mg	Vitamin A	530 IU
Iron	9 mg	Other vitamins	insignificant

Household Uses

Whole cloves, or the ground form of the spice, may be used with fruit or many sweet dishes, sweet vegetables, and vegetable juices, as well as with some meats. Some typical uses are the following: baked apple dishes, pastry spice, cakes, cookies, fruit soups, pickles, preserves, puddings, spicy sweet syrups, meats like baked ham, sausage, hamburger, pork shoulder roast, pot roasts, mincemeat, sauerbraten, and stews, sweet rolls, and on the following vegetables: beets, carrots, pumpkin, sweet potatoes, and winter squash.

Commercial Uses

Either whole or ground clove, or one of the extractives of clove has been used in baked goods, confections, tomato catsup, chili sauce, other condiments, preserves, chewing gums, ice cream mixes, beverages (both alcoholic and nonalcoholic), gelatin desserts, pudding mixes, poultry dressings, mouthwashes, germicides, perfumes, canned spiced fruits and prepared seasoned meats such as: bologna,

German bologna, boiled ham, head cheese, mortadella, spiced luncheon loaf, and pressed sausage. Except for pickling spice compound, whole spice is seldom used commercially. When clove is used in a seasoning compound, it is usually at a very low level because of its intense flavor. Less than 0.6 g (0.02 oz) of ground cloves or its equivalent in oil of cloves or the oleoresin is usually sufficient for 45.45 kg (100 lb) of meat in addition to the other spices usually used.

Oil of cloves has some antiseptic qualities and is recommended by some dentists as a dental analgesic. It is also used in toothpastes and by pharmacies as a flavoring aid.

Fig. 3.30
Coriander. Blossoming branch of the coriander plant.

Coriander
Coriandrum sativum L.
Family Umbelliferae

Historical/Legendary Background _____

According to early Sanskrit writings, coriander was known as far back as 5000 BC. Later records show it was placed in Egyptian tombs during the 21st Dynasty, between 1091 and 961 BC, or about 300 years after the ten commandments were presumably given to Moses on Mt. Sinai. Thebes' Medieval Papyrus, dated around 1550 BC. mentions the use of coriander seeds at burials. The eleventh chapter of Numbers, in the Old Testament, when the Israelites journeyed through the wilderness from Sinai to Paran refers to coriander in this way: "and the manna was as coriander seed, and the color thereof as the color of dellium." (Manna has been identified as a food miraculously supplied to the Israelites.) Coriander was ordered to be eaten during Passover as a remembrance of the Hebrews flight from Egypt. The Chinese have cultivated coriander since the fourth century and believed that those who ate the seeds during a spiritual trance would achieve immortality.

The Herbalist states that "the seeds are good to do away with the fevers that come from the third day and when drunken with honey will slay worms." Some considered coriander an aphrodisiac and fed it to animals during the mating season. In the Middle Ages the seeds were used to flavor wine, preserves, soups, and meat. An advertisement appeared in the *Boston Evening Post* in 1771 offering the seeds for sale.

Source

Coriander is a strong, odiferous, hardy annual plant of the parsley family, indigenous to the Near East and Mediterranean region of north Africa and southern Europe. It is now cultivated in Bulgaria, China, France, Great Britain, India, Italy, Morocco, Mexico, the Netherlands, Romania, Russia, Spain, Yugoslavia, Turkey, Argentina, and the United States.

Physical Description and Sensory Characteristics

The 60 cm (2 ft) tall plant produces a slender, erect, hollow stem with small, light-pink flowers in a compound umbell. The globular coriander fruit (improperly called seed), is brownish-yellow in color and about 4 mm in diameter with straight and curving indistinct ridges. The flavor resembles a mixture of caraway, cumin, sage, and lemon peel. Its odor may best be described as similar to bologna or

Fig. 3.31
Coriander seed.

frankfurters, since it is a principal flavoring ingredient for these items. The flavor could also be described as being warm, spicy, aromatic, sweet, fruity, slightly balsamic, roselike with a pleasant fruity aftertaste.

Extractives

As the oil of coriander makes up only about one percent of the seed, by weight, it is produced primarily overseas for obvious economic reasons. The oil consists of 60 to 70% d-linalool, d-α-pinene, β-pinene, β- and α-terpinene, geraniol, borneol, decyaldehyde, and acetic acids. The fixed oil represents about 20% of the total weight. Its fatty acids consists of oleic, petroselinic, palmitic, and linoleic. The essential oil from the smaller fruits is not only superior in flavor but much more plentiful.

The oleoresin is a brownish-yellow liquid with a minimum volatile oil content of 40 ml per 100 g. Approximately 1.36 kg (3 lb) of the oleoresin is equivalent to 45.45 kg (100 lb) of freshly ground coriander seed in odor and flavor characteristics.

Federal Specifications _____

Whole and ground coriander is the dried fruit of *Coriandrum sativum* L. The globular, yellowish-brown seeds shall have a slight, fragrant odor and a pleasant taste. It contains no more than 7.0% total ash, 1.0% acid insoluble ash, and 9.0% moisture. It contains no less than a trace of volatile oil. The ground spice must be uniformly ground to allow at least 95% to pass through a U.S. Standard No. 30 sieve.

Approximate Composition of Coriander Seed, 100 g, Edible Portion _____

Water	8.9 g	Iron	16 mg
Food energy	298 kcal	Magnesium	330 mg
Protein	12.4 g	Phosphorous	409 mg
Fat	17.8 g	Potassium	1267 mg
Total carbohydrate	55.0 g	Sodium	35 mg
Fiber	29.1 g	Zinc	5 mg
Ash	6.0 g	Riboflavin	2 mg
Calcium	709 mg	Other vitamins	insignificant

Household Uses _____

Ground coriander may be used to flavor confections, pastries, chili dishes, cream, cottage and other mild cheese dishes, fresh mushrooms, apple desserts, gingerbread, biscuits, cookies, cakes, pea soup, stews, and the vegetables corn and green beans. The young leaves may be used to flavor soups or used in salads. Coriander seed is used in many Spanish, Indian, Mexican, South American, Mediterranean, and North African dishes.

Commercial Uses _____

Coriander in one of its forms has been used commercially in baked goods, condiments, confections, ice cream mixes, chewing gums, alcoholic and nonalcoholic beverages, and meat seasonings. As mentioned earlier, coriander is used to flavor bologna and frankfurters. It is also used in seasonings for liver sausage, pork luncheon meat, and Polish sausage. The latter requires 141.75 g (5 oz) of freshly ground coriander or its equivalent in extractives of coriander to flavor 45.45 kg (100 lb) of meat whereas only 28.4 g (1 oz) is needed to flavor 45.45 kg (100 lb) of meat for bologna or frankfurters.

Fig. 3.32
Cumin. Umbels and stem of the cumin plant.

Cumin Seed
Cuminum cyminum L.
Family Umbelliferae

Historical/Legendary Background _____

As early as 5000 BC, Egyptians preserved the bodies of their kings by mummifying them with cumin, anise and marjoram. Later cinnamon and cassia were used. Marcus Aurelius of Rome was nicknamed Cumin because of his cupidity. Among ancient Greeks, cumin was the symbol of greed; Roman misers were said to have eaten it. At German medieval weddings, the bride and groom carried the spice along with some dill and salt in their pockets during the ceremony to ensure faithfulness to each other. In the New Testament, the twenty-third verse of the twenty-third chapter of Matthew, cumin is one of the three tithes mentioned: "Woe unto you, scribe and Pharisees, hypocrites! for ye pay tithes of mint and anise and cumin and have omitted the weightier matters of the law, judgement, mercy and faith." Ancient physicians claimed cumin made the face pallid in appearance.

Source

Cumin is the dried ripe fruit of an annual plant indigenous to Egypt. It is now cultivated in Argentina, Cyprus, Denmark, India, Iran, Lebanon, Malta, Mexico, Morocco, Russia, Sicily, Syria, and Turkey.

Physical Description and Sensory Characteristics

The small, slender herb grows to a height of about 60 cm (24 in.). It has finely dissected leaves, white or rose colored flowers and grayish bristly fruits about 6 mm long, tapering toward both ends, much like an oat seed. It is laterally compressed. The seed is yellowish-brown with a short stem. The aroma is strong and distinctive, resembling musty caraway, but according to some experts, more like "dirty socks" or bugs. The taste is warm, spicy, aromatic and pharmaceutical.

Extractives

Cumin seeds yield up to 4.5% volatile oil, of which 40 to 65% is cuminaldehyde. The odor is best described as strongly penetrating, irritating, fatty, overpowering, currylike, heavy, spicy, warm, and

Fig. 3.33
Cumin seeds.

persistent, even after drying out. The flavor is warm, heavy, spicy, and currylike, dominated by cuminaldehyde, not unlike that of caraway, but its heaviness lacks the pleasing freshness of caraway. The fixed oil content approximates 10%.

The oleoresin of cumin is brownish to yellowish-green in color; it contains 60 ml of volatile oil in 100 g. Five pounds (2.27 kg) of the oleoresin is equivalent to 100 lb (45.45 kg) of freshly ground cumin in aroma and flavor characteristics.

Federal Specifications

Whole or ground cumin shall be the dried seed of *Cuminum cyminum* L. The yellowish-brown seeds shall have a strong, distinctive, aromatic odor and a warm taste. It shall contain not more than 5.0% by weight of harmless extraneous matter; it shall have not more than 9.5% total ash, 2.0% acid insoluble ash and 9.0% moisture. It shall contain not less than 2.2 ml of volatile oil per 100 grams. 95% of the ground product shall pass through a U.S. Standard No. 30 sieve.

Approximate Composition of Cumin, 100 g, Edible Portion

Water	8.1 g	Phosphorous	499 mg
Food energy	375 kcal	Potassium	1788 mg
Protein	17.8 g	Sodium	168 mg
Fat	22.3 g	Zinc	5 mg
Total carbohydrate	44.2 g	Ascorbic acid	8 mg
Fiber	10.5 g	Thiamin	1 mg
Ash	7.6 g	Niacin	5 mg
Calcium	931 mg	Vitamin A	1270 IU
Iron	66 mg	Other vitamins	insignificant
Magnesium	366 mg		

Household Uses

Cumin is an essential ingredient and is the predominent flavor in most Egyptian, Indian and Turkish curries. It is used in many Mexican dishes along the Rio Grande where it was first introduced by Spanish explorers. It provides an exotic flavor when used sparingly with meat, poultry, and vegetable dishes. The flavor from 1.23 ml (¼ tsp) of ground cumin is sufficient for six servings of chicken stew, for example. It is good with mild, starchy foods like rice, potatoes, and bread. The Dutch and Swiss use it to flavor cheese; Germans use it to flavor breads and sauerkraut. The spice complements cheddar cheese canapes, salad dressings, and deviled eggs.

Commercial Uses

The oil of cumin is used in perfumery; it is one of the essential constituents of kummel liqueur and some German baked goods. Medicinally, it may be used as a stimulant, an antispasmodic, or a carminative. Its major use in the seasoning business is in the blending of curry powder blends. It is also used in seasonings for soups, stews, sausages, cheeses, pickles, meats, pungent mango pickles, and green mango chutney.

Fig. 3.34
Dillweed. Portion of flowering plant.

Dillseed—Dillweed
Anethum graveolens L.
Family Umbelliferae

Historical/Legendary Background

The word dill comes from the Norwegian word "dilla" meaning to soothe. It was cultivated by the ancient Babylonians and Assyrians for its magical and medicinal powers. Dioscorides described the medicinal value of the dill plant: "The decoction of the tops of dried dill and likewise of the feed being drunken, ingendreth milke in the breasts of nurses, allayeth the gripings and wind, provoketh urine increase and destroyeth the hiccups." The British Pharmacopoeia suggests adding it to water as a mild stomach medicine for children. Dill seeds were referred to as Meeting House Seeds because when they were brought to church generations ago, the congregation would nibble on them during prolonged sermons.

Source

The whole plant with immature seeds is called dillweed. The dried ripe fruits of the plant are dill seeds. Dill, a fennel-like annual is indigenous to France, Spain, and Russia. It is now cultivated in Canada, Denmark, Germany, Great Britain, Hungary, India, the Netherlands, Mexico, Pakistan, Romania, and the United States.

Physical Description and Sensory Characteristics

The plant grows to a height of about 1 m (3 ft), has deeply divided, green leaves and a large, lacy, compound umbelliferous crown of flowers and fruits. The seeds are flattened ovals, brown in color, with a lighter colored edge, measuring approximately ½ cm (¼ in.) in length. The aroma is warm, aromatic, reminiscent of caraway but sharper and less pleasant. Indian dill is derived from a closely related plant, native to northern India and is cultivated in Japan and southeast Asia. Due to different cultural practices in India, there is a wide variation in the aroma of this spice.

Fig. 3.35
Dillseed.

Extractives _____

The seeds yield up to 4.0% volatile oil consisting of 60% carvone, dihydrocarvone, *d*-limonene, α-phellandrene, α-pinene, and dipentene. The typical odor and flavor of the dillweed oil is chiefly due to α-phellandrene; the higher the content of this constituent the more nearly it resembles the freshly cut herb. Dillweed oils with 20% or less of carvone are preferred as having the finer and more appetizing herby flavor so appreciated in dill pickles. Dillweed oil is less abundant than that from the seeds, but it is strongly aromatic, though milder, with a different chemical composition. The *d*-carvone content is less than 40%, usually 34–36%, and the α-phellandrene content is higher than the oil from the seed.

The odor of dillseed oil has been described as sweet, fruity, fresh, carawaylike, medicinal, aromatic, and herbaceous. On the other hand, the oil distilled from the dillweed has been described as fresh, green, herbaceous, aromatic, warm, spicy, medicinal reminiscent of caraway, with a minty backnote and the flavor as being pleasantly aromatic, fresh, green, herbaceous, slightly burning with a fresh, herbaceous aftertaste.

The fruits of the Indian dill yield 1.2–3.5% of essential oil characterized by containing up to 40% dillapiole and a lower percentage of carvone.

Oleoresins are produced from dillseed primarily, fortified with dillweed oil to more closely resemble the flavor character of the whole herb. The color is light amber to green with a minimum volatile oil content of 70 ml per 100 g. Five pounds (2.27 kg) of the oleoresin is equivalent in flavor content to 45.45 kg (100 lb) of freshly ground spice.

Federal Specifications _____

Dillweed shall be the dried leaves of *Anethum graveolens* L. The bright green leaves have a pleasant, aromatic odor and possess a warm taste. It shall contain no more than 10% total ash, 2.0% acid insoluble ash and 8.0% moisture. There must be no less than 0.5 ml of volatile oil per 100 g. One hundred percent of the ground material shall pass through a U.S. Standard No. 30 sieve and 50% shall pass through a U.S. Standard No. 80 sieve with not more than 50% retained on the No. 50 sieve. There are no specifications for dill seed at this time.

Approximate Composition of Dillseed and Dillweed, 100 g, Edible Portion

	Dillseed	Dillweed
Water	7.7	7.3 g
Food energy	305	253 kcal
Protein	16.0	20.0 g
Fat	14.5	4.4 g
Total carbohydrate	55.2	55.8 g
Fiber	21.1	11.9 g
Ash	6.6	12.6 g
Calcium	1516	1784 mg
Iron	16	49 mg
Magnesium	256	451 mg
Phosphorous	277	543 mg
Potassium	1186	3308 mg
Sodium	20	208 mg
Zinc	5	3 mg
Niacin	3	3 mg
Other vitamins	insignificant	insignificant

Household Uses

The maximum flavor of dill is developed by cooking for about 10 min or by allowing at least 30 min to pass before using a marinade or dressing prepared with dill. Dillseed is excellent in pickles, sauerkraut, pickled green beans, cucumbers, sour cream based sauces, mayonaise, salad dressings, cheese spreads, any egg or cheese dish, potato salad, and garden salads. It goes well with fish, fish sauces, shellfish, tomato and vegetable juices, green apple pie, fruit soup, cauliflower, carrots, cabbage, turnip, and zucchini. It lends an interesting flavor to lamb chops, stews, and steaks. Six servings of potato salad can be seasoned with 2.46 ml (½ tsp) of ground or whole dillseed.

Dillweed is excellent in green salads, vegetable and seafood sauces, cucumber salad, egg salad, cottage and cream cheeses, poached salmon, and marinades for beef or fish. Some Europeans use chopped dillweed as a garnish for sandwiches. Twice as much of the fresh dillweed is required to equal the same flavor potential as that of the dried herb.

Commercial Uses

The essential oil of dill is used in baked goods, pickle products, ice creams, confections, gelatin desserts, chewing gums, condiments, beverages, both alcoholic and nonalcoholic, colognes, and in a few meat seasonings such as for liverwurst, summer sausage, pork sausage, bologna, and frankfurter.

Fig. 3.36
Fennel. Stem and umbels of fennel plant.

Fennel Seed
Foeniculum vulgare Miller
Family Umbelliferae

Historical/Legendary Background

Ancient scholars considered the leaves of the fennel plant to have aphrodisiac qualities and to be a fortifier, a rejuvenator and an aid to growing slim. It was said to sharpen the eyesight, stop hiccups, cure wheezing and improve a pallid face following a sickness. Others claimed that fennel seed assuaged stomach pains and comforted kidney pains. If it were taken with wine it would break the dropsy and all manner of swelling and it would fill the woman's breasts with milk. It was further claimed that the seed, herb and root were very good for the lungs, liver, and kidneys for it would open up any obstructions or stoppings of the same and comfort the inward parts.

Fennel is even described by Longfellow in his poem "The Goblet of Life."

Source

The fennel plant is native to southern Europe and Asia Minor. It is widely cultivated in Bulgaria, Denmark, Egypt, France, Germany, Great Britain, India, Italy, Japan, Morocco, the Netherlands, Romania, Russia, Syria, the United States, and Argentina.

Physical Description and Sensory Characteristics

The fennel plant is a pleasantly scented perennial herb about 0.6 to 1.2 m (2 to 4 ft) tall with erect stalks bearing finely divided green leaves, composed of numerous linear or awl shaped segments. The

Fig. 3.37
Fennel seeds.

grayish compound umbels bear clusters of small yellow flowers. The fruit or seeds are greenish-yellow-brown, varying in size up to 1 cm (⅜ in.) long, are laterally compressed, slightly curved, oval in shape with five ridges and a large single resin canal under each furrow. The aroma of fennel resembles anise or licorice but with a slight camphoraceous note. The flavor is similarly licoricelike, sweet with a slightly bitter aftertaste. Each part of the fennel plant is edible—the seeds, leaves, stalks and bulb.

Extractives

The dried fennel seeds yield up to 6% volatile oil rich in anethole, as in anise seed. The volatile oil contains 50 to 60% anethole, 15 to 20% fenchine, and minor quantities of α-pinene, camphene, d-α-phellandrene, dipentene, methyl chavicol and p-hydroxy phenyl acetone. The fixed oil content approximates 10%; it contains petroselenic, oleic, linoleic and palmitic acids.

The odor of the essential oil has been characterized as being aromatic, pleasantly fresh, warm, spicy, aniselike, slightly camphoraceous, changing to a heavier camphoraceous note when dried out, leaving an anetholic back note. The flavor has also been described as being warm, spicy, aniselike, aromatic, green, herbaceous, initially bitter, then sweet, with a fresh, slightly bitter, aftertaste.

The oleoresin is a brownish-green liquid with a minimum volatile oil content of 50 ml per 100 g. It is prepared from related species of fennel and not necessarily confined to just *Foeniculum vulgare,* Miller. Six and a half pounds (2.95 kg) of oleoresin of fennel is equivalent to (100 lb) 45.45 kg of freshly ground fennel seed in flavor and aroma characteristics.

Federal Specifications

Fennel is the clean, dried, ripe fruit of *Foeniculum vulgare* Mill. The green or yellow, tan-colored seeds have a pleasant aromatic odor and possess a sweet, aniselike taste. The seed must contain no more than 10.0% total ash, 1.0% acid insoluble ash and 8.0%

moisture. It must contain no less than 1.0 ml of volatile oil per 100 g. The ground product shall be uniformly ground to allow for a minimum of 95% by weight to pass through a U.S. Standard No. 25 sieve.

Approximate Composition of Fennel Seed, 100 g, Edible Portion

Water	8.8 g	Magnesium	385 mg
Food energy	345 kcal	Phosphorous	487 mg
Protein	15.8 g	Potassium	1694 mg
Fat	14.9 g	Sodium	88 mg
Total carbohydrate	52.3 g	Zinc	4 mg
Fiber	15.7 g	Niacin	6 mg
Ash	8.2 g	Vitamin A	135 IU
Calcium	1196 mg	Other vitamins	Insignificant
Iron	19 mg		

Household Uses

Fennel seed is used in English style soups, German breads, Polish borscht, Italian sausages and breads, and almost universally in meat balls, spaghetti, and tomato dishes. It also complements fish and seafood sauces and dishes, sweet pickles, sauerkraut, salads, chicken casseroles, roast pork, duck and chicken, apple and other fruit pie fillings, confections, and the following vegetables: cabbage, celery, cucumbers, onions, and potatoes. The Spanish use it abundantly in their baking and cooking.

Commercial Uses

Fennel seed or one of its extractives is used commercially to scent soaps and perfumes, to flavor carminative type medicines, nonalcoholic beverages, baked goods, condiments, ice creams, liqueurs like Anisette, and in seasonings for prepared meats, such as pepperoni, hot Italian sausage, and sweet Italian sausage.

Fig. 3.38
Fenugreek. Stem and umbels of the fenugreek plant.

Fenugreek Seed
Trigonella foenum-graecum L.
Family Leguminosae

Historical/Legendary Background _____

Fenugreek was grown for its medicinal value and for spring for-
age in India, western Asia and in the Nile Valley since remote
antiquity. It has been cultivated in Egypt since 1000 BC.

Source _____

Fenugreek is cultivated in Algeria, Argentina, Cyprus, Egypt, France, Germany, Greece, India, Italy, Lebanon, Morocco, Portugal, Spain, Yugoslavia and the United States.

Physical Description and Sensory Characteristics ___

Fenugreek is a small, slender, annual herb of the pea family. It grows to a height of about 76 cm (30 in.) bearing trifoliate, light green leaves, yellowish-white flowers, with leguminous-like fruit, containing small, deeply furrowed seed. The seeds constitute the spice. The color of the seed is light tan and has a flat shape about 5 mm long and 3 mm wide. Ground fenugreek seed has a very strong, maple sweetness, spicy and yet somewhat meatlike but bitter flavor. The aroma is that of burned sugar.

Fig. 3.39
Fenugreek seeds.

Extractives _____

The volatile oil content of the seed is very low, usually less than 0.02% but it is extremely odorous. The fixed oil content is 7.0% and has a very bitter taste, resulting from the presence of two alkaloids—trigonelline and choline. When ground fenugreek is extracted with alcohol, it yields an aromatic essence, which when compounded with other aromatic chemical extracts, may be used in the manufacture of an imitation maple flavored syrup. If the alcoholic extract is further processed to remove the solvent, the resulting oleoresin has a hydrolyzed vegetable protein flavor, reminiscent of meat.

Federal Specifications _____

Fenugreek shall be the clean, dried, ripe fruit of *Trigonella foenum-graecum* L. The hard, brownish-yellow colored seeds shall have a strong, pleasant, burned sugar odor and possess a farinaceous, slightly bitter taste. Fenugreek must contain not more than 5.0% total ash, 1.0% acid insoluble ash, and 8.5% moisture. Ninety-five percent of the ground product shall pass through a U.S. Standard No. 25 sieve.

Approximate Composition of Fenugreek Seed, 100 g, Edible Portion _____

Water	8.8 g	Magnesium	191 mg
Food energy	323 kcal	Phosphorous	296 mg
Protein	23.0 g	Potassium	770 mg
Fat	6.4 g	Sodium	67 mg
Total carbohydrate	58.4 g	Zinc	3 mg
Fiber	10.1 g	Ascorbic acid	3 mg
Ash	3.4 g	Riboflavin	2 mg
Calcium	176 mg	Other vitamins	insignificant
Iron	34 g		

Household Uses _____

Ground fenugreek seed may be used in curry powder blend, mango chutney, in stews and hearty soups. It is sometimes used in pickling brines for green beans and cauliflower and added to mayonaise for use with salads. It blends particularly well with the milder flavored spices.

Commercial Uses _____

Fenugreek seed or extracts prepared therefrom, have been used in syrups, pickles, baked goods, condiments, chewing gums, icings and a limited number of prepared meat seasonings. It is also used in the preparation of imitation maple and rum flavors and as an emollient and flavoring agent in pharmacy.

Fig. 3.40
Garlic. Garlic bulb and bulblet.

Garlic, Dehydrated
Allium sativum L.
Family Amaryllidaceae

Historical/Legendary Background _____

Garlic has been known for centuries before the Christian Era. In the long journey of the Ishmaelites to the Promised Land from Egypt, they developed a taste for garlic as we learn from the Book of Numbers, eleventh chapter, fifth verse: "We remember the fish we did eat in Egypt freely; the cucumbers and the melons and the leeks and the onions and the garlick." Subsequent generations of Jews had great praise for garlic. The Talmud recommended it highly because it killed intestinal parasites, multiplied the sperm, nourished and warmed the body and made the face radiant. Egyptians were known to use garlic when making a solemn vow. Medieval physicians recommended it as a disinfectant for numerous maladies. Ancient Romans believed it possessed magical powers and Mediterranean sailors carried cloves of garlic with them at sea believing it would prevent shipwrecks. The Roman poet, Horace, considered garlic odor as the "essence of vulgarity." Like Horace, the Greeks detested garlic but English parents would place garlic cloves in the stockings of their children who had whooping cough to prevent further infection.

Source

It is believed that garlic originated in the desert of Kirghiz in western Asia. It grows wild in Egypt, southern France, Italy and Sicily. It is cultivated almost universally in temperate and semi-tropical countries throughout the world. The better strains of garlic, certainly for dehydration purposes, are grown in the western United States, where extensive breeding programs have been in existence for several decades in California. High solids content, disease resistant strains, mechanical harvesting, maximum flavor and whiteness of color have been the major objectives in bulb selection.

Physical Description and Sensory Characteristics

Garlic is a small, hardy, perennial, bulbous plant of the amaryllidaceae family, closely allied to the common onion. There are white, pink and yellow varieties; each with a difference in flavor. For dehydration purposes, the white variety is used almost exclusively. The strong odored, pungent tasting bulb is composed of several bulblets, sometimes, though wrongly, referred to as cloves; the bulblets are enclosed within a tough, outer, whitish skin. Garlic is almost odorless until it becomes bruised or cut, at which time, the enzymes react very quickly to produce allicin (C_3H_5-S-S-C_3H_5) and this breaks down to allyl disulfide, the characteristic odor of garlic. If the enzyme is destroyed in processing the development of the characteristic odor of garlic would be prevented. The flavors of garlic and onion are complementary. The former is harsh and persistent while the latter is mild and sweet. Dehydrated garlic

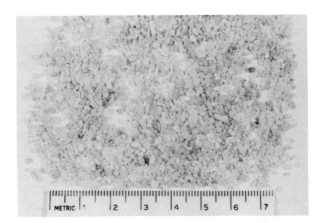

Fig. 3.41
Garlic, dehydrated, minced.

powder, or one of its many commercial forms, like diced, minced, or granulated, has a very strong, persistent aroma and taste. Garlic powder is extremely hygro-scopic and should be kept in tightly sealed containers. To prevent it from picking up moisture, and to keep it free flowing, less than 2% calcium stearate is sometimes added to the product.

One pound of dehydrated garlic is equivalent to 5 lb of fresh garlic. Dehydrated garlic is available commercially and in retail outlets in six different forms: powdered, minced, coarse, granulated, chopped, and diced. The moisture content of each should not exceed 6.75%. The difference between the types is primarily that of particle size. The hot water insolubles should not exceed 12.5% and the maximum optical index should not be in excess of 150.

Sieve Size Requirements for Dehydrated Garlic Products

Powdered Garlic
Not less than 98% shall pass through a U.S. Standard No. 45 sieve.
Not less than 75% shall be retained on a U.S. Standard No. 80 sieve.
Not less than 50% shall be retained on a U.S. Standard No. 100 sieve.

Granulated Garlic
Not less than 2.0% shall be retained on a U.S. Standard No. 35 sieve.
Not more than 5.0% shall pass through a U.S. Standard No. 100 sieve.
Not more than 1.0% shall pass through a U.S. Standard No. 140 sieve.

Coarse Garlic
Not more than 10% shall be retained on a U.S. Standard No. 35 sieve.
Not more than 10% shall pass through a U.S. Standard No. 100 sieve.

Ground Garlic
Not more than 20% shall be retained on a U.S. Standard No. 20 sieve.
Not more than 3.0% shall pass through a U.S. Standard No. 50 sieve.
Not more than 1.0% shall pass through a U.S. Standard No. 80 sieve.

Minced Garlic
Not more than 2.0% shall be retained on a U.S. Standard No. 8 sieve.
Not more than 3.0% shall pass through a U.S. Standard No. 20 sieve.
Not more than 1.0% shall pass through a U.S. Standard No. 35 sieve.

Chopped Garlic
Not more than 2.0% shall be retained on a U.S. Standard No. 4 sieve.
Not more than 5.0% shall pass through a U.S. Standard No. 12 sieve.

Extractives

The volatile oil of garlic amounts to less than 0.2% by weight of the fresh garlic. It is recovered by steam distillation of the freshly ground bulblets. Its color is brownish-yellow and its odor is pungent and disagreeable. The constituents of the oil are 60% diallyl disulfide, 20% diallyl trisulfide, 6% allyl propyl disulfide and smaller quantities of diethyl disulfide, diallyl polysulfide, allinin, and allicin. The true garlic odor is said to be derived from the diallyl disulfide.

Commercial oil of garlic, undiluted, has 200 times the strength of dehydrated garlic or 900 times the strength of fresh garlic. It may be purchased at different dilution levels; i.e., 5%, 10%, and so on, in vegetable oil to permit easier blending and mixing in seasoning mixtures.

Oleoresin of garlic is available in either water or oil dispersible forms; each one is a brownish-yellow liquid containing 5 g of volatile oil of garlic in each 100 g. Generally, 3.63 kg (8 lb) is equivalent to 45.45 kg (100 lb) of dehydrated garlic or 0.93 kg (2 lb) of oleoresin is equivalent to 45.45 kg (100 lb) of fresh garlic.

Federal Specifications—Garlic, Dehydrated _____

The fresh garlic used for dehydration shall be clean, mature, sound and wholesome. It shall be substantially free from damage caused by dirt or other foreign matter, moisture, cuts, disease, insects, mechanical, or other means. When specified, anti-caking agents approved by the Federal Food and Drug Administration may be included.

The garlic bulbs shall be cracked open to separate the individual bulblets, and the diseased, sprouted, or damaged bulblets discarded. The husks, root crowns, stems and skins shall be removed either before or after dehydration. The cloves shall be thoroughly washed to remove any adhering foreign material.

The dehydration conditions must be such that the product can not be scorched or otherwise damaged by heat or drying.

The dehydrated product must comply with the following requirements: It shall contain not more than 6.5% moisture, 0.02% by weight of acid insoluble ash and 10% by weight, or hot water insoluble solids. The optical density shall be 0.150, and the speck count shall be not in excess of 25 in 0.1 g.

Not less than 98% of the garlic powder shall pass through a U.S. Standard No. 35 sieve, not less than 95% shall be retained on and above a U.S. Standard No. 100 sieve and not less than 99% shall be retained on and above a U.S. Standard No. 140 sieve.

Two avoirdupois ounces of the product, when added to 16 fluid oz of water at 75°±5°F and allowed to soak for one hour shall possess a good characteristic, pungent flavor and odor, typical of fresh garlic.

Approximate Composition of Garlic Powder, 100 g Edible Portion

Water	6.5 g	Iron	3 mg
Food energy	332 kcal	Magnesium	58 mg
Protein	16.8 g	Phosphorous	417 mg
Fat	0.8 g	Potassium	1101 mg
Total carbohydrate	72.2 g	Sodium	26 mg
Fiber	1.9 g	Zinc	3 mg
Ash	3.3 g	Vitamins	insignificant
Calcium	80 mg		

Household Uses

Almost since history began, garlic has been used for flavoring Indian, Oriental, Mediterranean (European and African) dishes. If used sparingly, garlic may be used to enhance the flavor of most meats, salads, salad dressings (sauces), and any vegetable that is compatible with onion. It is customarily used with meat, poultry and seafood dishes, tomato dishes, soups, sauces, appetizers, Spanish, Mexican, and Italian style dishes, and with melted butter or margarine on French or Italian breads. Shrimp scampi would not exist without a touch of garlic. One clove or bulblet of fresh garlic is equivalent to 2 ml (⅛ tsp.) of garlic powder.

Commercial Uses _____

Dehydrated garlic is used extensively in condiments and meat seasonings. Like most other spice ingredients, it should be used with extreme caution because of its intense odor and disagreeable taste when used to excess. It is used in many canned, dehydrated and frozen prepared foods, bouillons, sauces, soups, gravy mixes, and a few baked goods.

Fig. 3.42
Ginger. Ginger plant with rhizomes.

Ginger
Zingiber officinale Roscoe
Family Zingiberaceae

Historical/Legendary Background _____

Ginger was one of the first oriental spices to reach southeastern Europe in the ancient spice trade. It has been told that around 2400 BC a baker on the Isle of Rhodes near Greece, prepared the first gingerbread. Shortly thereafter, the recipe found its way to Egypt where the Egyptians savored its excellent flavor and served it on ceremonial occasions. The Romans distributed it to all parts of their empire. Dioscorides reported that ginger was good with meat and in sauces for

> it is of an heating and digesting quality, it gently looseth the belly and
> is profitable for the stomach and effectively opposeth itself against all
> darkness of the sight answering the qualities and effects of pepper.

Marco Polo was the first European to write of actually finding ginger in China. In the Middle Ages, when ginger first appeared in Europe, a pound of ginger could buy a sheep. A San Domingo shipping manifest dated in the late sixteenth century indicated that ginger had been exported from this West Indian island to Europe. Obviously, the spice was either native to the region or had been introduced before that time by the Spaniards during their conquest of the islands.

Source

It is believed that ginger probably originated either in the tropical part of southern China or the nearby Pacific Islands. It is now cultivated in Australia, Sri Lanka, China, East Indies, Egypt, Greece, India, Indochina, Jamaica, Japan, Mexico, Nigeria, San Domingo, and Sierra Leone. The ginger from Jamaica is considered to be of the highest quality. Jamaica, India, Japan, and Africa produce the bulk of the world's supply of ginger today which totals over 25,000 tons.

Physical Characteristics and Sensory Attributes

The lilylike, herbaceous plant bears stems up to 120 cm (4 ft) tall with two vertical rows of narrow, glossy leaves and yellow-purplish flowers borne on leafless stems on conelike spikes at the end of the stems. The plant propagates by the splitting of the rhizomes. The fleshy rhizome is harvested when about a year old, washed and dried in the sun to a moisture content of less than 12%. This dried ginger is known as black ginger. If the outer layer of corky material

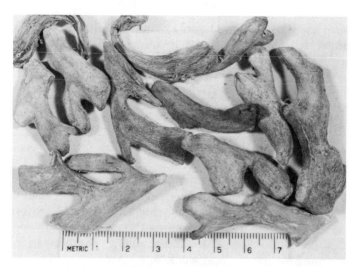

Fig. 3.43
Jamaica ginger, rhizomes.

is scraped off before drying, the product is known as white ginger. (A rhizome is an underground stem, not a root.) By harvesting young rhizomes early, about the sixth month, they are quite tender and may be used in the manufacture of preserved, or crystallized ginger.

Jamaica ginger is very light buff in color, 6 to 9 cm long, with an irregular, branched shape. Divested of its outer cork layer it is clean, hard, and fibrous. The odor is aromatic, agreeable, pungent, and spicy. The taste is also aromatic, pungent and biting. It has an average volatile oil content of 1.0% vol/wt.

African ginger, primarily from Sierra Leone, is darker in color, not peeled of its cork, lacking the fine aroma of Jamaican ginger but is excellent for use in meat seasonings. It has an average volatile oil content of 1.6% vol/wt.

Nigerian ginger is light in color, partially peeled and usually split. It is strongly aromatic and camphoraceous. Its volatile oil content is about 2.5% vol/wt.

Indian ginger (Cochin) is light brown in color, partially peeled on the flattened sides, has a strong lemon odor and contains about 2.2% volatile oil vol/wt. It also has a strong, aromatic, pungent taste.

Japanese ginger is pale, partially peeled, usually limed with calcium carbonate, resembles Cochin ginger, but is weaker in aroma. It contains an average volatile oil content of 2.0% vol/wt.

Chinese and Australian gingers are quite similar in that they are light brown in color and usually are unpeeled. Each contains approximately 2.5% volatile oil (vol/wt).

Extractives

The pungency of ginger is attributed to zingerone, shogaol, and gingerol. The primary flavoring constituents of the oil include cineol, borneol, geraniol, linalool, and farmasene. The oil from Jamaica ginger is very delicate in its aroma and flavor, whereas the oil from Cochin ginger is more aromatic and pungent. The African gingers are more pungent, harsh, and weak in aroma.

The oleoresin of ginger, of either African, Jamaican or Cochin origin is obtained by percolating ground ginger with acetone, alcohol, or petroleum ether, then evaporating off the solvent. The extract is an extremely dark, brownish-green, almost black, semi-solid containing 28 ml of volatile oil in each 100 g. Of the oleoresin 1.82 kg (4 lb) is equivalent to 45.45 kg (100 lb) of freshly ground ginger from the originating source in aroma and flavor characteristics. The oleoresin contains gingerol and zingerone in addition to the chemical constituents of the volatile oil.

Federal Specifications

Whole or ground ginger shall be the washed and dried, or decorticated and dried rhizome of Zingibar officinale, Roscoe. The roots (rhizomes) are irregular, varying from tan to pale brown in color, have an agreeable, aromatic, slightly pungent odor and a pungent, biting taste. The spice shall contain not more than 7.0% total ash, 1.0% acid insoluble ash and 12.0% moisture. It shall contain not less than 42.0% starch and 1.5 ml volatile oil per 100 g. The ground product must be uniformly ground to allow 95% of the product to pass through a U.S. Standard No. 30 sieve.

Approximate Composition of Ginger, 100 g, Edible Portion

Water	9.4 g	Magnesium	184 mg
Food energy	347 kcal	Phosphorous	148 mg
Protein	9.1 g	Potassium	1342 mg
Fat	6.0 g	Sodium	32 mg
Total carbohydrate	70.8 g	Zinc	5 mg
Fiber	5.9 g	Niacin	5 mg
Ash	4.8 g	Vitamin A	147 IU
Calcium	116 mg	Other vitamins	insignificant
Iron	12 mg		

Household Uses

The use of freshly ground ginger will add zest to almost any sweet meat, seafood or poultry dish. Chinese chefs use it often. They learned from their ancestors that a little ginger enhances even the most insipid dish. It is the principle flavoring ingredient in gingerbread, gingersnaps, New England Indian pudding, and gingered pears. It is also delicious on plain ice cream or made into a syrup for barbecue sauce, baked apples, apple compote, and ice cream. The spice goes well in pumpkin pie, macaroni and cheese, fruit desserts, mincemeat, cakes and cookies, steamed and baked puddings, pickles, sweet rolls, fried chicken, curries, poultry casseroles, oriental dishes and on most meats and marinades for beef, lamb, pork, veal, poultry, and fish. It is used in sauces for ham, pork, and tongue as well as on the following vegetables: winter squash, pumpkin, sweet potatoes, and carrots. The young green rhizomes may be preserved in syrup, or candied in sugar, as they are used in the West Indies and in China for a delicious confection.

Ginger has a tendency to round out some flavors while at the same time accenting others; it contributes a freshness to foods which other spices do not. The pungency potency of ginger increases with the application of heat.

Commercial Uses

Ginger, or one of its extractives, is used commercially as a flavoring ingredient in nonalcoholic beverages, liqueurs, ice creams, confections, baked goods, curry powder blends, sauces, condiments, and seasonings for meat. Ginger is used in the following prepared meat items: frankfurters, knockwurst, bologna, pork sausage, liver sausage, salami, pressed sausage, pressed ham, Dutch loaf, Braunschweiger liverwurst, baked liver loaf, fried chicken, and pork patties.

In pharmacy, ginger is used to reduce flatulence and colic, as an aromatic stimulant and as a carminative.

Fig. 3.44
Hops. Flowering vine of the hop plant.

Hops
Humulus lupulus L.
Family Urticaceae

Historical/Legendary Background _____

Ra, the Egyptian sun god, according to ancient legend, first taught man how to brew beer. Diodorus Siculus, in the first century BC claimed the Germans enjoyed their beer seasoned with hops, a secret learned from Finnish tribes. The Arabian physician, Mesue, in the middle of the ninth century claimed the use of hops would induce sleep and improve the nervous system. (There are many who believe in that theory today.) In the eighth and ninth centuries, the

Benedictine monks cultivated hops along with other herbs and spices in their gardens. The Romans used the shoots of the plant as a vegetable, cooked like asparagus, and in salads with a vinaigrette dressing. The cones (hops) were added to soups during the middle ages. In the sixteenth century, hops were used in France. From there it was introduced into England for cultivation purposes to be used in beer, although it had been growing wild among the rocky hedges of England for centuries. It was introduced into the United States early in the seventeenth century and has been cultivated here ever since.

Source

The bulk of the world's supply now comes from the United States, Germany, and Great Britain. Oregon, Washington, California, and Idaho produce most of the hops in the United States. West Germany produces about 25% of the world's supply, Great Britain about 33% and a small percentage is exported from Czechoslovakia. Other countries which cultivate hops are Argentina, Australia, Austria, Belgium, Brazil, France, the Netherlands, New Zealand, Japan, Poland, Russia, Spain, and Yugoslavia.

Physical Description and Sensory Characteristics

The common hop is a perennial, clockwise-twisting vine, that grows wild with stems up to 10 m (33 ft) in height. The plant has leafy greenish-yellow, conelike, catkins (female flowers) or imbricated heads (strobili) and ovoidal fruits surrounded by a calyx. The flowers are fragrant, spicy, bitter and contain from 0.3 to 1.0% volatile oil. Scales are scattered all over the plant with resinous, spherical glands called lepulin. The quality of the hops depends greatly on the amount of lepulin covering the plant. These sticky, yellowish granules develop to their maximum upon full maturation of the plant on the vine. The oleoresin of lepulin, contained in these glands, is a very brilliant yellow (light lemon) color, almost transparent, with a very strong, characteristic aroma and bitterness associated with beer.

The mature catkins are oblong to ovoid in shape, loose and paperlike, straw colored and up to 2 in. long. When cured they develop a strong characteristic odor peculiar to hops. The volatile floral notes are lost in the drying process.

The heads of the hops yield a green, light-acrid, oil of hops. The yield is about 0.5%. Its chief aromatic constituents are myrcene and humulene with minor quantities of lupulone, xanthohumol, ceryl alcohol, lactaric acid, dipentene, caryophylene, linalool, and methyl nonyl ketone.

The freshly harvested hops are dried in kilns at temperatures below 150°F (66°C) to a moisture content below 10%.

Household Uses

Hop shoots may be used as a vegetable when cooked like asparagus or in salads with vinaigrette dressing. The hops may be added to soups where bitterness may be desired.

Commercial Uses

In addition to its use as a beer flavoring agent, hops has been reportedly used to flavor tobacco, yeast, beverages, confections, baked goods, chewing gums, condiments, and in pharmacy as an aromatic bitter principle.

Fig. 3.45
Horseradish. Fleshy root portion with basal leaves and flowers.

Horseradish
Armoracia rusticana P. Gaertn., B. Mey. Scherb
Family Cruciferae

Historical/Legendary Background _____

Horseradish is the bitter spice eaten at the Passover ceremony of the Jews, to symbolize the bitterness of their enslavement by the Egyptians.

Source _____

Horseradish is indigenous to central, eastern and Mediterranean regions of Europe where it is now cultivated there extensively. It is also cultivated throughout most temperate zone countries including the United States. It has even become a troublesome weed in the agricultural areas of the United States.

Physical Characteristics and Sensory Attributes _____

Horseradish is a perennial, herbaceous plant of the mustard family grown for its pungent, white, fleshy, branched taproot and vertical rhizomes. The plant grows to about 1.2 m (4 ft) in height and thrives in deep, moist, fertile loams, found around Illinois, New Jersey, and Wisconsin. It bears small white flowers and oval shaped seed pods. The roots and rhizomes are hardy and may be harvested as needed by the processing plant. Once delivered to the plant, they are thoroughly washed and trimmed prior to grating. The grated rhizomes and roots are used in the making of horseradish sauce. Horseradish has a sharp, burning, pungent, aromatic flavor with a hot, mustardlike odor.

Extractives _____

Horseradish contains ascorbic acid and sinigrin which yields allyl isothiocyanate on hydrolysis with peroxidase or myrosinase (enzyme from black mustard.) The oil of horseradish contains sinigrin and sinigrin-derived allyl thiocyanate, diallyl sulfide, phenethyl, and phenyl propyl thiocyanate.

Household Uses

Grated horseradish sauce may be added to sharp, hot, piquant seafood cocktail sauces, prepared mustards, boiled beef, other seafoods and meat where its sharp, pungent characteristics are desired. It is good in salad dressings, appetizers, dips, and relishes. When mixed with whipped cream, it makes a delicious sauce for serving with ham, tongue, roast beef, corned beef, and broccoli.

Commercial Uses

Horseradish is used commercially in prepared seafood sauces and in specialty mustards. Allyl isothiocyanate is one of the active ingredients in Rasapan, a urinary antiseptic.

Fig. 3.46
Mace. Branch of nutmeg tree with fleshy fruit containing mace and nutmeg.

Mace
Myristica fragrans Houtt
Family Myristicaceae

Historical/Legendary Background _____

The history of mace is intertwined with that of nutmeg. Mace is derived from the reddish, lacy membranous tissue surrounding the nutmeg. It is believed that mace and nutmeg originated in the Moluccas Islands (part of the Spice Islands group, 1000 miles northeast of Java and almost equally distant east of Malaysia.) From these islands the spice was shipped to Java for export to Ceylon or India for reshipment to the port of Alexandria before being reshipped to

Venice for distribution throughout Europe, a distance of about 4000 miles. India recognized the value of these spices and began growing nutmeg trees but their quality never matched that grown in the Moluccas or Java. In fact, after the Europeans had become accustomed to the exquisite nuances of the far eastern products, they would not accept the merchandise from India. In the twelfth century, a pound of mace could buy three sheep or half a cow. Today, the world trade in mace is about $3 million, but in India the trees now grow wild and their fruit is practically, worthless, being odorless and tasteless, good only as an adulterant.

Source

As indicated above, the spice is indigenous to the Moluccas Islands but is now widely cultivated in the Banda Islands, Brazil, Granada, Java, Malaysia and Sumatra. The trees must be grown near the sea at an elevation of about 305 m (1000 ft) above sea level, in a tropical climate.

Physical Description and Sensory Attributes

The nutmeg tree is approximately 7.6–12.2 m (25–40 ft) tall when fully mature and bears fruit for 60 years or more. The leaves are glossy and very aromatic. The small blossoms are borne in clusters yielding yellow, peachlike fruit, which when fully ripe, have three distinct portions: the outer skin and fleshy portion, either eaten by the natives or discarded; the stringy, deep orange-red inner membrane called the arillus, which when dried in the sun for six to eight weeks, becomes the peachy-orange colored spice called mace. The innermost portion of the fruit is the nut, called nutmeg. The nut has a very hard outer shell, which is easily removed. The inner portion of the nut is actually the spice—nutmeg. By weight, the yield of nutmeg is ten times that of mace when both are dried. The wholesale price of mace is usually 20 to 25% higher than nutmeg. Mace is seldom used or sold commercially before grinding. The mace ob-

Fig. 3.47
Mace, dried and broken.

tained from Granada is not as aromatic or rich in color as that from
the East Indies. Mace is marketed under the name of its origin—
Granada, Penang or Banda. The genuine mace is very aromatic and
warm, spicy, slightly fruity and quite similar to nutmeg but
sweeter.

Extractives

The essential oil of mace is obtained by steam distillation of the
ground, dried inner membranes of the nutmeg fruit. The yield
ranges from 11 to 15% and consists of 87.5% monoterpenes, 5.5%
monoterpene alcohols and about 7.0% other aromatics. The oil is
derived primarily from East Indian sources whereas the oleoresin is
prepared from varieties grown in the West Indies. The aroma of the
oil is pinelike, terpeney, sweetly aromatic, warm, spicy, slightly
fruity, oily, with an oily, fruitlike backnote; the flavor is slightly
bitter, smooth, sweet, spicy, creamy-mellow, slightly pungent with a
lingering spicy aftertaste.

The oleoresin is a reddish-orange liquid containing 50 ml of volatile oil per 100 g. Generally, 3.18 kg (7 lb) of oleoresin is equivalent

to 45.45 kg (100 lb) of freshly ground West Indian mace in organoleptic characteristics.

Federal Specifications

Mace shall be the dried arillus of *Myristica fragrans,* Houtt, yellowish-tan to reddish-tan in color, made up of flat, hornlike, shiny branched pieces with a fragrant, nutmeglike aromatic odor and warm taste. The spice shall contain not more than 3.5% total ash, 0.5% acid insoluble ash, 6.0% moisture, 35% nonvolatile ether extract, and not less than 12 ml of volatile oil per 100 g, 20% nonvolatile ether extract, and not less than 95% shall pass through a U.S. Standard No. 20 sieve.

Approximate Composition of Mace, 100 g, Edible Portion

Water	8.2 g	Magnesium	163 mg
Food energy	475 kcal	Phosphorous	110 mg
Protein	6.7 g	Potassium	463 mg
Fat	32.4 g	Sodium	80 mg
Total carbohydrate	50.5 g	Zinc	2 mg
Fiber	4.8 g	Niacin	1 mg
Ash	2.2 g	Vitamin A	800 IU
Calcium	252 mg	Other vitamins	insignificant
Iron	14 mg		

Household Uses

Mace is excellent in flavoring bakery products such as pound cake, doughnuts, fruit cakes, fruit pies, cookies, and whipped cream toppings; it is delicious with cherry and chocolate dishes and almost any dish that calls for nutmeg. Mace has a fuller, spicier character than nutmeg. One should use 20% less mace than nutmeg. It is sometimes used in seafood chowders, fish sauces, soups, chicken casseroles, creamed vegetables, and in pickles and preserves.

Commercial Uses

Mace is used commercially in baked goods, ice cream, condiments, confections, chewing gum, icings, syrups, pickles, nonalcoholic beverages and in the following prepared meat product seasonings: pizza loaf, liver sausage, bologna, German bologna, bratwurst, frankfurter, boiled ham spice, pork sausage, mortadella, salami, liverwurst, and knockwurst. It is also used in some dehydrated soup mixes such as pea, beef, and chicken.

Fig. 3.48
Majoram, sweet. Flowering branched stem of plant.

Marjoram, Sweet
Origanum majorana L.
Family Labiatae

Historical/Legendary Background _____

The word marjoram, in Greek, means joy of the mountains. The plant is supposed to symbolize happiness. Newlyweds in Rome were crowned with it. It was a symbol of honor in Crete. In Sicily it was said to possess the gift of relieving sadness. It was planted on many gravesites to appease the souls of the dead and was used in funeral wreaths to honor loved ones. Marjoram was used by alemakers in the brewing of beer before hops were discovered. According to

Banckes's Herbal it would cure a cold if it were bound on the head; it was also good for bronchial coughs, asthmatic whooping coughs, and other respiratory ailments. Others believed that when it was made into a tealike brew it would remove obstructions in the alimentary tract, would hasten the eruption of measles and scarlet fever, and was an excellent nerve tonic.

Source

It is believed that marjoram originated in Arabia or other temperate countries in western Asia. It is a member of the mint family closely related to the more aromatic oregano. However, it is much sweeter and more delicate. The herb is cultivated in France, Germany, Granada, Great Britain, Hungary, Italy, Morocco, Portugal, Spain, South America, Tunisia, and to a limited extent in the United States.

Physical Description and Sensory Characteristics

The plant has groups of small, knobby flowers in knotlike formations and small, hairy, oval leaves that are grayish-green in color. The plant grows close to the ground, seldom exceeding 30 cm (1 ft) in height. The cut plant is field dried. The plant has a pleasant, aromatic aroma. The flavor is warm, aromatic, slightly sharp, bitter, and camphoraceous. The dried leaves and floral parts are used as a spice. The dried plant is distilled for its essential oil content.

Extractives

The essential oil is obtained by steam distillation. The yield is very low, in the neighborhood of less than 1.0%. It is a yellow or greenish-yellow extract with an aroma that is spicy, fragrant,

Fig. 3.49
Marjoram, sweet, chopped leaves.

warm, aromatic, sweet floral, and penetrating, resembling that of lavender. The taste is sharp, warm, spicy, slightly bitter, herbaceous, smoothly aromatic with a slightly bitter aftertaste. Chemically, it contains linalool, methyl chavicol, cineol, eugenol and terpinineol.

The oleoresin is a dark green, viscous, semisolid with a volatile oil content of 40 ml per 100 g. For a good quality oleoresin 1.14 kg (2½ lb) is equivalent to 45.45 kg (100 lb) of freshly ground marjoram in odor and flavor characteristics.

Federal Specifications

Marjoram shall be the dried leaves, with or without a small portion of the flowering tops of *Marjorana hortensis* Moench. The round, light green to light gray-green leaves possess a pleasant aromatic odor and have a warm, slightly bitter taste. The ground product shall contain not more than 10% of stems by weight; it must be uniformly ground to allow for a minimum of 95% by weight, to pass through a U.S. Standard No. 30 sieve. The product shall contain not more than 13% total ash, 4.0% acid insoluble ash, and 10.0% moisture. It shall contain not less than 0.8% volatile oil expressed as ml per 100 g.

Approximate Composition of Sweet Marjoram, 100 g, Edible Portion

Water	7.6 g	Magnesium	346 mg
Food energy	271 kcal	Phosphorous	306 mg
Protein	12.7 g	Potassium	1522 mg
Fat	7.0 g	Sodium	77 mg
Total carbohydrate	60.6 g	Zinc	4 mg
Fiber	18.1 g	Ascorbic acid	51 mg
Ash	12.1 g	Niacin	4 mg
Calcium	1990 mg	Vitamin A	8068 IU
Iron	83 mg	Other vitamins	insignificant

Household Uses

Like most spices, marjoram is deceptively potent and care should be taken not to use excessive amounts of this spice in seasoning a food product. Six servings of meat, fish or eggs require only ¼ to ½ tsp (1.2 to 2.5 ml) of sweet marjoram. The spice is excellent with lamb, mutton, roast pork, veal, beef, goose, and duck, stews, gravies, poultry stuffings, egg dishes, oyster stew, bean, pea and spinach soups, green leafy vegetables, and salads. It may be used sparingly with highly spiced foods like pizzas and many Italian, Greek, and French recipes for fish, creamed shellfish, and game fowl. It also goes well with eggplant, carrots, peas, spinach, summer squash, tomatoes, cauliflower, broccoli, and mushrooms.

Commercial Uses

Sweet marjoram, or one of its extractives, is used commercially in the formulation of liqueurs, vermouths, condiments, sauces, fried chicken seasoning, salad croutons and the following prepared meat item seasonings: pork sausage, German sausage, liverwurst, chicken loaf, head cheese and Braunschweiger liverwurst.

From earliest times, marjoram has been used in perfumes and unguents; it is still used in French and English soaps as an aromatic adjunct.

Fig. 3.50
Mint, peppermint. Single flowering stem of the peppermint plant.

Mint—Peppermint
Mentha x Piperita
Family Labiatae
Variety (a) Vulgaris—Black mint
Variety (b) Officinalis—White mint

Historical/Legendary Background ⎯⎯⎯⎯⎯⎯⎯

Dioscorides was the first to suggest that mint was an effective contraceptive. He even went so far as to claim it would reduce the swelling of tumors. Latin and French apothecaries claimed it was wholesome for the stomach; that it would stop the coughing up of blood when given with vinegar and water. Pliney recommended its application to the forehead or areas around the temples to eliminate headaches. Others suggested mixing it with salt for application to bites from mad dogs. Gerard's *Herbal* recalls other uses for mint: as a poultice to cure blotches on the face, for curing toothaches, and for preventing vomiting.

Mint was used in various ways during the Middle Ages; it was strewn on streets of cities to welcome triumphant gladiators; it was used by orators to make their voices more resonant; ladies used it to scent their baths, and it was used by apothecaries in the formulation of perfumes. It was grown in all the Roman monastery gardens; Jews called it the sage of Bethlehem. Cultivation in England did not begin until 1750.

Source

Mint grows wild throughout the temperate region and is culti-vated in Argentina, Australia, France, Germany, Great Britain, India, Italy, Japan, Yugoslavia, and the United States. The latter is the largest commercial source of peppermint in the world; most of it is grown in the pacific northwest.

Physical Description and Sensory Characteristics

The white mint variety is grown on a limited scale in southern England but because of its susceptibility to serious infections and the difficulty in growing it economically, it has been replaced with the hardier, black mint variety. Experts believe that white mint has the better flavor.

The black mint variety grows to a height of one meter (3 ft), bears bright green leaves measuring up to 45 mm long by 23 mm wide (1¾ in by ⅜ in). The plant is propagated by cuttings. The green leaves and tops are harvested when in full bloom and are partially dried

Fig. 3.51
Mint, peppermint, dried whole leaves.

with the leaf stalks attached. The aroma is very strongly mentholic, sweet, and cooling, with a taste that is fragrant, spicy, minty cool, sweet, and very slightly pungent. The aftertaste is sweet, minty, and cooling.

Extractives

The essential oil is obtained by steam distillation of the partially dried plant. The yield is slightly under 1.0%. The yield of oil per acre, in the United States, averages 54.5 kg (120 lb), whereas the yield in Great Britain is only one-sixth that amount. The oil is a pale yellow liquid with a characteristic peppermint odor. The principal constituents of the oil, after it has been rectified, are α- and β-pinene, limonene, cineol, ethyl amylcarbinol, l-menthol, menthone, menthyl acetate, piperitone, and other minor esters. All peppermint oils have these components but the ratio of one to another varies widely with oils from different geographical areas. From a sensory point of view, the oil has a fresh, strong, minty odor, sweet balsamic taste, with a pronounced cooling effect in the mouth. As the quality of the oil varies considerably in sensory attributes, depending on the source of supply, the technologist is advised to check samples from several suppliers before reaching a conclusion on purchasing specifications. The cost factor may also affect one's decision as there is a wide discrepancy in costs, depending again on the source of the material and the degree of rectification in its manufacture.

Federal Specifications

There are no Federal specifications for the procurement of this item.

Household Uses

Unless mint leaves are to be used simply as a garnish for fruit or beverages, they should be crushed just before using to obtain the optimum flavor. The crushed leaves may be used in juleps, jellies, beverages, sherberts, soups, stews, sauces, vinegar, lamb, veal, fish and beef dishes, as well as with yogurt, peas, spinach, carrots, and eggplant.

Commercial Uses

Peppermint oil is used in chewing gums, confections, ice cream, dentifrices, cordials, tobacco products and medicaments for indigestion. Mint is seldom used in seasonings for meat.

Fig. 3.52
Mint, spearmint. Single flowering stem of the spearmint plant.

Mint—Spearmint
Mentha spicata L.
Family Labiatae

Historical/Legendary Background _____

The same as peppermint.

Source _____

The United States accounts for most of the world output of spearmint. It is cultivated extensively in Russia, Japan, Great Britain, Germany, and the Netherlands. The state of Washington is the leading producer of this spice with yields of up to 36.74 kg (81 lb) of volatile oil per acre. Midwestern states like Indiana and Michigan yield only up to 18.1 kg (40 lb) of oil per acre.

Physical Description and Sensory Attributes _____

The plants resemble peppermint but they seldom grow higher than 62 cm (2 ft). Cultivation and harvesting procedures follow the same pattern as peppermint. The aroma is fresh, somewhat sickly sweet and minty, balsamic, and typically spearmint. The flavor is sharp, pleasantly pungent, herbaceous, sweet, and minty.

Extractives _____

The essential oil of spearmint is obtained by steam distillation. Approximately 0.6% is obtained from the leaves and flowering tops. The principal constituent is l-carvone, about 56% of the oil, but the characteristic spearmint notes are derived from the components: dihydrocuminyl acetate, dihydrocuminyl valerate and dihydrocarveyl acetate. The odor has been described by Heath as having a very strong impact with a sharp, fresh, penetrating minty, sickly-sweet, toffeelike, balsamic impression with a warm, smooth, pleasantly aromatic, sharp, herbaceous flavor.

Household Uses _____

Spearmint leaves may be used as a garnish for fruit cocktail or with beverages or in any dish that calls for mint leaves. As with peppermint, the leaves should be crushed just before using to obtain optimum flavor. The crushed leaves may be used in sauces, stews, soups, juleps, jellies, iced tea, and vinegar. It goes well with lamb, veal, fish, or beef and adds a fresh note to peas, eggplant, carrots, spinach, and yogurt.

Commercial Uses

Spearmint oil is used in confections, chewing gums, tooth pastes, baked goods, gelatin desserts, jellies, alcoholic and nonalcoholic beverages, and aids for digestion.

Fig. 3.53
Mustard, white. Flowering white mustard plant.

Mustard

Type I White or yellow (mild); *Brassica
hirta* Moench or Balba
Type II Brown (oriental); *Brassica juncea* (L) Cosson
Type III Black (hot); *Brassica nigra* (L) Koch
Family Cruciferae

Historical/Legendary Background _____

Mustard has been used in Europe since the earliest times, as a condiment with salted meats and as a digestive stimulant. Roman soldiers brought mustard seed to England as early as 50 BC. The

Greeks seasoned their fish and meats with mustard seed centuries before the Christian era. Even before the Greeks, the Chinese used the hot, pungent spice as a sauce to season most of their foods, much like today. They believed it enhanced the other flavors and they enjoyed its warm, hot flavor and aroma.

At the time of Christ, the lowly mustard seed was compared with the Kingdom of Heaven in one of Christ's parables as quoted from St. Matthew 13, 31 and 32.

> The Kingdom of Heaven is like to a grain of mustard seed, which a man took, and sowed in his field: which indeed is the least of all seeds: but when it is grown, it is the greatest among herbs and becometh a tree, so that the birds of the air come and lodge in the branches thereof.

Source

White or yellow mustard is native to southern Europe but is now cultivated widely in Austria, China, Chile, Denmark, India, Italy, Japan, Great Britain, the Netherlands, North Africa, Canada, and the United States (Montana and California). Brown mustard is grown only in the United Kingdom and the United States. Black mustard is grown in Argentina, Chile, Italy, the Netherlands, the United Kingdom, and the United States.

Physical Characteristics and Sensory Attributes

White or yellow mustard is an annual which grows to about 62 cm (2 ft) in height and bears a mass of bright yellow flowers. The seed is spherical and also pale yellow in color. The initial taste is slightly bitter but develops an agreeable, aromatic, warm pungency. Unlike the brown or black mustard seeds, when crushed, the white or yellow mustard seeds exhibit no odor although the taste is pungent.

Brown and black mustard seed are quite similar and are usually

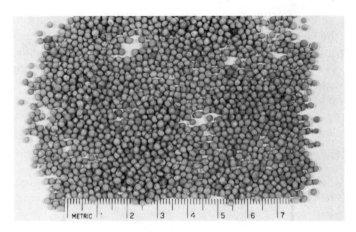

Fig. 3.54
Mustard seed, white.

called black mustard, although such a term is somewhat misleading as they really should be grouped together as brown mustard seed. The plants are similar to the white or yellow but with smaller flowers. The seeds are smaller and are dark red to brown in color. The crushed seeds give off a characteristic irritating odor which becomes intensely strong and irritating when moistened. The taste is initially bitter but becomes powerfully pungent.

Water or moisture activates the enzyme myrosin causing the glycoside sinalbin to yield p-hydroxy benzyl isothiocyanate, glucose and sinapine bisulfate. In the black or brown mustard seeds, the glycoside is sinigrin, which decomposes in a similar manner but the active constituent formed is allyl isothiocyanate, glucose, and potassium hydrogen sulfate. Allyl isothiocyanate is very pungent, has a very irritating odor, and a sharply acrid flavor.

The flavor or heat value of mustard can be enhanced or altered depending on the diluent used with the ground mustard flour:

	Diluent	Yield
Mustard flour	water	a sharp, hot taste
	vinegar	a mild, English style flavor
	wine	a pungent, spicy flavor
	beer	an extremely hot taste

Extractives

The cold pressed method is used to extract the fixed oil from the mustard seed. The fixed oil content amounts to 30 to 35% of the weight. The remaining product is called the press cake. The essential oil of mustard is obtained by steam distillation of this press cake after it has been hydrolyzed by the enzyme myrosinase to release the allyl isthiocyanate from the sinigrin glucoside.

The essential oil of white or yellow mustard is obtained by solvent extraction of the press cake because it contains little or no volatile oil. Again, the press cake must be first hydrolyzed to release the end products caused by the action of the enzyme. Hydrolysis, in either case, is brought about by maceration of the press cake with warm water.

The oleoresin of mustard seed is usually obtained from a blend of the three different types to provide for a balanced flavor effect. It is a yellow to light brown, oily type of liquid with a volatile oil content of 5 ml per 100 g. Two kilograms (4½ lb) is equivalent to 45.45 kg (100 lb) of the mustard spice.

Federal Specifications

These specifications classify mustard into three different types: whole, ground and flour.

Whole mustard is the seed of *Brassica hirta* Moench (white mustard). *Brassica Juncea* L. Cosson, or varieties, or closely related varieties of the types of *Brassica nigra* and *Brassica juncea*.

Brassica hirta Moench (white mustard) or yellow seeded varieties of *Brassica hirta* Moench shall be small, globular, yellow, clean looking hard seeds and shall not possess any volatile oil or "nose heat" when crushed and mixed with water.

Brassica juncea shall be small, globular, yellow to brown, or brown hard seeds. The seeds when ground and mixed with water on a one to three basis, must be capable of liberating a sharp, piercing, irritating odor and a very pungent taste.

Type I mustard shall contain not more than 5.0% total ash, 1.0% acid insoluble ash and 10.0% moisture.

Type II mustard, or ground mustard, shall be the powder prepared by grinding whole yellow mustard seed (*Brassica hirta* Moench.) The finished product represents the seed ground in its whole form and shall be without the outer cover hulls of husk (bran) removed and without the removal of any of the fixed oils. It shall be uniformly ground to allow for a minimum of 50%, by weight, to pass through a U.S. Standard No. 50 sieve. This form is widely used in the meat industry as an aid to emulsification, water binding, and texture in frankfurters and bologna. Ground mustard shall contain not more than 5.0% total ash, 1.0% acid insoluble ash and 6.0% moisture.

Type III mustard, or mustard flour, shall be a bright yellow powder, prepared from a blend of powders derived from milling the endosperm or interior portion of the seed of Type I-A and Type I-B whole mustard, after removal of the outer cover hulls or husk (bran) and with or without the removal of a portion of the fixed oil. The mustard seed must meet the requirements of grade 1, as defined in Grain Grading Guide for Mustard, established by the Department of Agriculture of the state of Montana. It shall be uniformly milled to allow for a minimum of 95% by weight to pass through a U.S. Standard No. 60 sieve. The product shall be practically free of black specks. In addition, the product, when mixed with water (1 to 8) shall have a fresh mustard odor. Mustard flour is an essential ingredient in mayonaise, salad dressing, baked beans, barbecue sauce, Chinese or hot English mustard, and related products.

Mustard flour shall contain not more than 5.0% total ash, 0.5% acid insoluble ash, 9.0% crude fiber, 10.0% moisture, and not less than 25% nonvolatile ether extract. The volatile oil content shall be not less than 0.4 and not more than 0.6 ml per 100 g.

Approximate Composition of Mustard Seed, 100 g, Edible Portion

Water	6.9 g	Fat	28.8 g
Food energy	469 kcal	Total carbohydrate	34.9 g
Protein	24.9 g	Fiber	6.6 g

Ash	4.5 g	Potassium	682 mg
Calcium	521 mg	Sodium	5 mg
Iron	10 mg	Zinc	5 mg
Magnesium	298 mg	Niacin	8 mg
Phosphorous	841 mg	Other vitamins	insignificant

Household Uses

Whole mustard seed is used in marinades, whole pickling spice mixes, pickled products, pot roasts, salad dressings, and on roasted meats.

Ground mustard and mustard flour is used in seafood cocktail sauces, barbecue sauces, cheese dishes, spice cakes and cookies, devilled eggs, baked beans, and ham dishes, roast pork, meat loaf, ham salad, salad dressings, chowders and bisques, Chinese dish accompaniments, and on beets, cabbage, and cucumbers.

Commercial Uses

Ground mustard is a principal ingredient in many prepared meat seasonings as it acts as an excellent binder, emulsifier, flavor enhancer, and inexpensive bulking agent. It is used in seasonings for bologna, German bologna, frankfurters, salami, liver sausage, pizza loaf, liverwurst, spiced luncheon loaf, knockwurst, and many others. It is also used in prepared salad dressings, pickle products, and condiments. Canned deviled ham owes much of its flavor and spreadable consistency, as well as color to the abundant use of mustard. People in Japan and Bengal use the oil of mustard in their illuminating lamps.

Fig. 3.55
Nutmeg. One nutmeg is sliced to show dark veins which contain the aromatic oil of nutmeg.

Nutmeg
Myristica fragrans Houtt
Family Myristicaceae

Historical/Legendary Background and Source _____

See Mace for complete details.

Physical Characteristics and Sensory Attributes _____

After very slow drying in the sun until the inner seed rattles when shaken, the hard shell is broken and discarded. The nutmegs are then sorted and graded by hand. The color is grayish brown and varies in size up to 3 cm long and 2 cm wide. The shape is oval. The appearance is wrinkled but smooth to the touch. Although it appears to be very hard, it is easy to cut or grate and reveals many brown veins which contain the strongly aromatic oil of nutmeg. The taste is bitter, warm, spicy, pungent, heavy, oily, and somewhat terpeney, while the odor is spicy, warm, slightly camphoraceous, sweet, and penetrating. The East Indian nutmegs are limed usually before export.

Extractives

The volatile oil of nutmeg amounts to about 16%. It is also called oil of myristica. It is yellowish to pale yellow with the odor and taste of nutmeg—spicy, warm, cineolic, camphoraceous, sweet, pungent, heavy, oily, penetrating, and somewhat harsh. Nutmeg yields from 24–30% of fixed oil, sometimes known as nutmeg butter. It is orange-red to reddish-brown in color with the consistency of butter at room temperature. The chief constituent is trimyristicin, the triglyceride of myristic acid, the glycerides of oleic acid and linoleic acid, unsaponifiable matter, volatile oil, and resins.

The oleoresin of nutmeg is a pale yellow oil with solids present. The minimum volatile oil content is 80 ml per 100 g. In general, 2.72 kg (6 lb) of the oleoresin is equivalent to 45.45 kg (100 lb) of freshly ground nutmeg in odor and flavor characteristics.

Federal Specifications

Nutmeg shall be the dried seed of *Myristica fragrans* Houtt deprived of its testa, with or without a thin coating of lime (calcium oxide). The surface of the seed kernels shall be furrowed in an irregular pattern; they shall be spheroidal (some nearly spherical nuts), grayish-brown to brown in color if unlimed; shall have a characteristic, strong aromatic odor; and an aromatic, warm, slightly bitter taste. The ground nutmeg shall have a dull brown color and must be uniformly ground to allow for a minimum of 95%, by weight, to pass through a U.S. Standard No. 20 sieve. The spice must contain no more than 3.0% total ash, 0.5% acid insoluble ash, 8.0% moisture, and not less than 7.5 ml of volatile oil per 100 g.

Approximate Composition of Ground Nutmeg, 100 g, Edible Portion _____

Water	6.2 g	Magnesium	183 mg
Food energy	525 kcal	Phosphorous	213 mg
Protein	5.8 g	Potassium	350 mg
Fat	35.3 g	Sodium	16 mg
Total carbohydrate	49.3 g	Zinc	2 mg
Fiber	4.0 g	Niacin	1 mg
Ash	2.3 g	Vitamin A	102 IU
Calcium	184 mg	Other vitamins	insignificant
Iron	3 mg		

Household Uses _____

Nutmeg is used usually in sweet, spicy dishes as banana bread, doughnuts, sweet yeast rolls and bread, pound cake, spice cakes, cookies, whipped cream desserts, apple and pumpkin pies, fruit sauces, eggnoggs, chocolate dishes, and custard puddings as well as with meat loaves, veal chops, chicken fricassee, chicken sauces, clam and oyster stews, Brunswick and vegetable stews, black bean, pea, tomato and potato soups, and sometimes with eggplant, onions, snap beans, tomatoes, beans, and corn. Ground nutmeg goes well with most custards, lemon desserts and is wonderful served over vanilla ice cream.

Commercial Uses _____

Nutmeg or one of its extracts is used commercially in baked goods, mincemeat, nonalcoholic beverages, liqueurs, ice creams, chewing gums, confections, icings, syrups, condiments, perfumery, and seasonings for dehydrated soups and processed meats such as bologna, frankfurter, mortadella, salami, liverwurst, pressed sausage, Dutch loaf, jellied corned beef, chicken loaf, baked liver loaf, bratwurst, Braunsweiger liverwurst, pork sausage, and pork patties.

Fig. 3.56
Onions.

Onions, Dehydrated
Allium cepa L.
Family Amaryllidaceae
Variety White Globe (Special strain)

Historical/Legendary Background _____

The true origin of onions is still unknown but it is believed that they originated either in Afghanistan or Persia in prehistoric times; onions are believed to be one of the world's oldest crops. An inscription on the Great Pyramid of Cheops indicates that "100 talents of silver had been spent on onions, garlic and radishes with which the slave labor were reimbursed, in lieu of money, for their part in building the pyramid in 2500 BC."

The advent of convenience foods late in this century greatly increased the demand for onions, particularly, dehydrated onions. Onion powder, or one of the many other popular types used in prepared mixed dishes like granulated, minced, chopped, diced, or sliced, could hardly meet the demand during World War II, and facilities were expanded several times in California and Idaho to meet the needs of the Armed Forces alone. After the war, the demand did not abate as their use was promoted and accepted by the civilian population as perhaps one of the best of dehydrated foods. It has been claimed, and rightfully so, that onion is used for flavoring more main dishes in America than any other spice or flavoring agent.

Source

The parent onion grew wild somewhere in western Asia but has been so widely modified into various varieties, due to climate, continuous cultivation practices, and hybridization techniques that there is little similarity between the original onion and those onions that we can purchase from any vegetable display counter today.

The Spanish Bermuda onion has been developed for its extremely mild flavor and solid bulb form. Other varieties have been developed for use as a green vegetable or for use in salads. Others have been specially produced for the small bulblets to be used for propagation purposes. Onions grown for dehydration purposes have been produced from specially selected strains of the White Globe variety, whose total solids, because of decades of breeding experiments, now approaches 20% while maintaining a highly pungent flavor. The United States, particularly California and Idaho, is the largest producer of dehydrated onions in the world. Japan, Egypt, Czechoslovakia, and Hungary follow in that order. Smaller quantities are produced in France, Great Britain, and the Netherlands.

Physical Description and Sensory Characteristics

Onion is a biennial plant of the Amaryllidaceae family. Inasmuch as we are more concerned with dehydrated onions than we are with the fresh, the descriptions that follow will be limited to the various types of dehydrated onions, as outlined in Federal Specification JJJ-0-533d.

The onions used for dehydration must be clean, sound, and wholesome, and shall be of the white or yellow varieties, having prominent pungent characteristics and high solids content. Varieties

Fig. 3.57
Onion, dehydrated minced.

which yield a bitter or mild dehydrated product must not be used. The onions should be free from soft rot, and from damage caused by dirt, or other matter, seedstems, moisture, sunburn, sunscald, disease, insects, mechanical, or other means.

The onions shall be washed thoroughly to remove soil, and sorted to remove any which are diseased or otherwise damaged. The root bases and tops shall be completely removed. The outer and discolored scales may be removed before or after dehydration. The dehydration conditions shall be such that the product will be scorched or otherwise damaged by heat or drying.

The product and package shall be free from insect infestation. Calcium stearate, or other anticaking agents in quantities permissable under the provisions of the Federal Food, Drug and Cosmetic Act, may be added to onion powder to prevent caking.

According to Basic-American's brochure on Dehydrated Onions, the product may be classified into twelve different types, with each type further subdivided into untoasted and toasted varieties. The specifications for the toasted varieties are the same as for the untoasted except for a lower moisture content for the former, 3.25% vs 4.5–5.0% for the latter, and a higher optical index range of 900–1700 vs 90–150. For each type, the total maximum plate count is 300,000 although specally treated and handled types, with less than 300,000 total plate count are available.

In general, 453.5 g (1 lb) of types 1 through 4, including powdered,

Table 3.1   Basic Specifications for Dehydrated Onions

Type	Maximum moisture (%)	Maximum color optical index	U.S. Standard size sieve Maximum %	Sieve size	Maximum hot water insolubles (%)
1. Powdered	4.5	105	2	45	20
			25	80	
			50	100	
Toasted	3.25	900–1700	The same req.		
2. Granulated	5.0	105	2	45	20
			95	100	
			99	140	
Toasted	3.25	900–1700	The same req.		
3. Coarse	5.0	150	10	35	20
			90	100	
Toasted	3.25	900–1700	The same req.		
4. Ground	5.0	90	20	20	20
			97	50	
			99	80	
Toasted	3.25	900–1700	The same req.		
5. Minced	5.0	90	2	6	
			97	20	
			99	35	
Toasted	3.25	900–1700	The same req.		
6. Chopped	5.0	90	2	4	
			40	8	
			90	12	
Toasted	3.25	900–1700	The same req.		
7. Chopped Special	5.0	90	2	4	
			30	8	
			90	12	
Toasted	3.25	900–1700	The same req.		
8. Large Chopped	5.0	90	5	.265	
			70	8	
			90	12	
Toasted	3.25	900–1700	The same req.		
9. Large Chopped Special	5.0	90	2	.265	
			30	6	
			97	12	
Toasted	3.25	900–1700	The same req.		
10. Random Chopped	5.0	90	5	.265	
			70	8	
			97	12	
Toasted	3.25	900–1700	The same req.		
11. Sliced	5.0	90	12	.265	
			92	12	
Toasted	3.25	900–1700	The same req.		
12. Diced (¼ in.)	5.0	90	2	.265	
			8	95	
			12	99	
Toasted	3.25	900–1700	The same req.		

granulated, coarse and ground, is equivalent to 4.53 kg (10 lb) of raw, prepared onion. For types 5 through 12, 453.5 grams (1 lb) is equivalent to 3.63 kg (8 lb) of raw, prepared onion.

Extractives _____

Onion contains a volatile oil, fixed oil, protein, cellulose, sugars, minerals, and so on. The volatile oil content of onion depends on the variety of onion used and the distillation processes employed. The extractives are, to some extent, water soluble. The average yield is 0.015% of a dark brown oil which has a tendency to crystallize upon standing. The chief constituents of the oil are d-n-propyl disulfide and methyl-n-propyl disulfide. Generally, 453.5 g (1 lb) has the flavoring strength of two tons of fresh onions or about 227 kg (500 lb) of dehydrated onion.

The oleoresin of onion may be either water or oil soluble, depending on the nature of the additive used to ease its handling; each is a brownish liquid containing 5 g of volatile oil in 100 g. In general, 453.5 g (1 lb) is equivalent to 182 kg (400 lb) of fresh onions or 45.45 kg (100 lb) of dehydrated onions.

It should be noted that freshly cut onions exhibit a lachrymatory property that is easily destroyed by heat and therefore is not present in either the dehydrated onion or its extractives.

Approximate Composition of Onion Powder, 100 g, Edible Portion _____

Water	5.0 g	Iron	3 mg
Food energy	347 kcal	Magnesium	122 mg
Protein	10.1 g	Phosphorous	340 mg
Fat	1.1 g	Potassium	943 mg
Total carbohydrate	80.7 g	Sodium	54 mg
Fiber	5.7 g	Zinc	2 mg
Ash	3.2 g	Ascorbic acid	15 mg
Calcium	363 mg	Other vitamins	insignificant

Household Uses

There are very few household vegetables, meat, or seafood dishes that are not enhanced by the use of dehydrated onion. It is a universal spice for these main dishes. It may be used also in most soups, gravies, canapes, vegetable juices, salads, and even on some baked goods. A touch of dehydrated onion in cream or cottage cheese, in sauces, omelets, or most egg dishes, adds a flavorful compatible taste. Onion powder is strong: 1 Tbs. is equivalent to one medium sized fresh onion (3 oz).

Commercial Uses

Dehydrated onion is used commercially in, or on, baked goods, pickles, tomato catsup, chili sauce, relishes, and other condiments and in a great many prepared meat seasonings, such as blood sausage, baked liver loaf, German bologna, bologna, head cheese, frankfurter, knockwurst, pizza loaf, Dutch loaf, meat loaf, meat balls, and rubs for roast beef. It is also used in prepared dry soup mixes, salad dressing mixes, gravy preparations, Chinese egg rolls, Mexican enchiladas, lasagna, cooked frozen food dishes, and french-fried onion rings.

Fig. 3.58
Oregano (wild marjoram). Flowering branched stem of the oregano plant.

Oregano (Wild Marjoram)
Origanum vulgare L. or *Origanum* spp.
Family Labiatae

Historical/Legendary Background _____

In the Middle Ages, physicians used oregano to cleanse the brain and improve the eyesight, as a cure for indigestion and the bites of spiders and scorpions.

Source _____

Oregano is indigenous to the sunny, sloping, hilly areas surrounding the Mediterranean, particularly Greece, Italy, and Spain. It is cultivated in Albania, France, Greece, Italy, Mexico, Spain, Turkey, and Yugoslavia. It also grows wild in Mexico where it is known as Mexican Sage. In the past 25 years or so, its use has multiplied rapidly due to the popularity of pizza.

Physical Characteristics and Sensory Attributes ___

Oregano is a perennial plant of the mint family. It has a branched, erect, reddish stem with ovate, opposite leaves. The purple flowers are arranged in heads. The color of the dried herb is pale, grayish-green while the aroma is strong, aromatic, and camphoraceous. The taste is piquant, spicy, warm, pungent, and slightly bitter. The plant contains volatile oil, a fixed oil, proteins, and minerals. The volatile oil contributes much of the flavor to oregano. In some oils of oregano, thymol is the principal flavoring ingredient, while in others, carvacrol is predominant. The plant is harvested when in full bloom. The spice consists of the dried leaves, stalks and floral parts of the plant.

Extractives ___

The Spanish type of oregano is the most important source of the essential oils. Origanum has often been confused with the thymus varieties but is readily distinguished from the latter which contains

Fig. 3.59
Oregano, chopped, dried leaves.

a high phenol content, mostly carvacrol. Part of the confusion exists because many other varieties of oregano contain varying percentage of thymol.

Spanish oregano oil has been profiled by Heath as having a very strong initial impact, strong but light, fresh and clean odor, warming but later cooling, eucalyptuslike, sweet, spicy, slightly floral, and strongly persistent, with a dry, spicy aftertaste. Its flavor is warming, astringent, very bitter, pleasantly aromatic, spicy with a bitter aftertaste changing to sweetness. Chemically, it contains up to 50% thymol, 7–8% α-pinene, cineole, linalyl acetate, linalool, dipentene, *p*-cymene and β-caryophyllene.

The oleoresin of oregano is made from *Coridothymus capitatus* Rchb. It is a dark, brownish-green, semi-solid to very viscous liquid with a volatile oil content of 17–20 ml per 100 g. Generally, 1.74 kg (4 lb) of the oleoresin is equivalent to 45.45 kg (100 lb) of freshly ground and dried oregano, in flavor and aroma characteristics.

Federal Specifications

Oregano shall be the dried leaves of *Origanum vulgare* L. or *Origanum spp.* The light green colored leaves, when crushed, shall have a strong, camphoraceous aroma and a warm, pungent, and slightly bitter taste. The spice shall contain not more than 9.5% total ash, 2.0% acid insoluble ash, 10.0% moisture, and not less than 3.0 ml of volatile oil per 100 g. 95% of the ground product shall pass through a U.S. Standard No. 30 sieve.

Approximate Composition of Oregano, 100 g, Edible Portion

Water	7.2 g	Fiber	15.0 g
Food energy	306 kcal	Ash	7.2 g
Protein	11.0 g	Calcium	1576 mg
Fat	10.3 g	Iron	44 mg
Total carbohydrate	64.4 g	Magnesium	270 mg

Phosphorous	200 mg	Niacin	6 mg
Potassium	1669 mg	Vitamin a	6903 IU
Sodium	15 mg	Other vitamins	insignificant
Zinc	4 mg		

Household Uses

The availability of oregano is a prerequisite in the preparation of Italian, Spanish, and most dishes of Mediterranean or Latin American origin. About 2.46 ml (½ tsp) is sufficient for 473 ml (1 pt) of food material. Oregano goes well with omelets, Italian sauces, tomato dishes, vegetable casseroles, any kind of pizza, hamburgers, pork dishes, beef, lamb and veal roasts, wild fowl, fried chicken, minestrone and bean soups, broths, cheese spreads, shrimp sauce, tossed salads, and the following vegetables: broccoli, eggplant, dried beans, cabbage, lentils, onions, tomatoes, and mushrooms.

The leaves, if possible, should be crumbled just before using, and should not be exposed to high temperature heat for more than ten minutes.

Commercial Uses

Oregano is used commercially in baked goods (pizzas), tomato sauces, condiments, and salad dressings. It is a favorite component of meatball seasoning and a few other Italian style meat preparations. It is seldom used in the usual delicatessen-type prepared meats.

Fig. 3.60
Paprika (pimiento). Flowering stem with long fruited peppers.

Paprika (Pimiento)
Capsicum annum L.
Family Solanaceae

Historical/Legendary Background _____

· None.

Source _____

Paprika grows throughout the world in temperate climates. Its origin is believed to have been the Caribbean region, from where it was taken to Turkey and thence to Hungary by West Indian explorers. It is widely cultivated in Argentina, Bulgaria, Canada, Chile, Hungary, Mexico, Portugal, Romania, Spain, Turkey, Yugoslavia, and the United States.

Physical Description and Sensory Characteristics ___

Paprika is a long, fruited, sweet, nonpungent species of capsicum. It is an annual, shrublike herb with a woody stem and single white flowers. The long fruits vary in color from a rich red to a dark red-brown. The spice is derived by drying and grinding the deseeded and destemmed ripe fruit which yields a mildly pungent, red colored powder, rich in vitamin C.

Hungarian paprika has a bright red color, a pleasantly hot but appealing taste, whereas Spanish paprika is less red and milder in flavor. The Spanish call it pimiento. The principal coloring matter of paprika is the caretenoid pigment—capsanthin. The outer, fleshy, pericarp carries the major portion of the coloring matter while the inner tissues and seeds contain the pungent chemical capsaicin. The color of paprika is reduced considerably and the delicate flavor disappears if the spice is stored for several months, particularly at temperatures above 20°C (68°F).

Hungarian paprika is classified commercially into five types.

Type I.   First Quality or Noble Sweet. It is made from pericarpal tissue only; it is rich red in color and sweet but slightly pungent in flavor.

Type II. Semi Sweet. This type is made from pericarpel tissue and placenta. It is less sweet than first quality paprika and slightly more pungent.

Type III. Rose Quality. This type is made from the whole fruit except for the calyx and peduncles. Its color is less red but more pungent than Types I or II.

Type IV. Pungent Quality. This type is really a second quality Rose. It is brick-red in color, pungent and is usually made from the whole fruit.

Type V.   Mercantile Quality. This type is a third quality Rose. It is brownish-red in color, very pungent and made from the whole fruit.

Spanish paprika is classified into three main types: Type I. Dulce or sweet; Type II Agridulce or semisweet and Type III. Piquante or pungent. Each is marketed in three qualities: extra—from pericarpal tissue only, select—from pericarpal tissue with about 10% seeds and is less red in color, and common—which may contain up to 30% seeds; it has a brick-red color.

Portugese paprika is classified into only two types: Type I. Doce Extra—first quality paprika, characterized by a rich red color and mild flavor. Type II. Doce Superior—less intensely red in color, contains a small quantity of crushed seeds but is still relatively mild in flavor.

It may be seen from the above descriptions that paprika is valued most for its high color and mildness of flavor. Its use in the home and commercially is for adding color to the finished product and to make the product more acceptable and pleasing to the eye. Its flavor qualities are secondary, though its slight pungency may be desirable. Paprika that has been stored under unfavorable conditions of high temperature and humidity conditions could add an unfavorable, stale, bitter flavor to foods and should be avoided.

Extractives

Paprika contains no volatile oil. Oleoresins must be prepared from carefully selected material so that the overall color value is maintained with the pungency kept at a minimum. Since the oleoresins generally will replace a certain quality of spice, the replacement value for each will be identical, as the spice to be replaced will vary in color in the same proportion as the corresponding extractive. High color value paprika is prepared by grinding only the fruit pods, whereas low color paprika is prepared by grinding the pods containing seeds. The seeds decrease the overall color value of the spice.

The customary oleoresins are dark red in color, nonpungent, and are sold either as 40,000 minimum color units, 50,000 color units, or 100,000 color units. Any other strength of color below 100,000 color units may be obtained by quantitative dilution with corn oil or other vegetable oil as a diluent. Color units may be measured by either the standard colorimetric methods or by standard spectrophotometric methods against known standards.

In general, 3.63 kg (8 lb) of oleoresin of paprika is equivalent to 45.45 kg (100 lb) of freshly ground spice. When ordering the oleoresin of paprika from a supplier, the technologist should specify the color value desired and know the type of ground paprika he is replacing.

Federal Specifications

Paprika is the sweet, nonpungent, or if specified, slightly pungent, dried, red ripe fruit of *Capsicum annum* L. It shall contain no more than 8.5% total ash, 1.0% acid insoluble ash, and 10.0% moisture. It shall contain not less than 100 ASTA color units (ASTA Method No. 20). 95% of the ground product shall pass through a U.S. Standard No. 30 sieve.

Nutritional Information

Paprika is a rich source of vitamin C, higher than some citrus fruits. It also contains bioflavanoids, claimed to be valuable in the treatment of frostbite and polio, according to Albert Szent-Gyorgyi, a Hungarian scientist. In 1932, the vitamin A content was established as being quite high.

Approximate Composition of Paprika, 100 g, Edible Portion

Water	9.5 g	Fat	13.0 g
Food energy	289 kcal	Carbohydrate	55.7 g
Protein	14.8	Fiber	20.9 g

Ash	7.0 g	Zinc	4 mg
Calcium	177 mg	Ascorbic acid	71 mg
Iron	34 mg	Thiamin	1 mg
Magnesium	185 mg	Riboflavin	2 mg
Phosphorous	345 mg	Niacin	15 mg
Potassium	2344 mg	Vitamin A	60,604 IU
Sodium	34 mg		

Household Uses

As paprika is usually used for its color-enhancing qualities, it is suitable for use as a garnish on appetizers, eggs, cheese dips, seafoods, and white vegetables. It improves the color of chicken dishes, sauces, salad dressings, goulashes, cole slaw, and prepared veal and other meat dishes.

Commercial Uses

It is used in seasonings for frankfurters, bologna, minced meat specialties, and some sausage products. Some processors have been known to add an antioxidant to the oleoresin of paprika to prevent its degradation in color by salt, light or subsequent heat treatment. Paprika is used in the manufacture of tomato sauces and Mexican chili powders. In addition to meats, paprika or its oleoresin, is used in condiments, baked goods, confections, soups, salad dressings, frozen desserts, and pickled products.

Fig. 3.61
Parsley. Entire parsely plant with spice portion separated.

Parsley
Petroselinum crispum (Mill) Nym.
Family Umbelliferae

Historical/Legendary Background _____

The early history of parsley is minimal even though the spice has been under cultivation for thousands of years. Theophrastus considered the plant to be good for persons with coronary conditions, naming it the coronary plant. Dioscorides claimed its consumption would provoke urine. It has been written that Juno's horses and Homer's heroes accelerated their speed after eating parsley. Early writers claimed its use would increase the blood, soothe the heart and stomach and was capable of absorbing the fumes of wine and thus ward off intoxication. For this reason, Greek and Roman heroes would wear it on their heads at ceremonial banquets. In the south, negroes used to consider it unlucky to transplant parsley from an old house to a newer one. The early Greeks decorated the graves of their loved ones; Egyptians threw it over the graves of their dead.

Charlemagne cultivated parsley in the early sixteenth century. French terms in the culinary arts refer to the use of parsley: "*bouquet garni* is a combination of parsley and other culinary herbs;

"aux fines herbs" refers to the use of parsley alone, although origi-nally it was a mixture of parsley with tarragon, chives, or chervil.

Source

Parsley is grown throughout the temperate and subtropical areas of the world. It is believed to be indigenous to Sardinia. It flourishes in the Mediterranean region of southern Europe, Algeria, and the United States (California and Louisiana.) It is also cultivated in Belgium, Canada, France, Germany, Greece, Great Britain, Italy, Japan, the Netherlands, Portugal, and Spain in addition to Algeria and the United States.

Physical Characteristics and Sensory Attributes

Parsley thrives in any good soil in the temperate and subtropical regions. It is a smooth biennial herb with much branched stems growing as high as 62 cm (2 ft) at times, bearing divided leaves which in some varieties are greatly curled and crisped. It is an aromatic plant widely grown for flavoring and for use as a garnish.

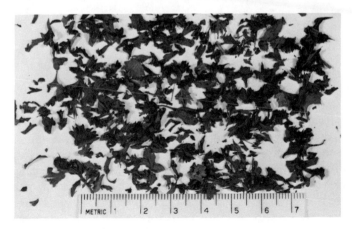

Fig. 3.62
Parsley, dehydrated chopped leaves.

The color of the dried herb is green. The aroma is pleasantly fresh, characteristic, fragrant and slightly spicy. The taste is agreeable, somewhat grassy and herbaceous.

Extractives

The plant yields two different types of essential oil: one from the whole plant and one from the seed. The yield of oil from the freshly harvested plant is not more than 0.06% whereas that from the seed is as high as 3.5%. The main constituent of the volatile oil is the phenol ether, apiole, to which parsley owes its odor and taste. Myristicin, α-pinene, and small amounts of aldehydes, ketones, and phenols are also present in the leaf oil. Parsley leaf oil is obtained by steam distillation of the leaves and flowering tops. The flavor is much harsher and more herbaceous than the seed oil which is somewhat viscous, yellow-amber in color and has a warm, bitter, aromatic taste.

The oleoresin of parsley provides a flavor characteristic of the entire plant and will enhance any composition containing even small percentages of it. It is a deep green, semiviscous liquid, containing 12–15 ml of volatile oil per 100 g. One hundred fifty grams (⅓ lb) is equivalent to 45.45 kg (100 lb) of freshly harvested parsley or 1.36 kg (3 lb) is equivalent to 45.45 kg (100 lb) of dehydrated parsley leaves.

Commercial Specifications

The product consists of the leaf portion of freshly harvested parsley, which has been washed, trimmed, diced, dried, and size classified. A maximum of 20% of the flakes may pass through a U.S. Standard No. 20 sieve. There shall be no foreign material in the dehydrated product, and it shall be practically free from yellow or discolored leaves. Its moisture content shall not exceed 4.5%. When reconstituted, its flavor shall be fresh, typical of fragrant parsley, and its color shall be uniformly bright green. To preserve its freshness, the dehydrated product should be packed in heat sealed, polyethylene lined, corrugated fiber cases and stored under dry, cool storage conditions at 70°F or below. Alternately, the product may be packed in either hermetically sealed metal containers or in 5 gal metal containers with friction top lids.

Approximate Composition of Dried Parsley, 100 g, Edible Portion

Water	9.0 g	Magnesium	249 mg
Food energy	276 kcal	Phosphorous	351 mg
Protein	22.4 g	Potassium	3805 mg
Fat	4.4 g	Sodium	452 mg
Total carbohydrate	51.7 g	Zinc	5 mg
Fiber	10.3 g	Ascorbic acid	122 mg
Ash	12.5 g	Riboflavin	1 mg
Calcium	1468 mg	Niacin	8 mg
Iron	98 mg	Vitamin A	23,340 IU

Household Uses

Parsley is suitable for use in almost any type of cuisine as a garnish on salads, meat, fish, and vegetable dishes, omelets, soups, and stews. When used more generously as a seasoning agent it blends well with meat balls, meat loaves, poultry seasoning, shad roe, and parsley butter. It is great in most soups and casseroles as a garnish or as added flavor.

Commercial Uses

Commercially, parsley is used in chicken and potato soup bases, vichyssoise, meat loaf seasoning, chicken loaf and meatball seasonings, salad croutons, salad dressings, baked goods, snacks and potato chips, and in condiments and nonalcoholic beverages.

Fig. 3.63
Black pepper. Climbing vine with spikes of black pepper.

Pepper, Black
Piper nigrum L.
Family Piperaceae

Historical/Legendary Background _____

The history of pepper is the history of the spice trade. Pepper began moving westward from India over 4000 years ago. Throughout recorded history, pepper has been considered the most precious of spices. Back in Biblical times, pepper was worth 4 denarii (70¢) per 453.5 g (1 lb). Twenty centuries later it could still be purchased for the same price per pound in New York. If one takes into consideration the differences in purchasing power between the two time periods one can visualize that it was a most expensive commodity at the time of Christ. Peppercorns were so costly they were used as a substitute for money. Taxes, dowries and other tributes were said to have included levies of pepper. Dockmen unloading pepper from ships were forbidden to have pockets in their clothing lest they hide a few corns.

Pepper was considered to be a stimulant and an aid to digestion. Hippocrates, as early as 400 BC declared it assisted the gastric juices to function. For centuries it has been used as a preservative and flavoring spice for meats.

Source

Black pepper is the dried, unripened fruit of a perennial climbing 6–7 m (20 ft) in height, indigenous to the hot, jungle forests of the far eastern tropics, twenty degrees on either side of the equator. Commercially, there are at least thirteen designated types of black pepper, usually named from the ports, from which they are shipped, not necessarily from the areas in which they are grown.

Alleppy, Brazil, Ceylon, Lampong, Malabar, Malagasy, Mangalore, Pandjung, Saigon, Sarawak, Siam, Singapore, and Tellicherry are among the better known types.

Lampong pepper is in greatest supply and is perhaps the most popular grade of pepper in the spice trade today. It is produced in the Lampong district of southern Sumatra but also comes from other parts of Indonesia, western Borneo, Riouw Archipelago, Banka, Billiton, northern Sumatra, and western Java. Tellicherry, the second most popular grade originates on the Malabar coast of southern India, as does Alleppy, Malabar, and Mangalore. Saigon type comes from Vietnam, Siam from Thailand, Sarawak from Malaysia, Ceylon from Sri Lanka, Malagasy from the Malagasy Republic, Brazil from Brazil, and Singapore from Malaysia, Cambodia, and Singapore.

Physical Characteristics and Sensory Attributes

The trunk of the black pepper shrub is knotted, elastic, with aerial roots. The leaves are broad and ovate. The spikes are 8 to 10 cm (3–4 in.) long and pendent. Each spike contains 20 to 30 pealike

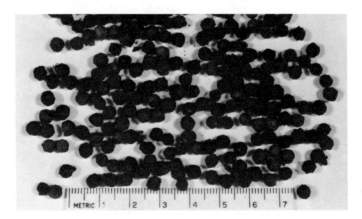

Fig. 3.64
Black pepper berries (Malaysian).

berries. Each berry has a thin pulpous layer, green in the early stages and when it begins to turn red it is ready to be picked. When dried, the color turns to dark brown or black. The shape is globular, small, and wrinkled. Black pepper has a penetrating, aromatic odor and a hot, biting, very pungent taste. Lampong peppercorns are small, somewhat gray in color and wrinkled. Their flavor is more pungent than aromatic. Singapore and Pandjung pepper resemble Lampong. High quality pepper is also produced in Thailand, Vietnam, Madagascar, India, Sri Lanka, Sumatra, Malaysia, and Brazil.

The total world crop is in excess of 70,000 metric tons per year, of which, the United States imports about one third of this supply. Black pepper represents about 25% of the total spice trade.

Extractives

Black pepper yields about 1.5% volatile oil and over 6% oleoresin. The distinctive odor and flavor of pepper overlie its pungency. The volatile oil of pepper has a moderate, initial impact and a fresh, irritating, terpinaceous, sweet odor with a musty, slightly woody note upon drying out. It has a warm flavor, sweetly spicy, woody, fruity, musty, with a pleasantly warm aftertaste. Pepper oil is primarily a mixture of hydrocarbons consisting of 70–80% monoterpenes, 20–30% sesquiterpenes, and less than 4% oxygenated compounds. The higher the percentage of monoterpenes, the fresher the pepper oil. The lower the α- and β-pinene content, the fresher the pepper oil also.

The high quality of pepper grown on the Malabar coast of India to the Malacca Coast and to the East Indian Archipelago is used for the preparation of oleoresin. There are several grades of oleoresin offered in the trade but the two principle grades are Indian, decolorized, oleoresin of black pepper and Indian, not decolorized, oleoresin. The decolorized product is light yellow-green in color, semisolid, and contains 55% piperine and 20 ml of volatile oil per 100 g. Piperine, an alkaloid, is the principal factor contributing to pungency and is used as one of the means for standardization. The volatile oil content is a measure of its flavoring strength. The nondecolorized product is deep green colored semisolid, containing 53–57% piperine and 23 to 30 ml of volatile oil per 100 g. Of either product, 2.38 kg (5¼ lb) is equivalent to 45.45 kg (100 lb) of freshly ground black pepper in organoleptic qualities.

Federal Specifications _____

Black pepper shall be the dried, immature berries of *Piper nigrum* L. deep dark brown to black, deep set wrinkled berries, and when ground shall have a distinctive, penetrating odor, a hot biting and very pungent taste and a light gray to a speckled black-gray color. The spice shall contain not more than 7.0% total ash, 1.0% acid insoluble ash, 12% moisture and 12.5% crude fiber. It shall contain not less than 2.0 ml of volatile oil per 100 g, 7.5% nonvolatile methylene chloride extract and 30% starch. At least 70% of the fine grind pepper shall pass through a U.S. Standard No. 30 sieve. The coarser grind shall be such that 95% shall pass through a U.S. Standard No. 16 sieve.

Decorticated black pepper shall be prepared from the dried, immature berries of *Piper nigrum* L., from which the outer and inner coverings have been removed. It shall contain not more than 3.5% total ash, 0.3% acid insoluble ash, 12% moisture and not less than 1.5 ml of volatile oil per 100 g. 95% of the ground product shall pass through a U.S. Standard No. 40 sieve.

Approximate Composition of Black Pepper, 100 g, Edible Portion

Water	10.5 g	Magnesium	194 mg
Food energy	255 kcal	Phosphorous	173 mg
Protein	11.0 g	Potassium	1259 mg
Fat (less piperine)	3.3 g	Sodium	44 mg
Total carbohydrate	64.8 g	Zinc	1 mg
Fiber	13.1 g	Niacin	1 mg
Ash	4.3 g	Vitamin A	190 IU
Calcium	437 mg	Other vitamins	insignificant
Iron	29 mg		

Household Uses

Because of its provocative aroma and irresistible flavor, black pepper has been sought and used for thousands of years for, and on, every conceivable food product. It is available in different grinds and forms: whole peppercorns, decorticated, cracked, coarse, medium, regular, or fine grind. Sausage makers have different names for some of these grinds, but essentially those six sizes prevail in the spice industry. Each size has its own specific use and the user usually has a preferred grind for his own particular use. The spice may be used with all meats, seafoods, vegetables, soups, egg dishes, salads, appetizers, some vegetable juices, baked goods, and pickles. Where the black specks may be objectionable in some products, one can substitute ground white pepper.

Commercial Uses

Black pepper or one of its extractives is used in dehydrated and canned soups, poultry dressings, pickles, condiments, pickling spice mixes, baked goods, confections, curry powder blends, nonalcoholic beverages, and practically all meat seasonings, like those for bologna, German bologna, frankfurter, knockwurst, fresh pork sausage, blood sausage, metwurst, Braunschweiger liverwurst, pepperoni, salami, mortadella, pressed ham, boiled ham spice, sweet Italian sausage, liver sausage, pizza loaf, pressed sausage, Dutch loaf, jellied corned beef, spiced luncheon loaf, meat loaf, meat balls, bratwurst, pastrami, and roast beef rubs. It is also used in seasonings for fried chicken, poultry dressings, gravy mixes, and meat sauces.

Malaysian Pepper

The Pepper Marketing Board of Malaysia has a brochure on Malaysian pepper that offers the reader a comprehensive story of pepper, its method of cultivation, production, statistics, methods of marketing and commercial grade specifications. We have included the article in its entirety because of the unusual importance of black pepper and white pepper in the overall food business, as well as the culinary field, in the home and in the spice business. The article may be found in the Appendix of this book.

Fig. 3.65
White pepper berries (Standard Malaysian).

Pepper, White
Piper nigrum L.
Family Piperaceae

Historical/Legendary Background _____

The historical and legendary background of white pepper is the same as that of black pepper. Both forms of the pepper come from the same climbing, perennial vine. The white pepper is the dried kernels of the fruits which are gathered after they have just turned slightly yellow, whereas the black pepper kernels were picked while still immature and green. The white pepper kernels are subsequently soaked in slow flowing water for about a week to soften and loosen the outer skin which is then more easily removed. The sun-bleached white peppercorns are smooth surfaced. White pepper is much less pungent than black pepper but of finer flavor with less harshness.

Source _____

The most important type of white pepper is Muntock, from the island of Banka, near Sumatra. Of almost equal importance commercially is the white pepper from Sarawak, followed by that from Brazil.

Extractives _____

White pepper yields about 1.5% volatile oil and about 7% oleoresin. A sensory assessment of the gas liquid chromatographic effluents from oil of Muntock white pepper vs. oil of Sarawak black pepper shows striking similarities in most all high peaks except for the floral note in white pepper oil, a mushroomlike note and a lesser corianderlike note, whereas the black pepper oil had a significant, clovelike note.

Household Uses _____

Many chefs, technologists, and Europeans prefer white pepper to black pepper for culinary use because they find the black specks of the latter objectionable to the eye in many food preparations.

It may be of interest to note that in Biblical times, white pepper was worth about 7 denarii or $1.25 per pound. In 1983 white pepper sold for $1.25 per pound on the wholesale market in New York. When one considers the differences in purchasing power between the two different time periods one begins to realize the extremely high price that was paid for pepper twenty centuries ago.

Approximate Composition of White Pepper, 100 g, Edible Portion _____

Water	11.4 g	Iron	14 mg
Food energy	296 kcal	Magnesium	90 mg
Protein	10.4 g	Phosphorous	176 mg
Fat (less piperine)	2.1 g	Potassium	73 mg
Total carbohydrate	68.6 g	Sodium	5 mg
Fiber	4.3 g	Zinc	1 mg
Ash	1.6 g	Vitamins	insignificant
Calcium	265 mg		

Fig. 3.66
Poppy seed plant.

Poppy Seed
Papaver somniferum L.
Family Papaveraceae

Historical/Legendary Background _____

Poppy seeds have been cultivated for over 3000 years. The Lake Dwellers of Switzerland knew about them; Homer referred to them in his writings; and early Greeks and Romans used them in their food and medicines. Mohammed's missionaries introduced poppy seeds into India in the seventh century where it was combined with sugar cane juice and made into a confection. Early physicians made a plaster of the seeds by mixing them with the white of an egg and mother's milk, and by applying the paste to the temples, assumed it would promote sleep. Some claimed that the juice of poppy seeds would remove warts. Rupert Brooke immortalized the poppy fields of Flanders in his poem entitled "Some Corner of a Foreign Field."

The filling for Jewish festive holiday cakes, known as *hamentachen* is made from crushed poppy seeds, honey, sugar, salt, lemon juice, beaten egg, and water or milk.

Source

Poppy seed is indigenous to China and Asia Minor. It is now cultivated in Canada, Czechoslovakia, Denmark, France, Germany, Great Britain, Hungary, India, Iran, the Netherlands, Poland, Turkey, Yugoslavia, and the United States.

Physical Description and Sensory Characteristics

Poppy seed plants grow to a height of 1 m (3 ft) and may be annual, biennial, or perennial. When the hairy plants, with small slender roots and erect sparsely branched stems, with central ribs are fully mature, the ovate globose fruit capsules open up, scattering thousands of minute, kidney-shaped, grayish-blue colored seeds that are nutty in aroma and taste. The bluish-black seeds are no larger than 1 mm in diameter. It has been estimated that it would take almost a million seeds to weigh 453.5 g (1 lb).

The seeds contain no volatile oil but have about 60% of fixed oil, which is yellow to pale yellow in color, odorless, and possesses an agreeable nutty taste.

The poppy seed plant differs from the poppy plant grown for the production of opium.

Fig. 3.67
Poppy seeds.

Federal Specifications

The whole poppy seed shall be the clean, dried seed of *Papaver somniferum* L. The hard, small, slate-blue, kidney shaped seeds shall have an agreeable, nutty taste, free from evidence of rancidity. Unlike most of the spice specifications, there are no chemical limitations on poppy seeds.

Approximate Composition of Poppy Seeds, 100 g, Edible Portion

Water	6.8 g	Iron	9 mg
Food energy	533 kcal	Magnesium	331 mg
Protein	18.0 g	Phosphorous	848 mg
Fat	44.7 g	Potassium	700 mg
Total carbohydrate	23.7 g	Sodium	21 mg
Fiber	6.3 g	Zinc	10 mg
Ash	6.8 g	Vitamins	insignificant
Calcium	1448 mg		

Household Uses _____

Poppy seed may be used for fillings in Hungarian cakes and pastries, on breads, rolls, pie crusts, buttered noodles or strudels, in cheese cake fillings, cream cheese and sour cream dips, with fruit or vegetable salads or cole slaw, in tuna fish and macaroni salad. When toasted, they go well with cheese dips, spreads, canapes, and over cooked vegetables such as green beans, cabbage, spinach, carrots, onions, zucchini, summer squash, and boiled white potatoes. They may be added to home made confections to give a slightly nutty taste and a desirable difference in texture. German households produce poppy seeds for home production of vegetable oil.

Commercial Uses _____

Poppy seeds are used commercially in or on baked goods and confections. The cold pressed, white poppy seed oil is used as a salad and cooking oil as well as in baked goods.

Fig. 3.68
Rosemary. Upper portion of rosemary plant.

Rosemary
Rosmarinus officinalis L.
Family Labiatae

Historical/Legendary Background

   Dioscorides claimed that if rosemary were boiled in water and drunk before one exercised it would cure anyone with yellow jaundice. After taking the liquid the patient would have to bathe and drink wine. Legend has it that the Virgin Mary washed her sky-blue cloak and spread it over a rosemary bush to dry; the flowers thenceforth were blue. The Arabians wrote that rosemary comforted the brain, the memory, the inward senses and restored speech to the dumb. Tragus wrote of rosemary as a desirable spice in German kitchens and in other cold country homes. Another legend that persists suggests that rosemary placed in clothes closets among clothes protects them from moths and other vermine. It was customary for French hospitals to burn rosemary with juniper to sanitize the air and prevent infections. The oil of rosemary was used by many apothecary dispensers as a means for preventing baldness. In the Middle Ages, it was used as an inexpensive incense material for funeral ceremonies. In Roman times, rosemary was a symbol of fidelity. The wine of Tiberius included rosemary in its preparation; it was recommended for various insect bites. Rosemary was used to perfume the baths of ladies in Turkey, Greece, and France. Shakespeare's Hamlet, Act IV, scene 5 refers to the spice in the passage, when Ophelia says to Laertes: "There's rosemary, that's for remembrance, pray love, remember."

Source

Rosemary is a small evergreen shrub indigenous to most European countries bordering on the Mediterranean Sea. It is cultivated in Algeria, France, Germany, Italy, Morocco, Portugal, Romania, Russia, Spain, Tunisia, Turkey, Yugoslavia, and in the United States.

Physical Description and Sensory Characteristics

The densely branched evergreen shrub, under the right conditions may grow as high as 2 m (6½ ft) but it is usually much shorter. It bears linear, leathery, dark-green leaves and light, sky-blue flowers. The entire plant, excluding the woody portions, may be used but normally only the leaves are considered suitable for spices. When dried, the leaves become rolled in appearance, dark-green to brownish-green in color and have a tealike fragrance. Their ap-

Fig. 3.69
Dried rosemary leaves. Note needlelike structure.

pearance has been likened to pine needles. When crushed, rosemary has an agreeable, fragrant, aromatic, eucalyptuslike aroma with a cooling, camphoraceous scent. The taste is somewhat peppery, spicy, astringent, warming, and herbaceous with a slightly bitter and camphoraceous after taste.

Extractives

Rosemary leaves yield up to 2% of an almost colorless, volatile oil with a camphoraceous characteristic odor. Chemically the constituents of the oil are 16–20% borneol, 27–30% cineole, 10% camphor, 2–7% bornyl acetate and small percentages of α-pinene, camphene, terpinol, and verbenone.

The borneol is responsible for the pungent, camphoraceous odor and burning taste; the cineole gives it a fresh, cooling eucalyptuslike aroma; the α-pinene is responsible for its warm, piney notes; the camphor contributes a cooling, penetrating, minty note; and the bornyl acetate accents the fresh, sweet piney notes while adding balsamic and herbaceous characteristics.

The oleoresin is a greenish-brown, semisolid containing 10–15 ml of volatile oil per 100 g. Generally, 2.5 kg (5½ lb) of oleoresin are equivalent to 45.45 kg (100 lb) of crushed and dried rosemary leaves.

Federal Specifications

Rosemary shall be the dried, clean, whole leaves of *Rosmarinus officinalis* L. The shiny, dark-green to brownish-green colored, rolled margined leaves shall have the shape and appearance of pine needles. Rosemary has a tealike fragrance; when crushed, the leaves have a slight camphoraceous odor; they have a somewhat bitter and slight camphoraceous taste. The product shall contain no more than 7.0% total ash, 0.5% acid insoluble ash, 7.0% moisture and not less than 1.1 ml of volatile oil per 100 g. 95% of the ground product must pass through a U.S. Standard No. 35 sieve.

Approximate Composition of Dried Rosemary Leaves, 100 g, Edible Portion

Water	9.3 g	Magnesium	220 mg
Food energy	331 kcal	Phosphorous	70 mg
Protein	4.9 g	Potassium	955 mg
Fat	15.2 g	Sodium	50 mg
Total carbohydrate	64.1 g	Zinc	3 mg
Fiber	17.7 g	Ascorbic acid	61 mg
Ash	6.5 g	Niacin	1 mg
Calcium	1280 mg	Vitamin A	3128 IU
Iron	29 mg	Other vitamins	insignificant

Household Uses

If used sparingly and with caution, rosemary enhances almost any food in which it is used. It is one of the most fragrant and pleasing of spices. It may be used with most any vegetable, particularly peas, green beans, asparagus, broccoli, cauliflower, potatoes, eggplant, summer squash, zucchini, spinach, and turnip. It adds a desirable flavor to scallops, tuna fish, fish chowder, chicken, scrambled or shirred eggs, omelets, stuffings for fish and poultry, savory breads, chicken, pea and potato soups, mushrooms, barbecued meats, salad croutons, fried chicken, chicken fricassee, meat stews, lamb and pork dishes.

Commercial Uses

Dried rosemary leaves, or one of its extractives, is used to season fried chicken, salad croutons, baked products, confections, non-alcoholic beverages, condiments, cheap perfumes, eau de colognes, and soaps.

Fig. 3.70
Saffron. Crocus plant showing a typical pistil, less the ovary, with the style branched into three tubular stigmas.

Saffron
Crocus sativus L.
Family Iridaceae

Historical/Legendary Background _____

In all probability saffron was first used by early civilizations as a dye because of its intense coloring feature. The Greeks and Romans, who called it *krokus,* used its fine quality scent as a perfume for their luxurious baths. According to the Song of Solomon, fourth chapter, thirteenth and fourteenth verses, saffron was among the most proclaimed spices:

Thy plants are an orchard of pomegranates, with pleasant fruits; cam-
phire, with spikenard, Spikenard and saffron; calamus and cinnamon,
with all trees of frankincense; myrrh and aloes, with all the chief
spices.

Oils scented with saffron, cassia, and cinnamon were used in the
days of the Egyptian Pharaohs to annoint their kings.

One of the later herbalists, John Gerard, quoting from earlier
works states: "For those at death's door and almost past breathing,
saffron will bringeth forth breath again." Near the end of the eighth
century, when the Moors conquered Spain, they brought with them
the yellow spice *zafran* to the Spanish people and for the past 1200
years it has been an essential component of their wonderful national, dishes. King Henry the VIII forbade the Irish to dye their
linen with saffron because the Irish believed it had a sanitizing
quality and they would not wash their linen as frequently as they
should.

Saffron is considered to be the most expensive spice on earth. In
1984, its wholesale market value was $600 per kilogram. Each
blossom of the crocus plant contains one pistil, consisting of three
stigma, a style, and an ovary. The stigmas and style make up the
saffron spice and contain most, if not all of the coloring matter. It
has been estimated that nearly 500,000 stigmas and styles would be
required to make 1 kg of spice.

Source _____

Saffron is indigenous to the countries of Asia Minor, Greece, and
Iran. It has been under cultivation for over 4000 years in such countries as Sicily, Kashmir, China, Greece, Italy, France, Great Britain, Persia (Iran), Portugal, and Spain. One hectare (2.5 acres)
yields only 6 kg (13 lb) of dried saffron.

Physical Description and Sensory Characteristics ____

The spice consists of the dried stigmas and style of the crocus bulb.
The plant seldom grows higher than 30 cm (12 in.), has bulbous
roots, with smaller fibrous roots, an erect, thin stem with purple

flowers each containing three stigmas. There are three varieties: a light yellow-orange saffron that is light in flavor; an orange saffron that is stronger in flavor; and the reddish-orange saffron that is the highest in flavor. The latter is grown only in Iran. In the Near East and in southern Europe, saffron is particularly well liked for its flavor as well as for its coloring properties; it is less expensive there and as a result is used more often than in the United States where its exorbitant cost prohibits its wide use. Although saffron is better known for its intense, yellowish coloring characteristics, it does have a very pleasant, sweet, spicy, delicate floral odor with a somewhat earthy, bitter, fatty, herbaceous flavor. The taste of saffron needs to be acquired as its initial reaction is one of bitterness, but once the taste has been acquired it becomes pleasurable.

So-called Mexican saffron bears no relationship to the genuine saffron, either in color, aroma or flavor.

Extractives

Saffron contains up to 1% volatile oil with an intense, spicy, rumlike odor. The oil contains 2, 2, 6-trimethyl-4, 6-cyclohexadienal and the glucocides: crocin and picrocrocin, which contribute to the characteristic color and bitterness of saffron. The flavor of the oil is reminiscent of weak iodine and is unpleasantly aromatic. The perfume industry has limited uses for such an oil because of its exorbitant cost. The coloring matter is crocin which yields on hydrolysis, crocetin, and d-glucose.

Approximate Analysis of Saffron, 100 g, Edible Portion

Water	11.9 g	Calcium	111 mg
Food energy	310 kcal	Iron	11 mg
Protein	11.4 g	Phosphorous	252 mg
Fat	5.9 g	Potassium	1724 mg
Total carbohydrate	65.4 g	Sodium	148 mg
Fiber	3.9 g	Zinc and Magnesium	insignificant
Ash	5.4 g	Vitamins	insignificant

Household Uses

Just a few strands of saffron are sufficient to color and flavor several servings of paella or rice. The famous Spanish dishes of *Arroz con Pollo* (chicken and rice) and *Bacalao Vizcaino* (codfish a la Biscay) depend on saffron for their color and unusual flavor. It is still used in parts of Scandanavia to color cakes, rolls, and pastries, as well as the usual chicken and fish casseroles. It may be used with lamb or veal casseroles, soups, sauces, and cheeses.

Because of its extremely high price, turmeric or a suitable U.S. Certified dye or food color is being substituted in the making of fancy baked goods, confections, paellas, chicken pot pies, and other similar products here in the United States.

Commercial Uses

Although saffron has been reportedly used in nonalcoholic beverages, baked goods, ice creams, confections, condiments, and meats, it is questionable whether such a practise exists very widely today because of the unfavorable economics associated with the spice. It may be used in the manufacture of exotic perfumes.

Fig. 3.71
Sage. Stem of sage plant showing leaves used for spice.

Sage
Salvia officinalis L.
Family Labiatae

Historical/Legendary Background _____

In French, the term sage means wise. The term sage advice probably originated in England where sage tea or some other brew made from sage was consumed regularly with the belief that it made one prudent and strengthened the memory. Many healing properties have been ascribed to this lowly herb by the ancient physicians. Until only a few centuries ago it was nearly always at the top of the list of household remedies for the relief of itching, the lowering of fevers and the relief of nervous headaches. Its botannical name salvia, means to save or heal. According to legend, sage grows according to the wealth of the family who owns the land and it only prospers where the wife rules. The Dutch used to acquire sage from France and ship it to China and receive four pounds of tea for each pound of sage in return.

Source

Sage is indigenous to the northeastern shores of the Mediterranean region, primarily Albania and Greece. It is cultivated in Albania, Cyprus, the Dalmatian Islands off the coast of Yugoslavia and adjacent areas of the Adriatic Sea, southern France, Great Britain, Italy, Portugal, Spain, Turkey, Yugoslavia, Canada, and the United States. The finest quality sage comes from the Dalmatian Islands followed closely by that from Albania. The chemical and sensory properties of sage vary considerably from one source of supply to another.

Physical Description and Sensory Characteristics

The slightly woody, white, wooly stems, about 30 cm (1 ft) long bear oblong leaves and numerous purple flowers; some are bluish or white, in whorls. The plant is a bitter, aromatic, perennial, semishrub of the mint family. The dried, whole, rubbed or ground, leaves are very aromatic, herbaceous and spicy with a unique balsamic, bitter taste, fragrant, warm, and astringent. The leaves are grayish-green to silvery-green in color and shiny, covered with short fine hairs; they are oblong in shape.

Fig. 3.72
Sage, dried leaves.

Extractives

The essential oil, to which the plant owes most of its flavor and character, is produced by steam distillation of the freshly harvested leaves. The yield is about 2.5%, though it could be much less depending on the climatic conditions of the growing and harvesting seasons and the country of origin. Its color is pale yellow to almost colorless. Its odor is strongly aromatic, sickly sweet, initially cooling then warming, spicy, herbaceous, camphoraceous, and very persistent with a burning flavor that is overpoweringly herbaceous, eucalyptuslike, sickly sweet with a lingering, bitter, sweet note. Chemically, the oil contains 40 to 60% thujone, 15% cineol, up to 16% borneol, up to 4% bornyl esters, α-pinene, salvene and d-camphor. The oil from Greek sage has a harsher, more eucalyptuslike aroma while English sage has an odor with more camphoraceous characteristics. Spanish sage has an odor that is somewhere in between the odor of the English and Greek sages.

The oleoresin of sage is usually prepared from the Dalmatian type of sage, *Salvia officinalis* L. The oleoresin has a warm, spicy taste, a very important attribute for sausage seasonings. The oleoresin is brownish-green and has a very heavy liquid consistency. It contains a minimum volatile oil content of 25 to 30 ml per 100 g. Of the oleoresin, 3.4 kg (7½ lb) is equivalent to 45.45 kg (100 lb) of freshly ground sage in aroma and flavor characteristics.

Federal Specifications

Sage shall be the dried leaves of *Salvia officinalis* L. The green to gray-green, oblong, lanceolate leaves, covered with fine, short hairs shall possess a strong, fragrant and aromatic odor, free of any camphoraceous note and free of objectionable terebinthic odor. It shall contain a maximum of 10%, by weight, of stems, excluding pedioles. The sage shall contain not more than 10.0% total ash, 1.0% acid insoluble ash, and 8.0% moisture. It shall contain not less than 1.0 ml of volatile oil per 100 g and not less than 95% of the ground sage shall pass through a U.S. Standard No. 20 sieve. For rubbed sage, 95% shall be retained on a U.S. Standard No. 40 sieve and at least 95% shall pass through a U.S. Standard No. 20 sieve.

Approximate Composition of Ground Sage, 100 g, Edible Portion

Water	8.0 g	Magnesium	428 mg
Food energy	315 kcal	Phosphorous	91 mg
Protein	10.6 g	Potassium	1070 mg
Fat	12.7 g	Sodium	11 mg
Total carbohydrate	60.7 g	Zinc	5 mg
Fiber	18.1 g	Ascorbic acid	32 mg
Ash	8.0 g	Niacin	6 mg
Calcium	1652 mg	Vitamin A	5900 IU
Iron	28 mg	Other vitamins	insignificant

Household Uses

Sage has a particular affinity for poultry stuffings and pork sausage dishes of every description; roasts, gravies, casseroles, or soups. It is also good with baked fish, liver sausage, cheese dishes, Spanish omelets, pasta, hamburgers, and in breads for making chicken or pork sandwiches. Its delightful aroma adds zest to tomatoes, eggplant, lima beans, onions, and other vegetables. One sage leaf or small pinch of rubbed sage is sufficient for one portion of meat, fish, or omelet.

Commercial Uses

Sage is used in seasonings for pork sausage products, fried chicken, meat loaf, meat balls, hamburger mixes, condiments, pickles, condiments, confections, chewing gums, nonalcoholic beverages, and a few specialty baked goods.

Fig. 3.73
Savory, sweet summer. Flowering shrublike plant.

Savory, Sweet Summer
Satureja hortensis L.
Family Labiatae

Historical/Legendary Background _____

Banckes's *Herbal* states: "It is forbidden to use it much in meats since it stirreth him to use lechery." Cresentius recommended it "as a purgative, as a remedy in complaints of the liver and lungs and as a bleach for a tanned complexion." It was included in medieval dishes 2000 years ago for its pleasant, appetizing, sharp, peppery flavor. It was claimed by Matthioli that savory stimulated the appetite, promoted digestion and caused liveliness of the body. Romans introduced the herb to England about 1000 years ago, where it was thereafter grown abundantly in all the individual herb gardens of the countryside. The Germans were known to have called savory the bean herb because it complemented green beans, dried beans and lentils so well.

Source

There are two main types of sweet savory: summer savory, an annual plant cultivated throughout France and the Mediterranean region, and winter savory (*Satureja montana* L.), a small hardy shrub which grows wild in southern Europe. Summer savory is now cultivated in France, Canada, Germany, Great Britain, Spain, and the United States.

Fig. 3.74
Savory, sweet summer, dried leaves and tops of stems.

Physical Description and Sensory Attributes _____

Summer savory is an annual, low growing plant about 20 to 30 cm (8–12 in.) in height which grows wild or may be cultivated. It has a well-developed tap root, an erect stalk, aromatic, narrow, opposite leaves dotted with glands and white flowers sprinkled with crimson dots. The flowering tops are used for oil extraction while the bright green leaves are used as the spice. The aroma is fragrant and spicy, herbaceous, and somewhat like disinfectant. The taste is spicy and peppery. It makes a good substitute for pepper.

Extractives _____

Savory contains a yellow to dark-brown volatile oil that has a spicy, aromatic odor resembling thymol or oregano. Its chief constituent is carvacrol, amounting to 30–45%. The other minor flavoring elements are α-pinene, 7–8%, *p*-cymene 30%, dipentene, thymol, borneol, *l*-linalool, terpineol, and *l*-carvone.

Federal Specifications _____

Savory shall be the whole or ground, dried leaves, and flowering tops of *Satureja hortensis*, L. The pale, brownish-green leaves shall have a fragrant, aromatic odor and a warm, slightly sharp taste. It shall contain no more than 10.0% total ash, 2.0% acid insoluble ash, and 10.0% moisture. It shall contain not less than 25 ml of volatile oil per 100 g and 95% of the ground product shall pass through a U.S. Standard No. 40 sieve.

Approximate Compositions of Sweet Summer Savory, 100 g, Edible Portion _____

Water	9.0 g	Iron	38 mg
Food energy	272 kcal	Magnesium	377 mg
Protein	6.7 g	Phosphorous	140 mg
Fat	5.9 g	Potassium	1051 mg
Total carbohydrate:	68.7 g	Sodium	24 mg
Fiber	15.3 g	Zinc	4 mg
Ash	9.6 g	Niacin	4 mg
Calcium	2132 mg	Vitamin A	5130 IU

Household Uses _____

Summer savory is one of the spices included in *fines herbes*. It is excellent with scrambled eggs, devilled eggs, and other egg dishes, chilled vegetable juices, salads, and dishes containing predominantly beans, lentils, or peas. The nuances of summer savory enhance the palatability of poultry dishes, hamburgers, pork and veal chops, boiled and baked fish dishes, fish chowders, most sausage products, soups, particularly pea and bean varieties, and many sauces. Summer savory should be added just before the end of the cooking cycle. Five milliliters (1 tsp) sufficient for four servings of a casserole. Summer savory blends well with cabbage, tomato soup, and sauces.

Commercial Uses _____

The spice, or the oil of summer savory is used in the manufacture of liqueurs, bitters and vermouths, some baked goods, condiments and, in very small proportions, in confections. It is used in commercial dry soup mixes and gravy mixes. It is seldom used in seasonings for prepared meat items.

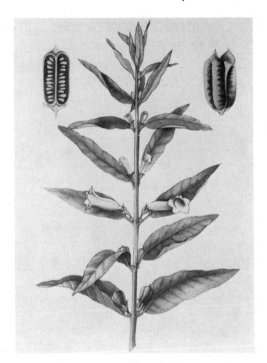

Fig. 3.75
Sesame. Flowering stem of sesame plant.

Sesame Seed
Sesamum indicum L.
Family Pedaliaceae

Historical/Legendary Background _____

Sesame is one of the world's oldest spice and oil seed crops. It has been said the Gods of the ancient Assyrians refreshed themselves with sesame seed wine before they began the horrendous task of creating the world. A 4000 year old drawing on an Egyptian tomb illustrates a baker adding sesame seeds to the dough. According to Brahma Purana, sesame was created by Yama, God of Death, after a long penitence; it was used in funeral and other ceremonies as a purifier and symbol of immortality. Sesame seeds were perhaps the first combat rations. They were used by Greek soldiers in the days of Cleopatra. Though little was known in those days of nutrition, especially good nutritional habits, they learned that the consumption of sesame seeds gave them much energy-giving strength to carry on their arduous tasks. African natives practically lived on them; they called them benne seeds. At the time of the slave trade, the Africans brought these seeds with them to Florida and Georgia where they introduced them for the first time. One can still find benne seed cookies and confections in the small shops of Savannah's waterfront. It was only in the latter part of this century that the baking industry brought them out of their humble state and began using them in bread, rolls, and cookies. American liked their nutty flavor and nutritionists extolled the nutritional benefits of high protein and fat and the prolonged shelf life of their marvelous oil. "Sesame" was the secret word in the story Ali Baba and the Forty Thieves.

Source

The sesame plant is indigenous to the Sunda Islands in Indonesia where it has been under cultivation for over 4000 years. From there, it was introduced into China, Japan, India, and Egypt. Subsequently other warm countries like Turkey, Lebanon, Greece, Ethiopia, Kenya, Sierra Leone, Tanganyika, Nicaragua, El Salvadore, Guatamala, Mexico, and the southern United States began cultivating this plant.

Physical Description and Sensory Characteristics

Sesame seed plant is an annual herb with branched stem which grows to a height of 0.6–1.2 m (2–4 ft), somewhat pubescent with opposite lower leaves and alternate upper leaves. Its 3 cm (1 in.) flowers are pale pink to white in color and the fruit are four-sided,

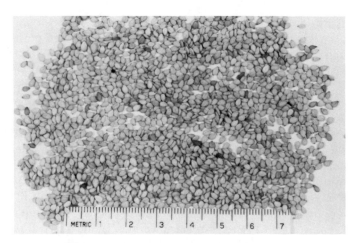

Fig. 3.76
Sesame seeds.

oblong shaped pods, containing small, creamy-white seeds, varying in size up to 3.5 mm (⅛ in.) in length and shaped like a compressed oval. The aroma is faintly nutty, as is the flavor, but these attributes are accentuated after the seeds are baked or toasted, at which time they take on a delicate, almondlike flavor and aroma. They are usually decorticated for the commercial trade.

Extractives

The bland odorless, pale yellow oil expressed from the seed, sometimes referred to as till oil is used extensively in foods. The fixed oil content of the seed ranges from 45 to 65%. It resists oxidative rancidity and contains 75% olein, stearin, palmitin, myristin, linolan, and sesamin. Sesame seed contains no perceptible volatile oil.

Federal Specifications

At the present time the specifications require that the whole sesame seed shall be the clean, dried seed of *Sesamum indicum* L. The slightly hard, flat, oval, small, smooth and shiny, dehulled, creamy-white seeds shall have a nutlike odor and an agreeable nutty taste. There are no analytical requirements specified.

Approximate Composition of Decorticated Sesame Seed, 100 g

Water	9.0 g	Magnesium	347 mg
Food energy	272 kcal	Phosphorous	776 mg
Protein	6.7 g	Potassium	407 mg
Fat	5.9 g	Sodium	40 mg
Total carbohydrates	68.7 g	Zinc	10 mg
Fiber	15.3 g	Niacin	5 mg
Ash	4.6 g	Vitamin A	66 IU
Calcium	131 mg	Other vitamins	insignificant

Household Uses

Sesame seed may be purchased either plain, decorticated, untoasted, or toasted. The decorticated may be used in quick breads, rolls, coffee cakes, cookies, or pies that are going to be baked, or on any food that will brown during the cooking. If they are to be used in salads, salad dressings, or confections, they should be lightly toasted to bring out the flavor. Toasted sesame seed and butter or margarine makes a tasty spread for bread. Sesame oil has excellent stability and makes an excellent frying medium for chicken and meats. It is a good replacement for peanut oil in fondue cooking.

Commercial Uses

Sesame seed is used by commercial bakeries for bread and rolls, crackers, and some cake products. It is also used by confectioners, salad dressing manufacturers, as well as salad oil and shortening suppliers. The flowers are pressed for perfume and toilet waters.

Fig. 3.77
Tarragon. Flowering stem with linear leaves.

Tarragon (Estragon)
Artemisia dracunculus L.
Family Compositeae

Historical/Legendary Background _____

Before the thirteenth century, not much has been recorded about
the origin of tarragon. Ibn Baithar, a famous Arabian botanist and

physician who lived in the thirteenth century, was the first to extol the virtues of this spice, claiming it was useful for sweetening the breath, for making bitter medicine more palatable and for curing insomnia. He called it *tarkhum*, the Arabic word for dragon. He also prescribed it for use as an antiseptic in times of pestilence. Later, the French began cultivating it for use as a salad green, a garnish for vegetables, and as a flavoring agent in their vinegar. They called it *estragon*.

Source

Tarragon is believed to be indigenous to southeastern Russia but is now widely cultivated throughout southern Europe and western Asia. Russia and France grow this spice for export though the Russian variety has an undesirable, harsh flavor, much coarser than the French variety, and should be avoided. The United States grows sufficient quantities for its own needs.

Physical Characteristics and Sensory Attributes

Tarragon is a vigorous, densely branched, perennial shrub, closely allied to the sage brush or mugwort cultivated for its flowering tops and light to dark-green leaves which are linear, lanceolate, and smooth. Tarragon is used primarily in the flavoring of vinegar, mustard, and pickles. It is propagated by root cuttings or division and grows to a height of approximately 100 cm (40 in.). The aroma is similar to that of anise or licorice and the taste is similarly flavored with sharp, aromatic undertones.

Extractives

The volatile oil content of tarragon ranges from 1 to 2% with its chief constituent being methyl chavicol. Other minor constituents

Fig. 3.78
Tarragon, broken leaves, dried.

are anethole—about 10%, pinenem phellandrene, ocimene and *p*-methoxycin namaldehyde. The yellowish-green liquid has an aroma similar to that of anise.

The oleoresin of tarragon is a dark green, viscous liquid prepared only from the French variety. It has a volatile oil content of 12–15 ml per 100 g. Generally, 1.13 kg (2½ lb) of the oleoresin is equivalent to 45.45 kg (100 lb) of ground, dried tarragon leaves in flavor and aroma characteristics.

Federal Specifications _____

Tarragon shall be the dried leaves of a perennial herb, *Artemesia dracunculcus* L. The light to dark green leaves shall have a pleasant, aromatic, licorice–aniselike odor and possess a bittersweet and herbaceous taste. The product shall contain not more than 15% total ash, 1.5% acid insoluble ash, 10.0% moisture, and not less than 1.3 ml of volatile oil per 100 g. 100% shall pass through a U.S. Standard No. 40 sieve.

Approximate Composition of Ground Tarragon, 100 g, Edible Portion

Water	7.7 g	Magnesium	347 mg
Food energy	295 kcal	Phosphorous	313 mg
Protein	22.8 g	Potassium	3020 mg
Fat	7.2 g	Sodium	62 mg
Total carbohydrate	50.2 g	Zinc	4 mg
Fiber	7.4 g	Niacin	9 mg
Ash	12.0 g	Riboflavin	1 mg
Calcium	1139 mg	Vitamin A	4200 IU
Iron	32 mg	Other vitamins	insignificant

Household Uses

Tarragon is the special ingredient in the world-famous Dijon mustard from France. Tarragon vinegar is said to be the choice vinegar among connoisseurs. It may be made at home by adding one or two sprigs of the fresh spice to a quart of wine vinegar and allowing the flavors to meld for 20 to 30 days. Tarragon is essential in the making of Béarnaise sauce, used with eggs and asparagus. Tarragon is excellent in leafy green salads, in pea, chicken, mushroom, tomato, and vegetable soups. The spice adds an interesting flavor to beets, asparagus, carrots, celery, green beans, onions, peas, summer squash, and zucchini. Tarragon complements poultry, veal, egg, cheese, stuffed shellfish, baked fish, and a host of other meat dishes. French and Armenian dishes favor the use of tarragon.

Commercial Uses _____

The oil of tarragon is widely used in perfumes and colognes, alcoholic and nonalcoholic beverages, confections, baked goods, vinegars, mustard and other condiments, salad dressings (sauces), soup mixes, and a few specialty baked goods. It is used occasionally in a few prepared meat seasonings.

Fig. 3.79
Thyme. Densely branched stem of thyme plant.

Thyme
Thymus vulgaris L.
Family Labiatae

Historical/Legendary Background _____

According to Dioscorides, thyme eaten with meat helps poor eyesight. He prescribed a mixture with honey for driving out the phlegmy matter from the thorax, for asthma, for expelling worms, for killing lice, and other curious maladies. Ancient Greeks considered thyme symbolic of courage. They relished the honey obtained from thyme blossoms which grew abundantly around Athens. To smell of thyme was the ultimate Greek compliment. Thyme was among the many herbs used in incantations and charms. Bees cannot resist its fragrance. The Egyptians used thyme for embalming their dead.

Source

Thyme is native to southern Europe and is widely cultivated in Bulgaria, France, Germany, Great Britain, Greece, Italy, Morocco, Portugal, Turkey, Russia, Spain, Tunisia, Canada, and the United States.

Physical Description and Sensory Characteristics

Thyme is a small, creeping, shrublike perennial with a pungent mintlike odor. It grows no taller than 50 cm (20 in.) in height. It has slender, densely branched, whitish branches, bearing narrow sessile leaves and dense clusters of purple flowers. The leaves and flowering tops are used as a spice but the entire plant, excluding the roots are used for the extraction of oil. The odor is warm, herbaceous, and reminiscent of sage; it has a slight, biting, spicy, rich taste with a lingering sharpness.

Extractives

The volatile oil of thyme is a pale, yellowish-red liquid with a rich, sweet, aromatic, warming, herbaceous odor yielding a sweet, phenolic, somewhat medicinal perception upon drying out. The taste is sharp, biting, warm, spicy, full bodied, and herbaceous. The chief constituent of the oil is thymol. Other components are carvacrol, *l*-linalool, *l*-borneol, geraniol, amyl alcohol, β-pinene, *p*-cymene, caryophyllene, terpineol and camphene. Thymol definitely characterizes *Thymus vulgaris* L. as opposed to other species that are not as favorably accepted in the trade.

The oleoresin of thyme is a dark green to brown, somewhat viscous, at times almost a semisolid, with a minimum volatile oil content of 50 ml per 100 g. Generally 1.81 kg (4 lb) of oleoresin is equivalent to 45.45 kg (100 lb) of freshly ground, dried thyme in flavor and aroma attributes.

Federal Specifications

The spice shall be the dried leaves and flowering tops of *Thymus vulgaris* L. The dried, brownish-green, curled leaves, when crushed, shall yield a fragrant, aromatic odor and have a warm, pungent taste. It shall contain not more than 11.0% total ash, 5.0% acid insoluble ash and 9.0% moisture, and no less than 0.9 ml of volatile oil (vol/wt) per 100 g. Not less than 95% shall pass through a U.S. Standard No. 30 sieve.

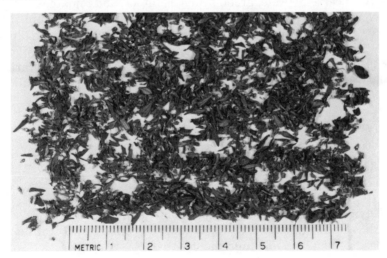

Fig. 3.80
Thyme, dried whole leaves.

Approximate Composition of Ground Thyme, 100 g, Edible Portion

Water	7.8 g	Magnesium	220 mg
Food energy	276 kcal	Phosphorous	201 mg
Protein	9.1 g	Potassium	814 mg
Fat	7.4 g	Sodium	55 mg
Total carbohydrate	63.9 g	Zinc	6 mg
Fiber	18.6 g	Niacin	5 mg
Ash	11.7 g	Vitamin A	3800 IU
Calcium	1890 mg	Other vitamins	insignificant
Iron	124 mg		

Household Uses

The creole cuisine of New Orleans depends on the use of thyme. Thyme and bay leaf are usually used together in French cuisine. Parsley, thyme, and bay leaf make up the French *bouquet garni*. Thyme is used in Burgundy sauce, turtle soup, meat loaf, and sparingly on carrots, beets, green beans, potatoes, and tomatoes. Thyme is very potent and should be used sparingly. Thyme is complementary to lobster, shrimp, clam and fish chowders, oyster stew, almost any shellfish dish, and in sauces for chicken, goose, or turkey stews or stuffings. It is desirable with creamed onions, beets, carrots, mushrooms, marinated beef, pork, lamb and veal roasts, fish fillets, ragouts, or pickles.

Commercial Uses

Thyme is used to season salad croutons, fried chicken, prepared poultry stuffings or dressings, and processed liver containing spreads. Its active oil ingredient—thymol—is an effective ingredient in cough drops, dentifrices, colognes, soaps, nonalcoholic beverages, baked goods, and canned soups. Benedictine liqueur is flavored with the extract of thyme. Thyme, or one of its extractives, is used in a few seasonings for prepared meats.

Fig. 3.81
Turmeric. The entire turmeric plant showing its rhizomes and thickened roots. The dried rhizomes, after cleaning and washing, are ground to make the spice.

Turmeric
Curcuma longa L.
Family Zingiberaceae

Historical/Legendary Background _____

Turmeric was used in ancient times as a culinary spice, a dye, a medicine, a ceremonial color, and as a magical symbol. It was used by the wearer to protect him against evil. It was called Indian Saffron by Europeans in medieval times. Hindu brides were painted with turmeric dye, and in many parts of India it was used as a general cosmetic.

Source

Wherever ginger grows, so does turmeric. It is cultivated in the East Indies, South Vietnam, China, India, Sri Lanka, Taiwan, and the West Indies. Originally the plant came from southern Asia and is now widespread throughout Japan, Malaysia, and Sri Lanka. It is also grown in Peru, Haiti, and Jamaica.

Physical Description and Sensory Attributes

Turmeric is an herbaceous, tropical plant with a perennial rootstock, or rhizome, related to the ginger family. The plant has climbing stalks reaching a height of 60–100 cm (24–40 in.) with leaves that are bright green, acute at both ends and somewhat broad. The flowers are pale yellow arising from two buds located in the axils or bracts. Reproduction occurs through the splitting of the rhizomes. The rhizomes have a characteristic, peppery, spicy aroma and a bitter, pungent taste. When used in conjunction with pepper, the pepper flavor is accentuated.

Turmeric is classified into Alleppey and Madras varieties. When the dried rhizomes are ground, Alleppey has an orange-yellow color while the Madras has a lemon-yellow color. Either one may be used in almost any curried dish, chow chow pickles, or mustard preparation. The coloring matter present is curcumin, *bis* (4-hydroxy-3-methoxy cinnamoyl) methane. Turmeric color is pH sensitive and its brightest yellow color exists in an acid medium.

Extractives

Turmeric yields about 5% essential oil which consists of turmerone, free acids, borneol, cineol, phellandrene, curcumin, and zingerone. It is orange-yellow in color and highly aromatic. It is usually a by-product of the decolorizing process in the manufacture of oleoresins. Its odor is earthy, spicy, warm, irritating, orientallike, and heavy, while its flavor is bitter, pungent, aromatic, spicy, metallic, and earthy.

The oleoresin of turmeric is a reddish-brown, heavy bodied liquid with a color value of 14 ± 1.0%. Oleoresins from different suppliers may be much higher or lower and even calculated differently. To determine the color value of oleoresin of turmeric see Chapter 6, section on Analytical Methods.

Generally, 3.86 kg (8½ lb) of oleoresin of turmeric are equivalent to 45.45 kg (100 lb) of freshly ground turmeric in color enhancing value and other sensory attributes.

Federal Specifications

Turmeric shall be the clean, sound, dried rhizome or bulbous root of *Curcuma longa* L. (A) Alleppey turmeric shall have the characteristics of the type grown in Alleppey regions. (B) Jamaica turmeric shall have the characteristics grown in the Jamaica regions. Ninety five percent of the ground product shall pass through a U.S. Standard No. 40 sieve. It shall contain not more than 7.0% total ash, 0.5% acid insoluble ash, 9.5% crude fiber, and 9.0% moisture. It shall contain not less than 3.5 ml of volatile oil per 100 g. The percent curcumin shall be between 5.0 and 6.6 (ASTA Method No. 18).

Approximate Composition of Turmeric, 100 g, Edible Portion

Water	11.4 g	Magnesium	193 mg
Food energy	1480 kcal	Phosphorous	268 mg
Protein	7.8 g	Potassium	2525 mg
Fat	9.9 g	Sodium	38 mg
Total carbohydrate	64.9 g	Zinc	4 mg
Fiber	6.7 g	Ascorbic acid	26 mg
Ash	6.0 g	Niacin	5 mg
Calcium	182 mg	Other vitamins	insignificant
Iron	41 mg		

Household Uses

Turmeric is used primarily for coloring poultry, egg, and meat dishes during the cooking process; it is also used in shellfish, pilafs, curried meat and poultry dishes, deviled eggs, potato and chicken salads, pickles, curry powders, salad dressings, and sandwich spreads.

Commercial Uses

Turmeric, or its oleoresin, has been used to color pickled products, soups, mustards, pudding mixes, condiments, and a few prepared seasonings for meat items.

4

4

Spice Blends

Chili Powder Blend

Physical Description and Sensory Characteristics ___

Chili powder is a blend of spices, predominantly ground chili pepper, cumin, oregano, and garlic powder. Other spices may be added to suit a particular local demand. The odor is warm, spicy, aromatic, hearty, persistent, and intense and the flavor is similar. The blend should be uniform in particle size and color, usually a dark reddish-brown.

A good, standard composition for a chili powder blend is as follows:

Spice	Percent by weight
Ground chili pepper	85
Ground cumin	8
Ground oregano	4
Garlic powder	1
Anti-caking agent	2
Antioxidant (Tenox 4 or 6)	100 ppm

Military Specifications ___

Chili powder seasoning specifications include the above formula and further require that the product shall possess a reddish-brown color with minimum extractable color of not less than 70 ASTA units (ASTA Method 19). The total ash content shall not exceed 13.0% by weight. The pungency shall be not less than 900 and not

225

Fig. 4.1
Chili peppers used in chili powder blend.

more than 2000 Scoville units (ASTA Method 20). The blended chili powder seasoning shall be free from lumps and not less than 95% shall pass through a U.S. Standard No. 20 sieve. (Mil. Spec. C-3394-C, 28 June 1968).

Approximate Composition of Chili Powder Blend, 100 g, Edible Portion

Water	7.8 g	Fiber	22.2 g
Food energy	314 kcal	Ash	8.5 g
Protein	12.3 g	Calcium	278 mg
Fat	16.8 g	Iron	14 mg
Total carbohydrate	54.7 g	Magnesium	170 mg

Phosphorous	303 mg	Ascorbic acid	64 mg
Potassium	1916 mg	Niacin	8 mg
Sodium	1010 mg	Vitamin A	34,927 IU
Zinc	3 mg	Other vitamins	insignificant

Household Uses

Chili powder blend is used in making the popular southwestern dish, chili con carne. It is also used in pickles, shellfish cocktail sauces, gravies, stew seasoning, Mexican dishes, hamburger sauces, and with frankfurters where a variation in flavor is desired. Some culinary experts have used it with egg dishes for a southwestern flair.

Commercial Uses

Chili powder blend is used commercially in processed chili con carne, pickles, and seafood cocktail sauces.

Curry Powder Blend

Historical/Legendary Background _____

The word curry is an English corruption of the shortened Indian word *turri* for the Hindustani word *turcurri*. In the Tamil dialect, curry means cookery but the term has become generic for sauces, which vary in composition from province to province. To an Indian family, curry is not a powdered blend of herbs and spices to be taken from a jar or other vessel for use on any type food but a special blend of selected spices, skillfully put together for a single dish. Each dish deserves its own particular creative blend of spices. Usually, several different curries are prepared for use at the same meal. In America curry powder blend is shaken out of a can or jar into a white sauce for chicken, meat, or seafood. The usual American curry powder is limited to about eight spices and in much different proportions than the Indian blend in order to make it blander for the less discriminating palate of Americans.

As early as the third century, the Greeks described curries as Indian food. The better Indian curries are skillfully blended mixtures of from nine to twenty five herbs and spices, fried together in a very hot clarified butter to bring out each of the individual rich bouquets and flavors. Milder flavored curries are preferred in the northern provinces of India while the southern provinces favor hotter, more pungent curries. The latter use higher percentages of chili peppers, ginger, black and white pepper, and mustard. The heat value of the hot chillies may be reduced by removing the seeds. When cumin, fenugreek, cardamom, and citrus peel are used in the curry blend they contribute a tanginess or sour taste, whereas coconut meat and milk, coriander, allspice, cloves, and sometimes sugar are added to give sweetness to the curry. It is the skillful blending of the proper spices that result in the highly exotic, taste sensations of curries.

The Hindus have promoted the use of curries for fifteen centuries or more since the high priests forbid the consumption of meat. It was forbidden because meat decomposed very rapidly in the extremely hot, humid climate of India and was usually unfit to eat. Today, however, with refrigeration facilities available to some of the population, and the gradual acceptance of some modern western customs, the Hindus are beginning to overlook the ancient restrictions and are consuming beef and lamb, but not pork, with their curries.

With the availability of so many native herbs and spices in the various provinces of India for centuries, it is little wonder that the culinary experts of the past experimented with different combinations of these aromatic and flavorful substances to make their limited vegetarian diets more palatable and less monotonous. Thus the turri or curry was conceived. Curried whole grain brown rice has been a stable part of the Indian diet for centuries.

Military Specification

Curry powder shall be uniformly blended and colored and appear as a semihomogenous mixture, possessing a fragrant, aromatic aroma and a warm, spicy, somewhat bitter taste. Ninety five percent of the mixture shall pass through a U.S. Standard No. 30 sieve and 100% shall pass through a U.S. Standard No. 40 sieve. Each spice shall conform to the quality standards established for each spice in Federal Specification EE-S-631H, dated June 5, 1975. (Specific requirements for each spice are outlined in Chapter 3 under each specific spice.) The formula shall conform to that shown in Table 4.1—U.S. Standard Formula.

Formulations

The following, freshly ground spices are used in various combinations in the compounding of curry powder blends: allspice, anise, bay leaves, capsicum, caraway, cardamom, cassia buds, chili peppers, cinnamon, cloves, coriander, cumin, fennel, fenugreek, garlic powder, ginger, mace, mustard seed, nutmeg, paprika, black or white pepper, poppy seed, saffron, sesame seed, and turmeric.

In order to protect the extremely hot, pungent spices from irritating the eyes while grinding, a teaspoonful of vinegar or lime juice may be added. Variations to any of the suggested formulas given in

Table 4.1 may be made by the enterprising chef, depending on the likes and dislikes of the consumer and the desired nuances in the final product. For individuality, one may serve a variety of different items with their curries, such as: chopped raisins, toasted almonds, grapes, peanuts, chunks of pineapple or other fruit, diced or minced onions, crumbled bacon bits or bacon flavored soy grits, diced radishes, chopped ripe or green olives, diced green peppers, mangoes or chutney. Desiccated coconut is a natural adjunct for curry.

Approximate Composition of Standard Curry Powder Blend, 100 g

Water	9.5 g	Magnesium	254 mg
Food energy	325 kcal	Phosphorous	349 mg
Protein	12.7 g	Potassium	1543 mg
Fat	13.8 g	Sodium	52 mg
Total carbohydrate	58.2 g	Zinc	4 mg
Fiber	16.3 g	Ascorbic acid	11 mg
Ash	5.6 g	Riboflavin	3 mg
Calcium	478 mg	Vitamin A	986 IU
Iron	30 mg	Other vitamins	insignificant

Household Uses

Curry powder blend may be used at the rate of about 14.8 ml (1 tbsp) for each 453.59 g (1 lb) of any meat, poultry, or seafood product or to 1 L (about 1 qt) of sauce for serving over rice. It may be used with chicken livers, shrimp, oysters, scallops, lobster, or any fresh fish dish. It goes well with noodles, rice, or boiled white potatoes, beets, dried beans, eggplant, carrots, parsnips, sweet potatoes, winter squash, onions, celery or turnips, in fish chowders or soups, salad dressings, cocktail dips, cottage or cream cheeses, breads, marinades for meat, apple pie, or in pea, turtle, tomato, or chicken soups. Curried beef, lamb, or chicken are the more popular American dishes.

Table 4.1   Formulations for Typical Curry Powder Blends

Freshly ground spices	U.S. Standard Formula No. 1[a]	General purpose curry formulas			
		No. 2[b]	No. 3[b]	No. 4[b]	No. 5[c]
	%	%	%	%	%
Coriander	32	37	40	35	25
Turmeric, Madras	38	10	10	25	25
Fenugreek	10	0	0	7	5
Cinnamon	7	2	10	0	0
Cumin	5	2	0	15	25
Cardamom	2	4	5	0	5
Ginger, cochin	3	2	5	5	5
Pepper, white	3	5	15	5	0
Poppy seed	0	35	0	0	0
Cloves	0	2	3	0	0
Cayenne pepper	0	1	1	5	0
Bay leaf	0	0	5	0	0
Chili Peppers, hot	0	0	0	0	5
Allspice	0	0	3	0	0
Mustard seed	0	0	0	3	5
Lemon peel, dried	0	0	3	0	0
	100	100	100	100	100

[a]From the U.S. Miliary Specification Mil-C-35042A, dated 30 Dec. 1964.
[b]From Heath 1978. Formula No. 2 is considered to be a mild curry, formula No. 3 a sweet curry, and formula No. 4 a hot type of curry.
[c]Formula No. 5 is a very hot, pungent Indian style curry more suited for use in the hot tropical areas of India.

Pickling Spice Blend

Pickling spice blends are used for pickling meats like corned beef, stews, vegetables, sauces, and cucumbers.

Three typical formulations that are used commercially, are shown in Table 4.2.

Household Uses _____

For household use, it is suggested that the usual 2 oz container of pickling spice be added to a quart of water or mild vinegar and brought to a simmering temperature, not over 200°F (93°C), for about 20 minutes to make a liquor, which may have many more uses

Fig. 4.2
Pickling spice blend (commercial pack).

Table 4.2 Pickling Spice Blend Formulations

Spice	A	B	C
Allspice, whole	—	5	5
Bay leaves, cracked	25	20	10
Chili peppers, whole	3	5	5
Cloves, whole	—	5	5
Coriander, whole	45	20	25
Dill seed, whole	7	10	15
Fenugreek, whole	—	5	5
Garlic, dehyd., minced	3	—	—
Mustard seed, whole	17	25	25
Pepper, black, whole	—	5	5
%	100	100	100

in home cooking than the dry spice mixture has in salad dressings, stews, sour cream dips, and many other preparations where a spicy lift might be desirable.

5

More Information on Spices

Some type of spice is grown in the more than 100 different countries that lie between 60° N latitude and 30° S latitude. The majority of exotic spices originate in the tropical regions between 20° N and 20° S latitude. A list of the primary sources of spices by country or geographical area follows. Countries that produce spices do not necessarily use them in their own ethnic dishes. On the other hand, some spices like capsicum, cinnamon, cloves, garlic, ginger, nutmeg, onion, parsley, and pepper are used for flavoring foods almost universally.

Table 5.1 lists the commonly used spices in the preparation of selected ethnic dishes in America. Europeans, Asiatics, and Orientals that migrate to America usually continue their traditional cultural, culinary habits for one or more generations before adapting their tastes for the foods to be found in their new homeland.

Spices have additional attributes other than the improvement of food flavor. Because of their low sodium content (see Table 5.2), many spices may be substituted for salt, in sodium-restricted diets, to relieve the monotony and blandness of salt-free meals. Suggested spice substitutes for salt in sodium restricted diets are given.

Some spices as shown in Table 5.3 contain antioxidants. Although these natural antioxidants will never compete with their synthetic counterparts, they nevertheless are regarded as beneficial and in some cases, significant.

Table 5.1 Commonly Used Spices in Preparation of Selected Ethnic Dishes in America

Spice	Armenian	Cambodian	Chinese[a]	Cuban	Danish	Dutch	Egyptian	Filipino	Finnish	French	German	Greek	Hungarian	Indonesian	Iranian	Iraqian	Italian	Japanese	Jewish	Korean	Lebanese	Mexican	Norwegian	Polish	Polynesian	Puerto Rican	Russian	Spanish	Swedish	Syrian	Turkish	Vietnamese
Allspice	X	X		X	X		X		X		X		X	X	X				X		X	X	X	X		X			X	X	X	X
Anise seed	X	X	X	X			X				X	X			X			X			X	X				X	X			X	X	
Anise, China star		X	X																													X
Basil, sweet			X	X	X	X			X	X	X	X	X		X		X		X		X	X	X	X		X	X	X	X	X	X	
Bay leaves			X	X	X	X			X	X	X	X	X	X	X		X	X	X		X	X	X			X	X	X	X	X	X	
Capers			X	X	X	X			X	X	X	X	X				X	X	X				X	X		X	X	X	X			
Capsicum (cayenne)	X	X	X	X	X		X	X						X		X			X		X					X	X			X		X
Caraway seed	X				X			X			X		X	X	X	X		X	X		X		X			X	X	X	X	X	X	
Cardamom	X				X			X						X	X	X			X		X		X	X		X	X	X	X	X		X
Cassia																X					X									X		
Celery seed					X				X	X	X				X		X		X		X		X				X		X		X	
Chervil		X			X	X				X	X						X	X	X				X				X		X			X
Chili pepper	X	X	X	X														X		X		X				X		X			X	X
Chives	X	X	X	X	X	X			X	X	X	X	X	X	X	X	X		X		X	X	X	X		X	X	X	X			X
Cinnamon	X	X	X	X	X	X	X		X	X	X	X	X	X	X	X	X	X	X		X	X	X	X		X	X	X	X	X	X	X
Cloves	X	X	X		X	X	X		X	X	X	X	X	X	X	X	X	X	X		X	X	X	X		X	X	X		X	X	
Coriander	X	X	X			X	X								X	X			X		X	X				X		X		X		X
Cumin	X	X	X			X	X								X	X			X		X	X				X		X		X		
Curry powder		X							X	X	X		X		X			X	X		X	X	X	X	X	X	X	X			X	X
Dillseed					X	X			X	X	X								X			X	X	X			X	X	X	X	X	
Dillweed													X						X				X	X			X		X			
Fennel	X	X	X	X	X		X			X	X				X	X	X	X	X		X	X	X	X		X	X	X		X	X	X

236

Fenugreek
Garlic
Ginger
Horseradish
Mace
Marjoram
Mint-peppermint
Mint-spearmint
Mustard
Nutmeg
Onion
Oregano
Paprika
Parsley
Pepper, black
Pepper, white
Poppy seed
Rosemary
Saffron
Sage
Savory
Sesame seed
Tarragon
Thyme
Turmeric

aSeasoning and spicing rituals vary with the region in China from which the Chinese may have emigrated; the north (Peking region) have their wine sauces; the east (Shanghai region) have their heavy soy sauces; the west (Szechwan region) use much hot pepper, garlic, ginger and green onions, whereas the south (Canton region) use milder spices.

MAJOR SOURCES OF SPICES BY COUNTRY OR GEOGRAPHICAL AREA

Albania
  Oregano
  Sage
Algeria
  Fenugreek
  Parsley
  Rosemary
Argentina
  Anise
  Coriander
  Cumin
  Fennel
  Fenugreek
  Hops
  Marjoram
  Mustard
  Paprika
  Peppermint
Australia
  Ginger
  Hops
  Peppermint
Austria
  Hops
  Mustard
Banda Islands
  Cloves
  Mace
  Nutmeg
Banka Island
  Black pepper
  White pepper
Belgium
  Basil
  Hops
  Parsley
Borneo
  Cinnamon
  Black pepper
Brazil
  Capsicum
  Cinnamon
  Hops

Mace
Nutmeg
Black pepper
White pepper
Bulgaria
  Anise
  Basil
  Caraway
  Coriander
  Fennel
  Paprika
  Thyme
Cambodia
  Cassia
  Black pepper
Canada
  Caraway
  Dill
  Mustard
  Onion
  Paprika
  Parsley
  Poppy seed
  Sage
  Savory
  Thyme
Chile
  Anise
  Mustard
  Paprika
China
  Anise
  Anise, Star
  Cassia
  Coriander
  Garlic
  Ginger
  Mustard
  Onion
  Poppy seed
  Saffron
  Sesame seed
  Turmeric

Comoro Islands
  Basil
Congo
  Capsicum
Costa Rica
  Caraway
Cyprus
  Anise
  Cumin
  Fenugreek
  Sage
Czechoslovakia
  Hops
  Poppy seed
Dalmatian Islands
  Sage
Denmark
  Cumin
  Dill
  Fennel
  Mustard
  Poppy seed
East Indies
  Ginger
Egypt
  Anise
  Cinnamon
  Coriander
  Cumin
  Fennel
  Fenugreek
  Garlic
  Ginger
  Onion
  Sesame seed
El Salvador
  Cardamom
  Sesame seed
France
  Anise
  Basil
  Bay leaves
  Capers

Celery seed
Chervil
Chives
Coriander
Dill
Fennel
Fenugreek
Garlic
Hops
Marjoram
Onion
Oregano
Parsley
Peppermint
Poppy seed
Rosemary
Saffron
Savory
Tarragon
Thyme
French Guiana
  Capsicum
French Indochina
  Cassia
  Cloves
Germany
  Anise
  Chives
  Dill
  Fennel
  Fenugreek
  Hops
  Horseradish
  Marjoram
  Onion
  Parsley
  Peppermint
  Poppy seed
  Rosemary
  Savory Thyme
Granada
  Mace
  Marjoram
  Nutmeg
Great Britain
  Caraway seed
  Celery seed
  Chives
  Coriander

Dill
Fennel
Hops
Marjoram
Mustard
Parsley
Peppermint
Poppy seed
Saffron
Spearmint
Thyme
Greece
  Anise
  Bay leaves
  Fenugreek
  Ginger
  Oregano
  Parsley
  Saffron
  Sage
  Sesame seed
  Thyme
Guatamala
  Allspice
  Bay leaves
  Capsicum
  Cardamom
  Sesame seed
Haiti
  Turmeric
Honduras
  Allspice
  Capsicum
Hungary
  Basil
  Celery seed
  Dill
  Marjoram
  Paprika
  Poppy seed
India
  Anise
  Basil
  Capsicum
  Caraway
  Cardamom
  Celery seed
  Cinnamon
  Cloves

Coriander
Cumin
Dill
Fennel
Fenugreek
Ginger
Mustard
Onion
Peppermint
Pepper, black
Pepper, white
Poppy seed
Saffron
Sesame seed
Turmeric
Indonesia
  Basil
  Caraway
  Cardamom
  Cassia
  Cinnamon
  Cloves
  Garlic
  Mace
  Nutmeg
  Pepper, black
  Sesame seed
Iran
  Basil
  Cumin
  Poppy seed
  Saffron
  Tarragon
Israel
  Bay leaves
  Garlic
  Onion
Italy
  Basil
  Capers
  Chervil
  Coriander
  Fennel
  Fenugreek
  Garlic
  Marjoram
  Mustard
  Onion
  Oregano

(*continued*)

Italy (*Continued*)
  Parsley
  Peppermint
  Rosemary
  Sage
  Saffron
  Thyme
Jamaica
  Allspice
  Cloves
  Ginger
  Turmeric
Japan
  Anise
  Capsicum
  Celery seed
  Fennel
  Ginger
  Hops
  Mustard
  Parsley
  Peppermint
  Sesame seed
  Spearmint
  Turmeric
Java
  Basil
  Cinnamon
  Mace
  Nutmeg
  Pepper, black
Kashmir
  Saffron
Kenya
  Sesame seed
Laos
  Cardamom
Lebanon
  Anise
  Cumin
  Fenugreek
  Onion
  Sesame seed
Leeward Islands
  Allspice
Malagasy Republic
  Anise
  Basil

  Cinnamon
  Cloves
  Pepper, black
Malaysia
  Cloves
  Mace
  Nutmeg
  Pepper, black
  Pepper, white
  Turmeric
Malta
  Cumin
Mexico
  Allspice
  Anise
  Bay leaves
  Capsicum
  Cinnamon
  Coriander
  Cumin
  Dill
  Garlic
  Ginger
  Onion
  Oregano
  Paprika
  Sesame seed
Moluccas Islands
  Cloves
  Mace
  Nutmeg
Mombassa
  Capsicum
Morocco
  Bay leaves
  Caraway
  Coriander
  Cumin
  Fennel
  fenugreek
  Marjoram
  Rosemary
  Thyme
The Netherlands
  Caraway seed
  Celery seed
  Chives
  Coriander

Dill
Fennel
Hops
Mustard
Onion
Parsley
Poppy seed
Spearmint
New Zealand
  Hops
Nicaragua
  Sesame seed
Nigeria
  Ginger
Pakistan
  Anise
  Dill
Peru
  Turmeric
Poland
  Basil
  Caraway seed
  Hops
  Horseradish
  Poppy seed
Portugal
  Bay leaves
  Fenugreek
  Marjoram
  Paprika
  Parsley
  Rosemary
  Saffron
  Sage
  Thyme
Riouw Archipelago
  Pepper, black
Romania
  Caraway seed
  Coriander
  Dill
  Fennel
  Horseradish
Russia
  Anise
  Bay leaves
  Caraway seed
  Celery seed

Chervil
Coriander
Cumin
Dill
Fennel
Garlic
Hops
Horseradish
Onion
Spearmint
Tarragon
Thyme
San Domingo
  Ginger
Sardinia
  Parsley
Seychelles Islands
  Basil
  Cinnamon
Sicily
  Capers
  Cumin
  Garlic
  Onion
  Saffron
Sierra Leone
  Ginger
  Sesame seed
Spain
  Basil
  Bay leaves
  Capers
  Celery seed
  Chervil
  Coriander
  Dill
  Fenugreek
  Hops
  Horseradish
  Marjoram
  Oregano
  Paprika
  Parsley
  Rosemary
  Saffron
  Sage
  Savory

Thyme
Sri Lanka (Ceylon)
  Cardamom
  Cinnamon
  Cloves
  Ginger
  Pepper, black
  Pepper, white
  Turmeric
Sumatra
  Cassia
  Cinnamon
  Mace
  Nutmeg
  Pepper, black
Sunda Islands
  Sesame seed
Syria
  Anise
  Caraway seed
  Cumin
  Fennel
Tanganyika
  Sesame seed
Tanzania
  Cloves
  Pepper, black
Thailand
  Pepper, black
Tunisia
  Marjoram
  Rosemary
  Thyme
Turkey
  Anise
  Coriander
  Cumin
  Oregano
  Paprika
  Poppy seed
  Sage
  Sesame seed
  Thyme
Uganda
  Capsicum
United States
  Anise

Basil
Capers
Capsicum
Caraway
Celery seed
Chervil
Chives
Coriander
Dill
Fennel
Fenugreek
Garlic
Hops
Horseradish
Marjoram
Mustard
Onion
Paprika
Parsley
Peppermint
Poppy seed
Rosemary
Sage
Sesame seed
Spearmint
Thyme
Vietnam
  Anise, Star
  Cassia
  Pepper, black
  Turmeric
Yugoslavia
  Bay leaves
  Coriander
  Fenugreek
  Hops
  Horseradish
  Oregano
  Paprika
  Peppermint
  Poppy seed
  Rosemary
  Sage
Zanzibar
  Capsicum
  Cloves

Although Table 5.1 may seem to be self-explanatory, several comments are worth mentioning.

1. Flavoring agents, other than the listed spices, may be added to the ethnic dishes to contribute to their distinctiveness. Items such as chocolate, fruit, lemon juice, lemon and orange rinds, nutmeats, rum, soy sauce, vanilla, and wine represent some of the adjuncts used. In some countries, shallots, because of their mildness or availability, may be used in place of onions; others may utilize fresh spices or uncommon herbs in preference to customary dried spices.

2. Because different climates and/or tribal customs exist within some countries like Russia, China, and those of the Mideast and Polynesia, one can expect to find different eating habits within each of these areas. Thus, only a fraction of the spices listed under each country may be used by some of the immigrants that come to this country.

3. Some areas depend more on seafood than animal food for their main course, while others may be strictly vegetarian. Religious preferences or prohibitions as well as climate and customs determine to a great extent the combination of spices to be used in flavoring specific foods.

SUGGESTED SPICE SUBSTITUTES FOR SALT IN SODIUM RESTRICTED DIETS

Good flavor, aroma, and appearance of food are particularly important in dietetic meals. Monotonous and insipid food in addition to the usual patient's lack of appetite make it extremely important that the dietitian be aware of the many attributes of spices for improving the acceptability of the meals and the ultimate recovery of the patient. What may be palatable for one patient may not be for another. It may be necessary to experiment by trial and error or by determining the patient's ethnic background or eating habits, resolve which spices are more apt to be acceptable than others. It must be pointed out again that most spices are quite potent in flavor-enhancing qualities and must be used with considerable discretion. Usually less than 2.5 g ($\frac{1}{8}$ to $\frac{1}{2}$ tsp) is sufficient to flavor 453 g (1 lb) of meat or 1 L (1 qt) of soup or chowder.

For patients having gastric problems, in addition to the need for a low salt diet, it is recommended that the following spices be avoided: ginger, allspice, clove, red pepper, mustard, horseradish, garlic, onion, nutmeg, mace, bay leaves, and curry powders. Sweet summer savory should be used in place of any of the peppers or pungent spices in such diets.

The following spices, containing less than 400 mg of sodium in 100 g of spice (0.40%) may be used safely in the flavoring of foods in place of salt. (See Table 5.2 for Sodium Content of Spices.) The average sodium content of the following spices approximates 50 mg per 100 g. Since only 2.5 g or less would be used to flavor a pound of food, sufficient for four servings, one serving would contain about 0.3 mg of added sodium, which is insignificant in 99% of the diets, yet significant in the acceptability of the food.

Table 5.2   Sodium Content of Dried Spices and Other Substitutes for Salt[a,b]

allspice	77 (mg/100 g)	mustard seed	5
anise seed	16	nutmeg	16
basil	34	onion powder	54
bay leaf	23	oregano	15
capsicum	30	paprika	34
caraway seed	17	parsley flakes	452
cardamom	18	pepper, black	44
celery seed	160	pepper, white	5
chervil	83	poppy seed	21
chili powder	1010	rosemary	50
cinnamon	26	saffron	148
cloves	243	sage	11
coriander seed	35	savory	24
cumin	168	sesame seed	40
curry powder	52	tarragon	62
dill seed	20	thyme	55
dill weed	208	turmeric	38
fennel seed	88	other substitutes	
fenugreek	67	almond	3 to 6 (*)
garlic powder	26	cocoa, undutched	5 (*)
ginger	32	lemon juice	1 to 2 (*)
horseradish root	8 (*)	mustard, prepared	4 (*)
mace	80	mustard paste	1300 (*)
marjoram, sweet	77	orange juice	1 to 2 (*)
mint	43 (*)	wine	4 to 10 (*)

[a]For reference purposes, the sodium content of table salt is 38,758 mg/100 g.
[b]Values marked with * refers to Table 25 in Merory 1978; All other data from USDA Handbook No. 8-2 1977.

Meats, Poultry and Seafoods_____

Beef	Bayleaf, capsicum, caraway seed, cardamom, celery seed, chives, cloves, cumin, curry powder blend, fennel, garlic, ginger, horseradish, mace, mustard, marjoram, nutmeg, onion, oregano, pepper, rosemary, sage, savory, and thyme
Eggs	Capsicum, chervil, chives, cumin, curry powder blend, dillweed, marjoram, mustard, onion, oregano, paprika, pepper, summer savory, and tarragon
Lamb	Cardamom, chives, cinnamon, curry powder blend, dill seed, garlic, ginger, marjoram, mint, mustard, onion, oregano, pepper, and rosemary
Poultry	Bayleaf, capers (not pickled), cardamom, celery seed, chives, cinnamon, cumin, curry powder blend, dill seed, fennel, garlic, ginger, mace, marjoram, nutmeg, onion, oregano, paprika, pepper, rosemary, sage, saffron, summer savory, and thyme
Pork	Cardamom, celery seed, chives, cinnamon, cloves, fennel, garlic, ginger, horseradish, mustard, onion, oregano, pepper, rosemary, sage, and thyme
Seafoods	Anise, bayleaf, chives, caraway seed, dill seed, ginger, horseradish, mace, marjoram, mint, mustard, nutmeg, onion, oregano, paprika, pepper, poppy seed, rosemary, saffron, sage, summer savory, tarragon, and thyme
Veal	Bayleaf, cardamom, chives, curry powder blend, garlic, ginger, mace, mint, marjoram, mustard, nutmeg, onion, paprika, pepper, and tarragon

Vegetables_____

Asparagus	Chervil, rosemary and tarragon
Artichokes	Basil
Beans, Green	Anise, basil, chives, coriander, dill seed, chervil,

	mace, marjoram, nutmeg, oregano, pepper, poppy seed, rosemary, tarragon, and thyme
Beans, Dry	Anice, basil, dill seed, mace, marjoram, nutmeg, oregano, and summer savory
Beets	Chervil, cinnamon, cloves, curry powder blend, mustard, and tarragon
Broccoli	Basil, chives, horseradish, mace, onion, oregano and pepper
Cabbage	Anise, chives, dill seed, fennel seed, marjoram, mustard, oregano, paprika, and poppy seed
Carrots	Cardamom, chives, cinnamon, cloves, chervil, curry powder blend, ginger, mace, mint, nutmeg, pepper and poppy seed
Cauliflower	Chives, dill seed, mace, nutmeg, paprika, and rosemary
Celery	Mace and nutmeg
Corn	Coriander, mace, nutmeg, and pepper
Cucumbers	Caraway seed, chives, dill seed, fennel, mustard, and pepper
Eggplant	Basil, cinnamon, curry powder blend, marjoram, mint, oregano, rosemary, and sage
Onions	Chervil, cinnamon, curry powder blend, mace, mustard, poppy seed, sage, and tarragon
Parsnips	Curry powder blend
Peas	Chervil, chives, mace, mint, nutmeg, onion, pepper, summer savory and tarragon
Potatoes, white	Chervil, caraway seed, chives, dill seed, fennel, mace, nutmeg, onion, pepper, poppy seed, and thyme
Potatoes, sweet	Allspice, cardamom, cinnamon, caraway seed, cloves, ginger, mace, and nutmeg
Pumpkin	Ginger and pepper
Squash, winter	Ginger, cardamom, cinnamon, cloves and curry powder blend
Squash, summer	Chervil, marjoram, poppy seed, rosemary, and tarragon
Tomatoes	Basil, bayleaf, capers, cinnamon, dill seed, fennel, marjoram, mace, nutmeg, oregano, sage, summer savory, and thyme
Turnip	Allspice, caraway seed, curry powder blend, pepper, and rosemary

Zucchini   Basil, chervil, poppy seed, rosemary, and tarragon

ANTIOXIDANT ACTIVITY OF SPICES

Although the natural antioxidants found in spices will never compete with their synthetic counterparts, they nevertheless are regarded as beneficial and in some cases, significant. The antioxidant activity of spices is given in Table 5.3.

Table 5.3   Antioxidant Activities of Spices[a]

Spice	Chipault et al. (1952)	Cort (1974)	Bishov (unpub.)	Spice	Chipault et al. (1952)	Cort (1974)	Bishov (unpub.)
Allspice	1.8	3.5	3.1	Ginger	1.8		
Anise seed	1.9			Mace	2.6	1.5	4.7
Basil	1.2			Marjoram	2.2	2.0	2.8
Bay leaf	2.1		1.8	Mustard	2.0		
Cardamom	1.3			Nutmeg	3.1	1.5	2.8
Caraway seed	1.8			Oregano	3.8		1.7
Cassia	1.4			Paprika	2.5		1.7
Celery seed	1.2		1.9	Pepper, black	1.4		1.0
Chili pepper	1.5			Pepper, red	1.5		1.9
Cinnamon	1.3		5.7	Pepper, white	1.2		1.0
Cloves	1.8	14.0	5.8	Poppy seed	1.2		
Coriander	1.3			Rosemary	17.6	3.0	3.2
Cumin	1.3			Sage	16.5	10.0	5.2
Dill	1.3			Savory	1.6		
Fennel	1.3			Thyme	3.0	1.5	2.1
Fenugreek	1.6			Turmeric	2.9	5.0	1.8

[a]Source: Peterson and Johnson 1978.

MICROBIOLOGICAL ASPECTS AND STERILIZATION OF SPICES

Spices were recognized by the Egyptians over 3000 years ago as having preservation possibilities. The antibacterial factors are present in the essential oils of the spices. Two of the most effective germicidal spices are cinnamon and clove. Cinnamon contains cinnamic aldehyde and cloves contain the ether eugenol.

Imported spices often have been accused of being heavily contaminated with microorganisms, insects, filth, and all manner of undesirable adulterants. When one considers the areas in which they are cultivated, the tropical or semitropical conditions required for their growth, and the semicrude methods of handling, packing, and transporting them half way around the world, it is little wonder that the bacteria counts may run well into the millions per gram.

Samples of ginger have been reported to contain 48 million total bacteria, 12 million yeasts and molds, 26 million spore formers, and over 700,000 anaerobic spore formers per gram (Tjaberg et al., 1972). Flannagan and Hui (1976) reported that 14 of 20 spices they examined contained Aspergillus flavus and four of these spices supported growth of this mold and the production of aflatoxin. Julseth and Diebel (1974) obtained standard plate counts of over 10 million per gram for black pepper, ginger, and paprika with over 10 million bacterial spores per gram. Without sterilization of these spices with either ethylene oxide or propylene oxide, these spices, when incorporated into food products, could easily pose a potential health hazard. The figures quoted above are not atypical of some spices, but neither are they representative of all spices. Growers overseas are becoming increasingly aware of their previous shortcomings and are cleaning up their operations, especially those that are controllable. Some of our own home-produced dehydrated onion products have unusually high bacteria counts but products processed in modern sanitary facilities under controlled conditions, containing 300,000 bacteria per gram or less are easily available for purchase.

The larger, technologically oriented, spice blenders have facilities for sterilizing spices and seasonings. The process adds about $0.02/lb to the cost of the spice or seasoning but is well worth it to the ultimate user.

The simplest type of equipment for sterilizing spices and seasonings consists of a heavy, steel walled chamber, about 8 to 10 ft deep, 4 ft high and 4 ft wide. The chamber is fitted with a lock-tight door with a recording temperature and pressure instrument. The chamber must be capable of withstanding at least 28½ in. of vacuum and 10 to 15 lb pressure. It is also desirable to have a heating unit within the chamber capable of raising the temperature 10 to 15 degrees above room temperature. The only other equipment needed is a tank of ethylene oxide fitted with a pressure gauge and a supply line to

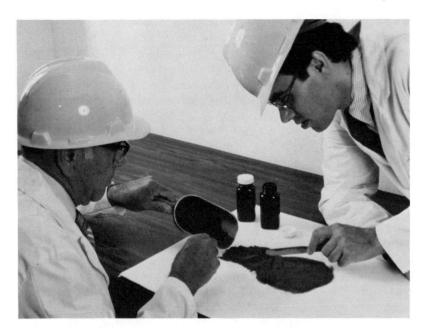

Fig. 5.1
Visual inspection of dry mixture. Courtesy of Baltimore Spice Company.

the chamber. The chamber briefly described is capable of holding ten, 200-lb poly-lined fiber drums or about twenty 100-kg sacks of spices.

After loading the chamber with the filled drums or sacks of spices or seasonings, the door is securely locked and the chamber evacuated to at least 28½ in. of vacuum, the vacuum is held for about 10 minutes and then released, replacing the evacuated chamber with ethylene oxide gas up to a preassure of 5 to 10 lb. The heat is turned on to a recorded reading of 90°F and the chamber held under these conditions for 8 to 10 hours. The sterilizing process is usually scheduled for over-night in order to have the materials ready for the production crew the next morning. After the required conditions have been met, the supply of gas is shut off and the gas within the chamber penetrates the gas permeable packaging materials and begins killing off the bacteria present. Such a process destroys 95–100% of the total bacteria present, all of the pathogenic organisms, yeasts and molds, insect eggs and insects, and all other forms of living matter. Obviously, the process does not remove the evidence of insect fragments, larvae, etc.; but once the product has been treated and used within a reasonable time, the spice or seasoning will no longer be a significant health hazard as its untreated product might have been.

The exact mechanism by which the bacteria, yeasts, and mold are inactivated is still unknown. Presumably, the essential metabolizing components of the cells contain chemical bonds that react with the ethylene oxide forming alkyl hydroxyethyl groups, which cannot be utilized by the cells in their metabolic cycle and thus they die.

Upon completion of the sterilizing cycle, the chamber is vented and any residual ethylene oxide remaining in the products is easily dissipated in subsequent mixing and blending operations.

The use of ethylene oxide has been questioned by many investigators. Ethylene oxide is chronically toxic at levels not detected by smell. It is a skin irritant producing erythema and edema with a potential for sensitization. Various toxic effects of ethylene oxide, including death, were discussed by White (1977). Embree et al. (1977) reported mutagenic effects of ethylene oxide on various cells, including mammalian cells. Wesley et al. (1965) reported that ethylene oxide reacts with chlorides in food to form chlorohydrins. These are toxic, nonvolatile, and persist in the food during processing. They reported levels of 1 mg per gram of ethylene chlorhydrin present in spices sterilized with ethylene oxide.

The use of ethylene oxide to control microorganisms and insects is still permitted in ground spices or other natural seasoning materials except mixtures containing salt. The residue cannot exceed 50 mg per gram of spice. This method of sterilization should be used only when other techniques are not practical.

Propylene oxide is used like ethylene oxide, but its penetrating ability is weaker. It is microbiocidal. It requires a higher temperature or longer treatment to accomplish the same microbial kill as ethylene oxide. Propylene oxide can also react with chlorides to form chlorohydrins in foods. Some countries are considering restricting its use, while others may ban its use completely.

The only known effective and safe alternative technique is the use of radiation suggested by B. E. Proctor et al. of M.I.T. back in 1950. Since industry has not responded very favorably to the possibilities of radiation in the past 30 years, it is not likely we will see any less resistance within the next decade, unless the government determines there is a definite health hazard involved and prohibits, or restricts, the use of ethylene oxide as a means of fumigating (sterilizing) spices.

Bibliography Part II

American Spice Trade Association, 1972. Your Spice Shelf Cookbook. Englewood Cliffs, New Jersey.

Anderson, J. 1975. The Doubleday Cookbook. Doubleday Co., Garden City, New York.

Anon. 1980. "When Is an Herb a Spice." American Spice Trade Association, Englewood Cliffs, New Jersey.

Anon. 1976. Mustard Flour, Industrial Products Division, R. T. French Co., Rochester, New York.

Anon. 1974. Symposium on the Spice Industry in India. Assoc. Food Scientists and Technologists, Mysore, India.

Ashurst, P. R. *et al.* 1972. A new approach to spice processing. *Tropical Prod. Inst. Conf. Proc., London,* pp. 209–214.

Ayres, J. C., and Kirschman, J. C. 1981. Impact of Toxicology on Food Processing. AVI Publishing Co., Westport, Connecticut.

Baldry, J. *et al.* 1974. Chemical composition and flavor of nutmegs of different geographical origins. *Proc. 4th Int. Cong. Food Sci. Technol.* **1a,** 38–40.

Baldry, J. *et al.* 1976. Composition and flavor of nutmeg oils. *Int. Flavors, Food Additives* **7,** 28–30.

Banwart, G. J. 1981. Basic Food Microbiology. Abridged Textbook Ed. AVI Publishing Co., Westport, Connecticut.

Basic-American Food Co. 1980. Dehydrated onions and garlic. San Francisco, California.

Berner, D. L. *et al.* 1973. Spice anti-oxidant principle. (Assigned to Campbell Soup Co.) U. S. Patent 3,732,111, Oct. 1, 1973.

Bhalla, K., and Punekar, B. D. 1975. Incidence and state of adulteration of commonly consumed spices in Bombay city. II. Mustard, black pepper and asafoetida. *Indian J. Nutr. Diet.* **12,** 216–222.

Bishov, S. J. unpublished. Antioxidant Index by retardation of oxygen uptake by 2 freeze-dried CMC-stripped corn oil emulsion.

Carson, J. F., and Wong, F. F. 1961 The volatile flavor components of onions. *J. Agric. Food Chem.* **9,** 140–143.

Cartwright, L. C., and Nanz, R. A., 1948 Comparative evaluation of spices. *Food Technology* **2**, 330–336.

Central Food Technology Research Institute 1974. A select bibliography on spices (1966–1972). Mysore, India.

Chipault, J. R., Mizuno, G. R. Hawkins, J. M., and Lundberg, W. O. 1952. The antioxidant properties of natural spices. *Food Res.* **17**, 46.

Claibourne, C. 1970. Cooking With Herbs and Spices, Rev. Edit. Harper & Row Publishing Co., New York,

Collins, R. P., 1967. A World of Curries—An International Cookbook. Harper & Row Publishing Co., New York.

Coretti, K., and Inal, T. 1969. Residue problems with the cold treatment of spices with T-gas (ethylene oxide). *Fleischwirtschaft* **49**, 599–604.

Cort, W. M. 1974. Percentage of BHT activity in retarding oxygen depletion in hemoglobin catalyzed stripped sunflower oil emulsion. *Food Technol,* **28**, 61.

Cripps, H. M. 1972. Spice oleoresins, the process, the market, the future. *Tropical Prod. Inst. Conf. Proc. London* pp. 237–242.

Cranwell, J. P. 1975. The Hellfire Cookbook. N.Y. Times Book Co., New York.

Day, A. S. and Stuckey, L. 1964. The Spice Cookbook. D. White Co., Port Washington, New York.

Desrosier, N. W., 1978. Rietz Master Food Guide. AVI Publishing Co., Westport, Connecticut.

Du, C. T., and Francis, F. J. 1975. Anthocyanins of garlic *(Allium sativum* L.) *J. Food Sci.* **40**, 1101–1102.

Eiserle, R. J. 1981. The Oleoresin Handbook, 3rd Ed., Fritzsche, Dodge & Olcott Inc., New York.

Eiserle, R. J., and Rogers, J. A. 1972. The composition of volatile oils derived from oleoresins. *J. Am. Oil Chem. Soc.* **49**, 573–577.

Embree, J. W., Lyon, J. P., and Hine, C. H. 1977. The mutagenic potential of ethylene oxide using the dominant-lethal assay in rats. *Toxicol. Appl. Pharmacol.* **40**, 261–267.

Encyclopedia of Herbs, 1977. Marshall Cavendish Co., London.

Ernst, R. B. 1974. Ethylene oxide gaseous sterilization. *In* International Symposium on Sterilization and Sterility Testing of Biological Substances, R. H. Regamey, F. P. Gallardo, and W. Hennessen (editors). S. Karger, Basel.

Farkas, J., Beczner, J., and Incze, K. 1973. Feasibility of irradiation of spices with special reference to paprika. *In* Radiation Preservation of Food. Int. Atomic Energy Agency, Vienna.

FDA. 19 Spices defined. 21-Code of Federal Regulations 1.12(a): U.S. Food and Drug Administration, Washington, D.C.

Federal Register. 1961. Spices, Essential Oils, Oleoresins and Natural Extractives Generally Recognized as Safe. 26 F.R. 5221, June 10.

Federal Specification 1967. Onions, Dehydrated. JJJ-0-533d. Feb. 16.

Federal Specification 1975. Spices, Ground and Whole, and Spice Blends -EE-S-631H. June 5.

Fenaroli, G. 1975. Handbook of Flavor Ingredients, 2nd Edition. T. E. Furia and N. Bellanca (Editors). The Chemical Rubber Co., Cleveland, Ohio.

Flannigan, N., and Hui, S. C., 1976. The occurrence of aflotoxin-producing strains of *Aspergillus flavus* in the mold floras of ground spices. *J. Appl. Bacteriol.* **41**, 411–418.

Gaulke, J. A. 1975. Cooking with Spices and Herbs. Lane Magazine and Book Co., Menlo Park, California.

Gerard, J. 1975. The Herbal or General History of Plants. Rev. 1633 Ed. Dover Publications Inc., New York.

Gilbert, J., and Nursten, N. E. 1972. Volatile constituents of horseradish roots. *J. Sci. Food Agric.*, **23**, 527–539.

Good Housekeeping Institute, 1975. Good Housekeeping Cooking with Herbs and Spices, Ebury Press, London.

Green, R. J. 1975. Peppermint and spearmint production in the United States—progress and problems. *Int. Flavors, Food Additives* **6**, 246–247.

Grieve, M. 1974. A Modern Herbal. The Medicinal, Culinary, Cosmetic and Economic Properties, Cultivation and Folklore of Herbs, Grasses, Fungi, Shrubs and Trees, With All Their Modern Scientific Uses. Hafner Press, New York.

Gross, A. F., and Ellis, P. E. 1969. Lipase activity in spices and seasonings. *Cereal Sci. Today* **14**, 332–335.

Guenther, E. 1948. The Essential Oils, 6 vols. D. Van Nostrand Co., New York.

Hadlok, R., and Toure, B. 1973. Mycological and bacteriological studies of "sterilized" spices. *Arch. Lebensmittelhyg.* **24**, 20–25. (German)

Hall, R. L., and Oser, B. L., 1965. Recent progress in the consideration of flavoring ingredients under the food additives amendment: 3 gras substances. *J. Food Tech.* **19**, 253.

Hardman, R. 1973. Spices and herbs; Their families, secretory tissues and pharmaceutical aspects. *Tropical Products Inst. Conf. Proc., London.*

Harper, R. S. 1974. Pepper in Indonesia. *World Crops* **26**, 130–133.

Heath, H. B. 1978. Flavor Technology: Profiles, Products, Applications. AVI Publishing Co., Westport, Connecticut.

Heath, H. B. 1972. Herbs and Spices for Food Manufacture. *Tropical Sci.* **14**, 245–259.

Heath, H. B. 1973. Herbs and Spices—A Bibliography. Part I. *Flavour Ind.* **4**, 24–26.

Heikal, H. A. *et al.* 1972. A study on the dehydration of garlic slices. *Agric. Res. Rev.* **50**, 243–253.

Hemphill, R. 1977. Cooking with Herbs and Spices. Angus & Robertson, London.

Hodgson, M. 1977. The Hot and Spicy Cookbook. McGraw Hill Book Co., New York.

Hogsted, C. Malmquist, C. N., and Vadman, B. 1979. Leukemia in workers exposed to ethylene oxide. *J. Am. Med. Assoc.* **241**, 1132.

International Trading Center. 1977. Spices—A survey of the world market. Geneva, Switzerland.

Jones, L. W., 1956. A Treasury of Spices. American Spice Trade Assoc. Pridemark Press, Baltimore, Maryland.

Julseth, R. M., and Diebel, R. H., 1974A. Microbial profile of selected spices and herbs at import. *J. Milk Food Technol.* **37**, 414–419.

Julseth, R. M., and Diebel, R. H. 1974B. *Indian Spices* **11**, 6–11.

Kalamazoo Spice Co., 1980. Brochure on oleoresins and aquaresins. Kalamazoo, Michigan.

Komarik, S. L., Tressler, D. K., and Long, L. 1982. Food Products Formulary, Vol. I. 2nd Edition. Meats, Poultry, Fish and Shellfish. AVI Publishing Co. Westport, Connecticut.

Kreuger, J. 1980. Dehydrated ingredients: availability, advantages disadvantages, use and cost. *Proc. Prep. Foods* 3

Krishnaswamy, M. A. *et al.* 1974. Microbiological quality of certain spices. *Indian Spices* **11**, 6–11.

Law, D. 1973. The Concise Herbal Encyclopedia. St. Martin's Press, New York.

Lewis, Y. S. 1973. The importance of selecting the proper variety of a spice for oil and oleoresin extraction. *Tropical Prod. Inst. Conf. Proc., London.*

Little, A. D. Inc. 1957. Flavor Research and Food Acceptance. Reinhold Publ. Corp., New York.

Lowenfeld, C. 1978. The Complete Book of Herbs and Spices. 2nd Ed. Rev., David & Charles Publ. Co., New York.

Macleod, A. J., 1973. Spices. *Chem. Ind.* No. 19, 778-780.

Magra, J. A., 1975. Capsicum. *Crit. Rev. Food Sci. Nutri.* **6**, 177–199.

Malaysian Pepper Marketing Board. 1980. Malaysian pepper. Kuching Grading Center, Sarawak, Malaysia.

Masada, Y. *et al.* 1974. Studies on the constituents of ginger (zingibar officinale Roscoe) by GC-MS. *J. Pharm. Soc. Jpn* **94**, 735–738. (Japanese). See also *Proc. 4th Int. Congr. Food Sci. Technol.* **la**, 84–86.

McCormick & Company, 1979. Spices of the World Cookbook, Rev. Ed. McGraw Hill Book Co., New York.

McKernan, W. M. 1972–1973A. Microencapsulation in the flavor industry. Part I. *Flavour Ind.* **3**, 596–598, 600. Part II. *Flavour Ind.* **4**, 70, 72–74.

Menuti, W. 1980. Freeze dried chopped chives. G. Armamino & Son, Inc. San Francisco, California. Personal communication.

Merck Index, 1976. 9th Ed. Martha Windholz, editor. Merck & Co., Inc. Rahway, New Jersey.

Military Specification Mil-C-3394C. June 28, 1968. Chili Powder Seasoning.

Military Specification Mil-C-35042A. Dec. 30, 1964. Curry Powder Seasoning.

Military Specification Mil-C-35008B. Mar. 21, 1967. Garlic, Dehydrated.

Nearle, M. W., 1963. Spices in food product manufacture. *Canner/Packer* **132**, 41–47.

Parry, J. W., 1969. Spices, Vols. I and II. Chemical Publ. Co., New York.

Pearson, A. M., and Tauber, F. W. 1984. *Processed Meats.* 3rd Ed. AVI Publishing Co., Westport, Connecticut.

Peterson, M. S. and Johnson, A. H. 1978. Encyclopedia of Food Science. AVI Publishing Co. Inc. Westport, Conn.

Pfeiffer, E. H., and Dunkleberg, H., 1980. Mutagenicity of ethylene oxide and proplyene oxide and of the glycols and halohydrins formed from them during the fumigation of foodstuffs. *Food Cosmet. Toxicol.* **18**, 115.

Powers, E. M. *et al.* 1975. Microbiology of processed spices. *J. Milk Food Technol.* **38**, 683–687.

Proctor, B. E., Goldblith, S. A., and Fram, H., 1950. Effect of supervoltage cathode rays on bacterial flora of spices and other dry food materials. *Food Res.* **15**, 440.

Pruthi, J. 1976. Spices and Condiments. National Cook Trust, New Delhi, India.

Rosenkrantz, S., Carr, H. S., and Rosenkrantz, H. S. 1974. 2-Haloethanols mutagenicity and reactivity with DNA. *Mutation Res.* **26**, 367.

Russell, G. F., and Olson, K. V. 1972. The volatile constituents of oil of thyme. *J. Food Sci.* **37**, 405–407.

Sabel, W., and Warren, J. D. F. 1973. Theory and practise of oleoresin extraction. *Tropical Prod. Inst. Conf. Proc., London* pp. 109–192.

Salzer, U. J. 1975. Analytical evaluation of seasoning extracts (oleoresins) and essential oils from seasonings. I. *Int. Flavours Food Additives* **6**, 151–157; II. 206–210, 253–268.

Silberstein, O., Galetto, W., and Henzi, W. 1979. Irradiation of onion powder; effect on microbiology. *J. Food Sci.* **44**, 975.

Staniforth, V. 1973. Spices or oleoresins: A choice? *Tropical Prod. Inst. Food Conf. Proc.,* London pp. 193–197.

Stobart, T., 1973. The International Wine and Food Society's Guide to Herbs, Spices and Flavorings. McGraw Hill Book Co., New York.

Sulc, D. *et al.* 1974. Development of technological procedures for production of new spice concentrates and extracts from paprika. *Conf. Proc. 4th Int. Conf. Food Sci. Technol.* **8b**, 34–36.

Tassan, C. G., and Russell, G. F., 1975. Chemical and sensory studies on cumin, *J. Food Sci.* **40**, 1327–1332.

Ter Heide, R. 1972. Qualitative analysis of the essential oil of cassia (*C. cassia* Blume). *J. Agric. Food Chem.* **20**, 747–751.

Tjaberg, T. B., Underdal, B., and Lunde, G., 1972. The effect of ionizing radiation on the microbiological content and volatile constituents of spices. *J. Appl. Bacteriol.* **35**, 473.

Todd, R. D. 1970. Microencapsulation and the flavour industry. *Flavour Ind.* **1**, 768–771.

Tropical Products Institute, 1972. Conference on spices, London, England.

USDA. 1977. Composition of Foods: Spices and Herbs, Raw, Processed, Prepared. Agricultural Handbook No. 8-2 Rev. U.S. Dept. Agriculture, Washington, D.C.

United States Pharmacopeia, 1980. National Formulary XV, 20th Edition. Mack Publishing Co., Easton, Pennsylvania.

Vajdi, M., and Pereira, R. R. 1973. Comparative effects of ethylene oxide, gamma radiation and microwave treatments on selected spices. *J. Food Sci.* **38**, 893.

Veek, M. E., and Russell, G. F., 1975. Chemical and sensory properties of pimento leaf oil. *J. Food Sci.* **38**, 1028–1031.

Wahlroos, O., and Virtanen, A. I., 1965. Volatiles from chives. *Acta Chem. Scand.* **19**, 1327–1332.

Walford, J. 1976. Solubilizers for essential oils in flavour formulations. *Food Manuf.* **51**, 35–37.

Warmbrod, F., and Fry, L. 1966. Coliform and total bacterial counts in spices, seasonings and condiments. *J. Assoc. Off. Anal. Chem.* **49**, 678–680.

Wesley, F. *et al.* 1965. The formation of persistant toxic chlorohydrins in foodstuffs by fumigation with ethylene oxide and propylene oxide. *J. Food Sci.* **30**, 1037–1042.

White, J. D. 1977. Standard aeration for gas sterilized plastics. *J. Hygiene Cambridge* **79**, 225–232.

Winton, 1945. Analysis of Foods. John Wiley & Sons, New York.

PART THREE

Soluble Spices

Extractives of Spices

HISTORY

Spices have been known for sixty centuries or more, but it was not until food technology became a serious field of study in the late 1930's that the conception of soluble spices first originated.

At the turn of the century, spices were not an important commodity. Spices may have arrived at their destination years earlier than in the days of the Romans but not in much better condition. They were still adulterated with filth, insect eggs, and larvae; microorganism counts were in the millions; quality at the source was uncontrolled; and processed foods in which spices were used were often subject to spoilage in a matter of days.

Spices were no longer being used to mummify the deceased or to hail the conquering heroes, but they were still being harvested by hand, dried in the sun, exposed to the elements of nature, shipped in burlap or paper bags of unknown origin, transported to all corners of the earth in the holds of ships where contamination from sea-going rodents and other pests were not the exception, stacked on wharfs in New York or San Francisco for further exposure to all sorts of local contaminations, and finally stored in warehouses near the docks until purchsed by the unsuspecting spice grinders who knew little more about the products than the field hands who harvested the crop 10,000 miles away.

Harvey W. Wiley's personal crusade against the exploitation of adulterated foods, and for more stringent government regulation of such practices, witnessed the realization of his endeavors in 1906 when Congress enacted the first pure food and drug law. It was not until a few decades later that the importers, the exporters and the growers of spices were to feel the effects of such a law. Unwholesome spices were being confiscated and destroyed without reimbursement. Today, spices are examined and graded at the source before they are shipped. They are examined again at their destination and must comply with stringent regulations for wholesomeness before being accepted by government inspectors.

OLEORESINS

Assisted immeasurably by the flavoring extract manufacturers in America, companies like the Stange Company and Griffith Laboratories in Chicago pioneered the development of oleoresins and ultimately soluble spices. The oleoresins of black pepper and ginger were more or less laboratory curiosities in the thirties, technologists began to explore means for improving them and utilizing them in foods as they would the natural spices from which they were derived.

The original oleoresins were first developed by extracting ground spices with a solvent, removing the solvent under vacuum and disposing of the inert material. The resulting oleoresin was a heavy, asphalt-looking mass of material, rich in aromatics, some of them not always pleasant (due to traces of the solvent), unappetizing in appearance, and because of the viscosity, difficult to work with. Many of the solvents used initially were dangerous; they were flammable and even explosive if not handled with care. Acetone, hexane, and various alcohols were examples of such hazardous solvent materials. These media were not complete solvents because they did not extract out the hydrophilic components of the spice, which also contribute to the overall flavor. The industry turned to chlorinated hydrocarbons, like methyl dichloride because it has a low boiling point, is nonflammable, is easy to recover, and is a complete solvent; it produces a full bodied oleoresin, rich in all of the flavoring components of the original spice.

All spices, however, are not of the same composition, and combinations of solvents had to be employed to determine the specific mixture best suited for each spice. With the improvement in extraction techniques and technological expertise in solvents, the demand for oleoresins of pepper and ginger grew, which prompted the development of oleoresins from the remaining spices. One should bear in mind, that while this development work was going on, the art of sensory analysis was still in its infancy also, and without suitable organoleptic methods for comparing the oleoresins with their corresponding spices, the laboratory technologists had to devise their own testing procedures. With the advent of sophisticated colorimeters, spectrophotometers, gas chromatography, and the like, the laboratory could trace the complete flavor profile of a spice or its extractive and relate its findings to the palate-sensitive, sensory panel's results. Thus, the laboratory could finally determine the true equivalency of an oleoresin to its parent spice. In taste testing oleoresins vs. natural spices, one should bear in mind that the flavor effect of the former is immediate and complete whereas the flavor cells of the spice are not always readily available.

Essentially, oleoresins consist of essential oil, organically soluble resins and other related materials present in the original spice, as well as many nonvolatile fatty acids. The amount of fatty oil present is dependent on the raw material and the type of solvent employed. Spice seeds will yield more fatty oils than spice constituents from other parts of the plant.

The nonvolatile components, such as those that contribute to pungency in black pepper, are almost as important as the volatile essential oils, if one desires a full, rounded, flavor of black pepper. The components must be in the same relative proportion as they exist in the original spice. The resins and fatty oils act as natural fixatives for the more volatile essential oil components. Some solvent-free oleoresins are difficult to handle because of their heavy viscosity or tackiness. In such cases, propylene glycol or a fatty oil is added to make the item more flowable.

Some oleoresins are altered to yield more specific advantages to the end product. For example, Fritzsche Dodge & Olcott Inc. produces a Superesin which is essentially a blend of oleoresin and essential oil from the same spice, standardized to yield a more potent product, a more complete product, and one that most closely resembles the natural spice in aroma and flavor characteristics when used on the basis of its recommended spice equivalency. (See Table 6.1 for spice equivalencies of oleoresins of spices.) The same company produces a trademarked item called Bakeresins prepared specifically for use in baked goods. The essential difference in this latter product is the type of essential oil utilized. It is claimed to be better suited for baked goods and more equal to the quality of spice used in the baking industry.

Kalsec, Inc. has recently introduced a new series of oleoresins under the trademark Aquaresin. These are dispersible in water and other polar carriers with agitation, as well as being dispersible in oil and other nonpolar carriers. They are designed to be used as liquid seasonings rather than being dispersed on dry edible carriers. These Aquaresins are standardized with mono-, di-, and triglycerides, lecithin, and lactic acid, all derived from natural sources.

Production of oleoresins, superesins, aquaresins, and the like, is not limited to the two companies mentioned. Several other reputable suppliers provide comparable products to the food industry and should not be overlooked in seeking a source of supply.

In the manufacture of seasonings for prepared meat products, instant soups, gravies or sauces, many of these extracts are blended together in formulated proportions by the seasoning manufacturer to yield a density of flavor equivalent to that of a freshly ground spice mixture, and incidentally, at a much lower cost.

Needless to say, such oleoresins are very concentrated flavoring compounds; some are most difficult to weigh accurately and mix with other ingredients; food scientists foresaw the need to disperse such compounds on a carrier if they were to be used extensively in manufacturing operations. Thus, the idea of soluble spices was born.

ESSENTIAL OILS

Although several volumes have been written on essential oils, suffice to say, essential oils are the principal, but not sole, flavoring constituents of spices. The major portion of a fresh spice, whether it be a leaf, a stem, a bud, a fruit, the bark, a seed, a rhizome, or the entire plant, consists of water and fibrous tissue, neither of which, contributes to the aroma or flavor of the spice. With the possible exception of cayenne pepper, paprika, poppy seeds, and sesame seeds, spices are dependent on their essential oil content for their characteristic aromatic profile.

The first reference in the literature to essential oils of spice appears in the latter part of the thirteenth century, at which time, Arnold de Villanova steam distilled the aromatic essences from the leaves of rosemary and sage. However, it was not until great advances had been made in organic chemistry that the technology of essential oils really developed. Some essential oils are dry distilled, vacuum distilled, or expressed cold. A few are dependent upon purified solvents or selectively extracted with a series of solvents.

Some oils are distilled (rectified) more than once to remove undesirable fractions or to increase their concentration. Some oils are cooled after extraction to remove the natural waxes and improve their clarity. Many oils are extracted near the source of the raw material and subsequently reprocessed at destination in more modern distilleries. Some spices are distilled from the fresh state, others may be partially dried or completely dried, depending on the economics of the process in the location where the distillation is accomplished. The essential oil of a given species or variety of spice is generally uniform in flavor quality regardless of the quantity present in the spice. In general, the flavor intensity of the essential oil should be at least as potent as the reciprocal of the yield, based on the dried spice. Essential oils are sterile, free from extraneous materials, soluble in liquid fats or oils, emulsifiable in other liquid solutions, stable under good storage conditions, and represent up to 98% savings in weight and storage space.

Essential oils do have limitations as complete flavoring agents in that they do not contribute the hydrophyllic flavoring substances or the fixed oils found in oleoresins, nor do they contain the natural antioxidants of spices. Some are easily oxidized due to the presence of terpenes. Because of their high concentration, difficulty may be encountered in weighing out minute quantities for dispersion in mixtures. A small error in weighing could result in a major error or change in the flavor of the end product.

For a complete dissertation on essential oils, one should consult Guenther (1948).

Encapsulated Oils

Microencapsulation is the usual term and technique applied to the encapsulation of spice essential oils. It is accomplished by making an emulsion of the essential oil with one of the modified starches, developed for the purpose, or a soluble gum like gum acacia, and spray drying the emulsified product under controlled temperature and humidity conditions. The starch or gum must be of food grade if the encapsulated product is to be used for food purposes; it also must be water soluble to allow the flavor to be liberated uniformly throughout the product in which the encapsulated oil is to be used. The average particle size should be uniform and approximately equal to the size of fine salt or dextrose to allow for uniform distribution in a dry seasoning mix and to minimize separation from the other granular materials during the blending, filling, and other handling procedures.

DRY AND LIQUID SOLUBLE SPICES

Although most soluble spices are of the dry type, it should be noted that two other forms exist that have limited applications.

Liquid soluble spice flavorings are simply blends of essential oils and oleoresins, diluted to a specific spice strength with the addition of a suitable solvent like propylene glycol or glycerol. Polysorbate 80 is added to make them water soluble, and if emulsions are desired, an edible gum is used as a vehicle. The solvent is the probable limiting factor in the use of this type of soluble spice, which is used primarily for pickle brines and canned soups.

The other type of soluble spice is known as fat-based soluble spice, so named, because the oils and oleoresins are blended with either liquid or melted solid vegetable oils. Such spices are designed for oil phase products such as mayonaise or some specialty instant soup mixes. Some bakers use such a spice for spraying onto freshly baked goods as a flavored glaze.

The more common soluble spice type, known in the trade as "Dry Soluble Spice" but referred to in government publications as "Spice Flavorings, Soluble" appear at first to be quite simple products. A fixed amount of oleoresin (see Table 6.1) is dispersed on a predetermined amount of salt, dextrose, sugar, corn syrup solids, or some other dry, edible innocuous substance and blended until the product is completely and uniformly dispersed throughout the product. A well-trained eye will tell the blending foreman when the process is complete. Before such experience can be obtained, however, time and particle distribution studies should be made with the particular type of mixing equipment to be used.

Almost any type of good mixing equipment, with stainless steel parts in contact with the mix, is suitable for blending dry, soluble spices. Cost, efficiency, durability, capacity, and other factors must be considered before purchasing decisions are made. A small but efficient plant may have only two mixers—one capable of mixing up to 200 lb of seasoning and a second unit with a 700–1200 lb mixing capability. Obviously, the bulk density of the mix is one of the major factors in estimating the capacity of a mixer. In some cases, it may be necessary to facilitate the blending process by making an initial premix of all the oils and oleoresins to be blended with a small fraction of the base, in a smaller blender and then blending this concentrated premix into the remainder of the base. This procedure eliminates the "balling up" of some ingredients. Anyone who has experienced this balling up of ingredients in a large blender can appreciate the difficulty in trying to break up these hard, pealike, balls of flavor, once they have formed. In some cases, the entire batch must be "dumped," screened, and returned to the blender at considerable expense in time and labor. In the larger spice blending plants that utilize several mixers with capacities of 2000 lb or more each, one can well imagine the difficulties encountered when the process is interrupted.

As a final step in the preparation of dry soluble spices, it is usually necessary to add a drying agent to the mix to assure it is free-flowing when it is used. Such an agent may be tricalcium phosphate, calcium stearate, sodium silicate, or some other similar compound approved for such use by the Food and Drug Administration. Such use is limited to not more than 2% by weight of the total mix.

In commercial production, the figures shown in column four of Table 6.1, for the percentage extractives on a soluble dry edible carrier, are added to dextrose or salt, to make up 100% dry soluble spice. Such a blend will have the flavor and aroma equivalency of the natural spice, pound for pound. This is true for the Superesins and some of the oleoresins, but not for the essential oils. Some essential oils are converted to dry, soluble spices but they are limited in their usefulness by the limitations of the essential oil's flavor and aroma values.

SPICE EQUIVALENCY DEFINED

Essential oils, oleoresins and other extractives are standardized by reputable manufacturers to yield the same aroma and flavor, year after year, for the specific spice, from a specific area in the world. All manufacturers do not produce products to the same strength as others, nor do they procure their raw materials from the

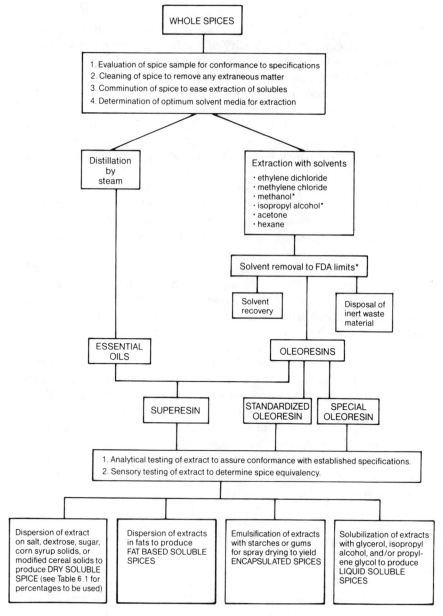

Fig. 6.1
Oleoresins and soluble spices from fresh whole spices

same country of origin. Suppliers usually determine the ground spice equivalency of their particular extracts, and as they are apt to differ, the technologist must check his supplier's product with the particular spice he has been working with, to assure for himself, that the spice equivalency is representative of his findings.

Spice equivalency of extracts is defined as *the number of pounds of oleoresin, required to equal 100 lb of freshly ground spice, in aroma and flavor characteristics.* This weight of oleoresin is added to sufficient salt, sugar, dextrose, or other edible dry material as a carrier, to total 100 lb of dry soluble spice. One pound of such dry, soluble spice is then equivalent to 1 lb of the corresponding freshly ground spice.

Table 6.1 outlines the spice equivalencies of extracts produced by Fritzsche, Dodge & Olcott Inc. Such equivalencies are shown in column four. For example, 5 lb of oleoresin of allspice containing 40% volatile oil is equivalent to 100 lb of freshly ground allspice in flavor and aroma; or 4½ lb of the Superesin containing 60% volatile oil is also equal to 100 lb of freshly ground allspice.

The figures in column three are useful in formulating seasonings as we shall see in Part 5. Using the same illustration, 1.418 g of oleoresin of allspice is equivalent to 1 oz of freshly ground allspice. Mathematically, the equations look like this:

$$1.418 \text{ g oleoresin} = 1.000 \text{ oz ground spice}$$
$$\frac{1.418 \text{ g} \times 16 \times 100}{453.5} = \frac{1.0 \times 16 \times 100}{16}$$
$$5 \text{ lb OR} = 100 \text{ lb ground spice}$$

The last two columns in the table represent the requirements of the federal specifications. Although some of the Superesins do not appear to be equal to or better than the government's minimum standards, they all are in compliance with the 1981 edition of the *Food Chemical Codex*. It is probable that the government standards will be revised to comply with the *Codex*. Where government standards do not exist, soluble spices may be made using the figures shown in columns four and five for the respective oleoresins. Federal Specifications - EE-S-645B dated June 20, 1966.

In addition to the analytical requirements shown in Table 6.1, Soluble Spice Flavorings shall be the flavoring constituents of the natural spices incorporated on a soluble, dry, edible carrier. They are intended for use as alternatives for natural spices in foods procured by agencies of the federal government.

Table 6.1   Spice Extractives-Equivalencies to Fresh Spices-Soluble Spices[a]

(1)	(2)	(3)	(4)	(5)	(6)	(7)
					Federal specifications	
Extractive	Type[b]	g/Type equivalent to 1 oz ground spice	% Extractives on soluble dry, edible carrier	Minimum % vol. oil in extractive vol/wt.	Extract on dry carrier (%)	Vol. oil in extract vol/wt. (%)
Allspice (Pimenta)						
leaf	E.O.	0.710	2.504	100	—	—
berry	O.R.	1.418	5.000	40	—	—
berry	S.R.	1.276	4.500	60	4.5	40
Anise seed	E.O.	0.710	2.504	100	—	—
	O.R.	2.339	8.250	15	—	—
Bay leaf (laurel)	E.O.	0.284	1.000	100	—	—
	O.R.	1.418	5.000	15	—	—
	O.R.	0.851	3.000	28	—	—
Basil	S.R.	0.213	0.750	40	2.0	40
Capsicum (Cayenne)						
1,000,000 Scoville H.U.	O.R.	1.701	6.000	0	—	—
480,000 Scoville H.U.	O.R.	1.701	6.000	0	5.0	0
Caraway seed	E.O.	0.710	2.504	100	—	—
	S.R.	1.418	5.000	60	5.0	60
Cardamom	E.O.	0.851	3.000	100	—	—
	S.R.	1.134	4.000	70	4.0	50
Cassia	E.O.	0.430	1.517	100	—	—
Celery seed	E.O.	0.567	2.000	100	—	—
	O.R.	1.347	4.750	9	—	—
	S.R.	0.851	3.000	12	3.0	10
Cinnamon	S.R.	0.567	2.000	65	6.0	50
Clove	E.O.	4.260	15.026	100	—	—
	S.R.	1.701	6.000	70	6.0	70
Coriander	E.O.	0.142	0.500	100	—	—
	S.R.	0.851	3.000	40	—	—
Cumin	S.R.	1.418	5.000	60	—	—
Dill seed	E.O.	1.142	4.028	100	—	—
	O.R.	1.418	5.000	10	—	—
	S.R.	1.418	5.000	70	5.0	60
Dill weed	E.O.	0.284	1.000	100	—	—
Fennel	E.O.	1.418	5.000	100	—	—
	S.R.	1.843	6.500	50	5.0	50

Table 6.1 (Continued)

(1)	(2)	(3)	(4)	(5)	(6)	(7)
					Federal specifications	
Extractive	Type[b]	g/Type equivalent to 1 oz ground spice	% Extractives on soluble dry, edible carrier	Minimum % vol. oil in extractive vol/wt.	Extract on dry carrier (%)	Vol. oil in extract vol/wt. (%)
Garlic Oil		0.142	0.500	100	—	—
Garlic (Special)[c]	O.R.	0.567	2.000[d]	5g	—	—
	O.R.	2.268	8.000[e]	5g	—	—
Ginger, African	O.R.	1.134	4.000	28	4.0	25
Cochin	O.R.	1.134	4.000	28	4.0	25
Ginger	S.R.	1.134	4.000	28	4.0	25
Mace	E.O.	1.418	5.000	100	—	—
	O.R.	1.985	7.000	40	—	—
	S.R.	1.985	7.000	50	7.5	50
Marjoram, sweet	E.O.	0.140	0.494	100	—	—
(Special)	O.R.	2.268	8.000	4	—	—
Marjoram, sweet	S.R.	0.709	2.500	40	3.0	40
Mustard	O.R.	1.276	4.500	5	—	—
Nutmeg	E.O.	1.134	4.000	100	—	—
(Special)	O.R.	2.552	9.000	60	—	—
Nutmeg	S.R.	1.701	6.000	80	6.0	80
Onion oil		0.012	0.0425	100	—	—
Onion (Special)	O.R.	0.071	0.250[d]	5g	—	—
	O.R.	0.284	1.000[e]	5g	—	—
Oregano	E.O.	0.212	0.748	100	—	—
(Special)	O.R.	1.134	4.000	17	—	—
	O.R.	0.851	3.000	27	—	—
Paprika (2500 color units)	O.R.	2.268	8.000	0	—	—
(1,000 color units)	O.R.	2.268	8.000	0	—	—
Parsley (Special)	O.R.	0.094	0.333[d]	12	—	—
	O.R.	0.851	3.000[e]	12	—	—
Pepper, black, Indian	O.R.	1.488	5.250	23[f]	4.5	150
Indian de-colorized	O.R.	1.488	5.250	23[f]	—	—
Rosemary	E.O.	0.142	0.500	100	—	—
(Special)	O.R.	1.559	5.500	10	—	—
Sage, Dalmatian	E.O.	0.350	1.235	100	—	—
(Special)	O.R.	2.126	7.500	25	—	—
Sage, Dalmatian	S.R.	0.710	2.500	65	5.4	65

(continued)

Table 6.1   (*Continued*)

(1)	(2)	(3)	(4)	(5)	(6)	(7)
					Federal specifications	
Extractive	Type[b]	g/Type equivalent to 1 oz ground spice	% Extractives on soluble dry, edible carrier	Minimum % vol. oil in extractive vol/wt.	Extract on dry carrier (%)	Vol. oil in extract vol/wt. (%)
Tarragon (Estragon)	E.O.	0.035	0.123	100	—	—
	O.R.	0.709	2.500	12	—	—
Thyme	S.R.	1.134	4.000	50	4.0	50
Turmeric						
standard 7% curcumin	O.R.	4.394	17.500	0	—	—
super 14% curcumin	O.R.	2.410	8.500	0	—	—

[a]Spice equivalencies are based on oils and oleoresins produced and supplied by Fritzsche, Dodge & Olcott, Inc., New York. Materials from other suppliers may differ considerably in their values.
[b]E.O. = Essential Oil. O.R. = Oleoresin. S.R. = Superesin.
[c]Special = A selective diluent has been added (propylene glyco' or a fatty oil) to ease the dispersibility of the oleoresin. Onion and garlic oleoresins come in water or oil dispersible forms.
[d]= Fresh spice equivalent.
[e]= Dehydrated spice equivalent.
[f]= 53% piperine content minimum.

All material used shall be of edible grade, clean, sound, whole-some, of good quality, and free from evidence of insect infestation, foreign matter, off-odors, and off-flavors. All spices used, shall com-ply with the applicable requirements of EE-S-631 except that the analytical requirements shall not apply. (See Part II of this book, under each of the individual spices for the federal specifications for each.) Anticaking agents may be used provided the type and amounts meet the requirements of the Federal Food, Drug and Cos-metic Act and Regulations promulgated thereunder.

Salt shall be white, refined, sodium chloride, with or without anti-caking agents. Iodized salt shall not be used.

Sugar shall be white refined cane or beet sugar, or a combination thereof.

Dextrose shall be anhydrous dextrose and of food grade.

In column six, the term extract means: the total extractives of the spice (the sum of the nonvolatile ether extract and volatile oil content (vol/wt) of the flavoring.) The minimum volatile oil content required is shown in column seven.

ADVANTAGES AND DISADVANTAGES OF VARIOUS SPICE TYPES _____

Fresh Spices

Advantages

Slow flavor release in high temperature processing.

Easy to weigh and handle.

No particular labelling problems.

Disadvantages

Bulk of weight is devoid of aroma and flavor.

Variable flavor quality and strength, depending on age, source, and storage conditions.

Presence of tannins could discolor some manufactured products.

Dried herbaceous spices develop off-flavors and aromas.

Presence of lipase enzymes could affect taste of products in storage.

Loss of volatile oils or constituents, particularly in ground spices within days or weeks.

Easily adulterated with exhausted material or inferior spices.

Subject to contamination at source, in transport, and in storage.

Greater warehouse facilities required for storage.

Warehouse, plant, and offices contaminated with spice dust during grinding operations.

Some spices have extremely high bacteria counts.

Ground spices contribute undesirable specks in finished products.

Poor flavor distribution results in some finished products.

Even "sterilized" spices contain the remains of dead insects, larvae, or eggs.

Essential Oils of Spices _____

Advantages
Uniform, standarized flavor, consistent with source of raw material.
Free from enzymes, tannins, bacteria, and filth.
Does not contribute moisture to final product.
Does not contribute color significantly to final product.
Good storage stability under normal storage conditions.

Disadvantages
Loss of volatiles under high temperature processing conditions.
Flavor and aroma is not completely typical of the natural spice.
Readily adulterated or sophisticated.
Some oils are readily oxidized
Naturally occurring antioxidants have been removed in processing.
Not easily dispersible on dry, edible carriers.
Very concentrated, making them difficult to handle and weigh accurately.

Oleoresins of Spices _____

Advantages
Uniform, standardized, complete flavor, equal to the natural spice.
Hygienic, free from bacteria, filth, and other contaminants.
Free from enzymes and contain natural antioxidants.
More complete, full-bodied flavor than comparable essential oil.
Approximately 50% lower in cost than corresponding spice on a flavor cost basis.
Low moisture content, relatively insignificant.
Long shelf life under normal and semi-adverse conditions.
Losses from volatilization of essential oils minimized due to presence of resins.
Less warehouse space required to store equivalent amount of natural spice flavor.

Disadvantages

Highly concentrated and sometimes quite viscous, making them difficult to weigh accurately.

Because of their viscous nature, some of the material may be left in the original containers and subsequently lost.

Flavor affected by source and quality of raw material which may not be the same source as that of the spice it is intended to replace.

Some tannins may be present unless treated for their removal.

Possibility exists for solvent contamination unless very carefully controlled at the source of manufacture.

All oleoresins do not have the same viscosity and each must be handled quite differently to avoid "hot spots" in the seasonings.

Aquaresins

Advantages

Uniform, standardized flavor, consistent with source of raw material.

Free from tannins, enzymes, bacteria and filth.

Relatively low moisture content.

Complete well rounded flavor of spice from which it was derived.

Better adapted for liquid seasonings.

Less viscous than some oleoresins, generally uniform viscosity for different spices.

Complete compatability with all other aquaresins.

Easier to weigh and handle than some oleoresins.

Easily dispersible in water, brines and syrups.

Disadvantages

Spice equivalency about 50% lower than oleoresins. Thus, higher in cost per pound of flavor solids.

Possibility of solvent contamination unless very carefully controlled.

Some tannins may be present unless treated for their removal.

Flavor affected by source and quality of raw material and may not be the same source as that of the spice it is intended to replace.

Encapsulated Spice Oils or Oleoresins _____

Advantages
Flavor protected from losses in strength over long storage periods.
Free flowing and easily weighed, handled, and mixed.
Free from enzymes, tannins, bacteria, and filth.
Easy to incorporate into dry mixes.
Free of salt, dextrose, and other fillers, except starches and/or gums used to encapsulate the oils or oleoresins.
Nonhygroscopic with good storage stability.

Disadvantages
Very expensive, contains only about 20% essential oil or oleoresin, therefore, only 20% as potent.
Not appropriate for liquid or baked products.
Could result possibly in a layering effect, or separation from the mix if all ingredients are not uniform in particle size.

Dry Soluble Spices _____

Advantages
Standardized color and flavor quality.
Free from filth, adulteration, impurities, and other contaminants.
Easily weighed and handled without difficulty.
Readily dispersed in food seasonings or food products.
Free of off-color food specks or sediment.
Low moisture content.
Free from enzymes.
Contain natural antioxidants.
Commercially sterile.
Approximately 30% or more lower in cost than corresponding spice.
Immediate flavor impact.
More uniform seasonings at reasonably stabilized prices, not subject as much to the wide, weekly fluctuation of the world market prices for spices.
Do not contribute unwanted and undesirable spice specks or color to the end product.

When desired, contribute uniform color to the finished product, as when oleoresin of paprika is used.
Free from dust in handling.

Disadvantages
Loss of some volatiles in long storage at high temperatures.
Tendency to "cake" unless protected with anticaking agents.
Allowances must be made in final formulations for the carrier used in dispersing the oils and oleoresins, i.e., salt, dextrose
Some are not resistant to high temperature processing, as in open kettle cooking.

ANALYTICAL METHODS

Tolerances for Solvent Residues in Oleoresins_____

The following are excerpts from the regulations of Part 21 CFR of the Federal Food, Drug and Cosmetic Act which pertain to solvent residues in Oleoresins.

173.210 Acetone Residues   A tolerance of 30 ppm is established for acetone in spice oleoresins when present therein as a residue from the extraction of spice.

173.230 Ethylene Dichloride Residues   A tolerance of 30 ppm is established for ethylene dichloride in spice oleoresins when present therein as a residue from the extraction of spice; Provided, however, that if residues of other chlorinated solvents are also present, the total of all residues of such solvents shall not exceed 30 ppm.

173.240 Isopropyl Alcohol Residues   Tolerances are established for residues of isopropyl alcohol resulting from its use as a solvent in the manufacture of spice oleoresins at 50 ppm (0.005%).

173.250 Methyl Alcohol Residues   A tolerance of 50 ppm is established for methyl alcohol in spice oleoresins when present therein as a residue from the extraction of spice.

173.255 Methylene Chloride Residues   Methylene chloride may be present in food under the following conditions: In spice oleoresins as a residue from the extraction of spice, at a level not to exceed 30 ppm (0.003%): Provided that, if residues of other chlorinated solvents are also present, the total of all residues of such solvents shall not exceed 30 ppm.

173.270 Hexane Residues   A tolerance of 25 ppm is established for hexane in spice oleoresins when present therein as a residue from the extraction of spice.

Determination: Residual Solvents (Official FCC Method)

NOTE: This procedure is for the determination of acetone, ethylene dichloride, hexane, isopropanol, methanol, methylene chloride, and trichloroethylene solvent residues in oleoresins.

Equipment and Materials
1. Distilling Head. Use a volatile oil determination apparatus designed for use with oils heavier than water.
2. Toluene. The toluene used for this analysis should not contain any of the solvents determined by this method. The purity may be determined by gas chromatographic analysis, using one of the following columns or their equivalent: (1) 17% by weight of Ucon 75-H-90,000 on 35/80-mesh Chromosorb W; (2) 20% Ucon LB-135 on 35/80-mesh Chromosorb W; (3) 15% Ucon LB-1715 on 60/80-mesh Chromosorb W; or (4) Porapak Q 50/60 mesh. Follow the conditions described under Procedure, and inject the same amount of toluene as will be injected in the analysis of the solvents. If impurities interfering with the test are present, they will appear as peaks occurring before the toluene peak and should be removed by fractional distillation.
3. Benzene. The benzene used for this analysis should be free from interfering impurities. The purity may be determined as described under Toluene.
4. Detergent and Antifoam. Any such products that are free from

volatile compounds may be used. If volatile compounds are present, they may be removed by prolonged boiling of the aqueous solutions of the products.

5. Reference Solution A. Prepare a solution in Toluene containing 2500 ppm of benzene. If the toluene available contains benzene as the only impurity, the benzene level can be determined by gas chromatography and sufficient benzene added to bring the level to 2500 ppm.

6. Reference Solution B. Prepare a solution containing 0.63% v/w of acetone in water.

Sample Preparation

1. Method A (all solvents except methanol). Place 50.0 g of the sample, 1.00 ml of Reference Solution A, 10 g of anhydrous sodium sulfate, 50 ml of water, and a small amount each of Detergent and Antifoam in a 250-ml round bottom flask with a 24/40 ground-glass neck. Attach the Distilling Head, a 400-mm water-cooled condenser, and a receiver, and collect approximately 15 ml of distillate. Add 15 g of anhydrous potassium carbonate to the distillate, cool while shaking, and allow the phases to separate. All of the solvents except methanol will be present in the toluene layer, which is used in the Procedure. Draw off the aqueous layer for use in Method B.

2. Method B (methanol only). Place the aqueous layer obtained from Method A in a 50-ml round-bottom distilling flask with a 24/40 ground-glass neck, add a few boiling chips and 1.00 ml of Reference Solution B, and collect approximately 1 ml of distillate, which will contain any methanol from the sample, together with acetone as the internal standard. The distillate is used in the Procedure.

Procedure

Use a gas chromatograph equipped with a hot-wire detector and a suitable sample-injection system or on-column injection. Under typical conditions, the instrument contains a ¼-in. (od) × 6- to 8-ft column maintained isothermally at 70° to 80°. The flow rate of dry carrier gas is 50 to 80 ml per min. and the sample size is 15 to 20 μ (for the hot-wire detector). The column selected for use in the chromatograph depends on the components to be analyzed and to a certain extent, on the preference of the analyst. The columns 1, 2, 3, and 4, as described under Toluene, may be used as follows: (1) This column separates acetone and methanol from their aqueous solution. It may be used for the separation and analysis of hexane, acetone, and trichloroethylene in the toluene layer from Method A. The elution order is acetone, methanol, and water, or hexane, acetone, isopropanol plus methylene chloride, benzene, trichloroethylene, and ethylene dichloride plus toluene. (2) This column separates methylene chloride and isopropanol, and ethylene dichloride. The elution order is hexane plus acetone, methylene chloride, isopropanol, benzene, ethylene dichloride, trichloroethylene, and toluene. (3) This is the best general purpose column, except for the determination of methanol. The elution order is hexane, acetone, benzene, ethylene dichloride, and toluene. (4) This column is used for the determination of methanol, which elutes just after the large water peak.

Calibration

Determine the response of the detector for known ratios of solvents by injecting known mixtures of solvents and benzene in toluene. The levels of the solvents and benzene in toluene should be of the same magnitude as they will be present in the sample under analysis.

Calculate the areas of the solvents with respect to benzene, and then calculate the calibration factor F as follows:

$$F(\text{solvent}) = \frac{\text{wt \% solvent}}{\text{wt \% bezene}} \times \frac{\text{area of benzene}}{\text{area of solvent}}$$

The recovery of the various solvents from the oleoresin sample, with respect to the recovery of benzene is as follows:

Hexane	52%	Trichloroethylene	113%
Acetone	85%	Ethylene dichloride	102%
Isopropanol	100%	Methanol	87%
Methylene chloride	87.5%		

Calculation

Calculate the ppm of residual solvent (except methanol) by the formula

$$\text{Residual solvent} = \frac{43.4 \times F(\text{solvent}) \times 100}{\text{\% recovery of solvent}} \times \frac{\text{area of solvent}}{\text{area of benzene}}$$

in which 43.4 is the ppm of benzene internal standard, related to the 50 g oleoresin sample taken for analysis. Calculate the ppm of residual methanol by the formula $[0.87 > \text{times frac} <' \text{ area spc of spc methanol } '> \text{ over } <' \text{ area spc of spc acetone } ' >,! \times$

in which 100 is the ppm of acetone internal standard, related to the 50-g oleoresin sample taken for analysis.

Volatile Oil Determination (Clevenger Method) ____

Weigh sufficient oleoresin (to obtain approx. 5 ml of oil) into a 500 ml flask. Add 250 ml of water, boiling chips or magnetic stirring bar. Reflux for 6 hours or until no more oil collects. Allow to cool to room temperature. Water droplets adhering to the oil layer may be dislodged by using a thin wire. Read the volume of oil to the nearest 0.02 ml and calculate the percentage of oil by volume. Concentration is expressed as ml per 100 g.

NOTE: For oleoresins cinnamon, clove, and allspice, where fractions of oil both lighter and heavier than water are obtained, draw from trap into a 100 ml cassia flask and add NaCl to the water layer to raise the oil level into the graduated portion of the flask.

The oil may be separated and dried and examined by optical rotation, refractive index, and gas liquid chromatography.

Determination of Color Value: Oleoresins Capsicum, Paprika (Official FCC Method) ____

Apparatus
1. Spectrophotometer-capable of accurately measuring absorbance (A) at 460 nm.
2. Absorption cells-1 cm square matched cells with stoppers.
3. Standard glass filter-(Standard reference material 2030 from the National Bureau of Standards).
4. Volumetric flasks-100 ml with ground glass stoppers.
5. Pipettes-transfer type.

Reagents
Acetone-reagent grade.

Procedure
1. Mix sample well by shaking.
2. Accurately weigh 70 to 100 mg of sample and transfer it to a

100 ml volumetric flask.

3. Fill to mark with acetone, stopper it tightly and shake well.

4. Allow the solution to stand for 2 min.

5. With a 10 ml pipette, transfer 10.00 ml of the solution into another 100 ml volumetric flask, and dilute to mark with acetone, stopper tightly, and shake well.

6. Transfer a portion of the solution to the spectrophotometric cell and measure the absorbance (A) at 460 nm with an acetone blank.

7. Determine the absorbance of the standard glass filter at 465 nm.

Calculations

1. Instrument correction factor

$$(I_f) = \frac{\text{NBS } A \text{ for glass filter at 465 nm}}{A \text{ of glass filter at 465 nm}}$$

2. Extractable Color

$$\text{Color} = \frac{A \text{ of acetone solution} \times 164 \times I_f}{\text{Sample weight in g}}$$

Notes

1. The A of the glass filter need only be determined once per day.

2. The recommended range of A values is $A = 0.30$ and $A = 0.70$. Extracts having A greater than 0.70 should be diluted with acetone to one-half the original concentration. Extracts having A less than 0.30 should be discarded and the extraction performed with a larger sample.

Determination of Percent Curcumin: Oleoresin Turmeric (Official FCC Method)

Equipment

A suitable spectrophotometer, preferably a double beam, capable of reading absorbance at 420–425 nm.

A pair of matched cells (1 cm).

50 ml, 100 ml volumetric flasks.

Procedure

1. Weigh accurately approximately 0.5 g of well-mixed sample of oleoresin into a 100 ml volumetric flask, record the weight as w. Add enough acetone and shake until the sample is completely dissolved. Bring to volume and mix thoroughly. Pipette 1 ml of the solution into a 100 ml flask and dilute to mark with acetone. Mix thoroughly. Pipette 5 ml of this solution into 50 ml volumetric flask and bring to volume with acetone. Mix thoroughly. Read the absorbance (A_u) of this solution at a wavelength of 420–422 nm using acetone as the blank.

2. Repeat the above procedure using pure curcumin. Record the weight as W. The absorbance (A_s) for pure curcumin is approximately 1600. It will vary slightly depending on the type of instrument used. A_s should be determined for each instrument as a precise value to include in the final equation to calculate % curcumin. Pure curcumin has a melting point of 183°C.

3. Both determinations should be made as rapidly as possible to avoid color loss.

Calculation

$$\% \text{ Curcumin} = 100 \times \frac{W}{w} \times \frac{A_u}{A_s}$$

Determination of Scoville Heat Units: Oleoresin Capsicum (Official FCC Method) _____

Materials and Procedure

A. 200 mg of oleoresin is weighed into a 50 ml volumetric flask. Ethyl alcohol (95%) is added to volume and the mixture thoroughly shaken. (Insolubles present should be allowed to settle.)

B. Sucrose Solution: Prepare a suitable volume of 10% w/v solution of sucrose in water.

C. Standard Solution: 140 ml of the sucrose solution from Part B is mixed with 0.15 ml of the alcoholic solution described in Part A (equivalent to 240,000 Scoville Heat Units. Before proceeding further, check label statement and make appropriate dilution.) After thorough mixing, 5 ml of this solution is given to each of 5 panel members. The panelist swallows the solution and notes whether a pungent or stinging sensation is perceived in the throat. A sensation which is just perceptible at this dilution is equal to 240,000 Scoville Heat Units.

The following chart indicates the dilution ratio of the Standard Solution and its corresponding Scoville Heat value. The volume of the Standard Solution in Column A from Part C above, is mixed with the volume of sucrose solution in Column B to yield the total volume of testing solution in Column C; 5 ml of this solution is given to each of the 5 panel members. The panelist notes whether a pungent or stinging sensation is perceived as outlined in Part C.

A ml Standard Solution	B ml Added Sucrose Solution	C Total Volume Testing Solution	Scoville Heat Units
20	10	30	360,000
20	20	40	480,000
20	30	50	600,000
20	40	60	720,000
20	50	70	840,000
20	60	80	960,000
20	70	90	1,080,000
20	80	100	1,200,000
20	90	110	1,320,000
20	100	120	1,440,000
20	110	130	1,560,000
20	120	140	1,680,000
20	130	150	1,800,000
20	140	160	1,920,000
20	150	170	2,040,000

Note

If the oleoresin sample is claimed to contain less than 240,000 Scoville Heat Units, prepare one or more dilutions according to the following table. Proceed with testing as outlined above.

Oleoresin Solution From Part A Above	Sucrose Solution (ml)	Scoville Heat Units
0.15	60	100,000
0.15	70	117,500
0.15	100	170,000
0.15	120	205,000

Comments
1. The stinging sensation described in Parts C and D above, must be at a perceptible level. Various dilutions should be made until this point is reached.
2. Where value is known, initial dilution should be made accordingly.
3. Three out of five members of the panel must agree to the pungency at the indicated level.
4. In some cases where the oleoresin is extremely pungent, it is recommended that the test be repeated after an interval of at least one-half hour to duplicate the results.
5. It is recommended that the individual be thoroughly experienced in this method before becoming a member of the panel.

Spectrophotometric Determination: Capsaicin in Oleoresin Capsicum

Instrument
Beckman DK-2 or equivalent.

Reagents
Purified Capsaicin, Reagent grade ethylene dichloride.

Calibration
Prepare a graph of concentration vs. absorbance for 4 or 5 capsaicin solutions, ranging from 0 to 10 mg/100 ml.
Use ethylene dichloride for a reference solvent, and 1 cm silica cells.
Record the UV spectrum from 320–250 nm.
Draw a base line tangent to the minima at 260 nm and 255 nm.
Measure absorbance from peak height (280 nm) to the base line.
Plot this absorbance vs. concentration.

Determination
Weigh 20–50 mg of sample into a 100 ml volumetric flask, dilute to 100 ml with ethylene dichloride, dissolve and record immediately.
Scan from 320–255 nm using 1 cm silica cells. Draw a base line tangent at the minima and determine the absorbance by measuring from the peak to the base line.

Calculations
Determine capsaicin conc in mg/100 ml from the graph.

$$\% \text{ Capsaicin} = \frac{(\text{capsaicin mg/100 ml}) \times 100}{\text{Sample wt. mg/100 ml}}$$

Note
There is no established correlation between observed pungency by the organoleptic procedure and this instrumental procedure. An instrumentally determined percent of capsaicin does not relate to a constant Scoville unit measurement.

Determination of Piperine: Oleoresin Black Pepper

Total Nitrogen by Kjeldahl Method
(AOAC No. 2.23 Modified)

Distillation
The Kjeldahl flask used in the digestion is fitted with a rubber stopper through which passes the lower end of an efficient bulb or trap to prevent NaOH being carried over mechanically during distillation. Connect upper end of bulb tube to condenser tube by rubber tubing.

Method
Weigh accurately 1 g sample oleoresin black pepper and place into a 800 ml Kjeldahl flask. Add 0.65 g metallic Hg, 17 g Na_2SO_4, 25 ml conc H_2SO_4 (93–98%), and a few boiling chips. Place flask in inclined position and heat gently until frothing ceases (if necessary, add small amount of paraffin to reduce frothing); boil briskly until solution is clear and then continue for 1 additional hour. Cool, add 250 ml H_2O and shake well to dissolve solid sulfates, add 50 ml Na_2S (40 g/liter) to precipitate Hg. Then add 80 ml aqueous NaOH (450 g/liter) and connect quickly to condenser without agitation, distill at least 150 ml into a 500 ml Erlenmeyer flask containing 50.00 ml $0.1N$ HCl and 100 ml H_2O (make sure that the end of the condenser is immersed in the standard acid solution in the receiver). Titrate excess HCl with 0.1 N NaOH using methyl red indicator (1 g/200 ml alcohol) to yellow end point.

Calculation
Calculate % of total nitrogen, using the formula:

$$\% \text{ Nitrogen} = \frac{0.1401 \text{ (ml N/10 HCl consumed)}}{\text{wt. of sample}}$$

Calculate % Piperine using the formula:

$$\% \text{ Piperine} = \frac{2.851 \text{ (ml N/10 HCl consumed)}}{\text{wt. of sample}}$$

ml N/10 HCl used = (ml blank − ml run) × factor of HCl

Note
All reagents used must be Nitrogen Free.

Instrumental Method
(Official FCC Method)

Instrument
A Ratio Recording or other UV Spectrophotometer suitable for scanning from 400 nm to 270 nm.

Reagents
Piperine—m.p. 129–130°C purified by repeated crystalizations from isopropanol.
Ethylene dichloride solvent.

Calibration
Prepare a graph of concentration vs absorbance for 4 to 5 piperine solutions ranging from 0 to 1 mg piperine per 100 ml ethylene dichloride, using 1 cm silica cells. Plot absorbance at 341 to 342 nm vs concentration of piperine in mg/100 ml.

Determination
Weigh 100 mg oleoresin taken from a 25 g representative sample that has been heated to 100°C in a steam bath or oven (not a hot plate) and stirred well with a glass rod. Dilute to 100 ml with ethylene dichloride and dissolve. Take a 1 ml aliquot and dilute to 100 ml with ethylene dichloride and run at once using 1 cm silica cells. Read the absorbance at 341–342 nm and determine the piperine concentration from the graph. Calculate % piperine as follows:

$$\% \text{ Piperine} = \frac{\text{Piperine concentration from graph mg/100 ml}}{\text{Sample weight mg/100 ml}} \times 100$$

Proper Storage Conditions _____

Oleoresins are generally packed in 25 or 35 lb double coated phenolic pails with crimped on covers with pouring spout.

When stored in full containers, in a cool place at approximately 68°F, the contents will remain in good condition for at least one year. Partially full containers should either be repackaged into smaller containers or used as quickly as possible to prevent possible deterioration.

Extreme cool conditions may tend to produce a semisolid or tarry substance which will require heating on a steam bath to return it to a fluid condition for easier use. In no case should the container with the viscous substance be heated on a hot plate.

Labeling Requirements _____

Oleoresins are considered natural flavors by definition. The labels of some products describe not only the title, but any additional non-flavoring ingredient which might be present, such as vegetable oil, propylene glycol, etc. When such ingredients are present, the main title of the product it carries the word "Special" as part of it.

The term "natural flavor" or "natural flavoring" means the essential oil, oleoresin, essence or extractive, protein hydrolysate, distillate, or any product of roasting, heating or enzymolysis, which contains the flavoring constituents derived from a spice, fruit or fruit juice, vegetable or vegetable juice, edible yeast, herb, bark, bud, root, leaf or similar plant material, meat, seafood, poultry, eggs, dairy products, or fermentation products thereof whose significant function in food is flavoring rather than nutritional.

Bibliography Part III

Anon, 1980. Aquaresins. Kalsec Co., Inc. Kalamazoo, Michigan.

Ashurst, P. R. *et al.* 1972. A new approach to spice processing. *Tropical Products Inst. Conf. Proc.*, London, pp. 209–214.

Berner, D. L. *et al.* 1973. Spice anti-oxidant principle. (Assigned to Campbell Soup Co.) U.S. Patent 3,732,111, Oct. 1.

Bhalla, K., and Punekar, B. D. 1975. Incidence and state of adulteration of commonly consumed spices in Bombay city. II. Mustard, black pepper and asafoetida. *Indian J. Nutr. Diet.* **12**, 216–222.

Cripps, H. M. 1972. Spice oleoresins, the process, the market, the future. *Tropical Products Inst. Conf. Proc.*, London, pp. 237–242.

Eiserle, R. J., 1981. The Oleoresin Handbook. 3rd Edition Fritzsche, Dodge & Olcott, Inc., New York.

Eiserle, R. J., and Rogers, J. A. 1972. The composition of volatile oils derived from oleoresins. *J. Am. Oil Chem. Soc.* **49**, 573–577.

Federal Register, 1968. Residual Solvents Permitted in Spice Extractives. Food Additives Regulation 121.1040–121.1045.

Federal Specification 1966. Spice Flavorings, Soluble EE-S-645B, June 20.

Fox, H. M., 1933. Gardening with Herbs for Flavor and Fragrance. The McMillan Co., New York.

Guenther, E. S. 1944. *Essential Oils*, Vols. 1–6. D. Van Nostrand and Co., New York.

Hadlok, R. and Toure, B. 1973. Mycological and bacteriological studies of sterilized spices. *Arch. Lebensmittelhyg.* **24**, 20–25. (German)

Heath, H. B., 1978. Flavor Technology: Profiles, Products, Applications. AVI Publishing Co., Westport, Connecticut.

Lewis, Y. S. 1973. The importance of selecting the proper variety of a spice for oil and oleoresin extraction. *Tropical Products Inst. Conf. Proc.*, London, pp. 183–188.

McKernan, W. M. 1972–1973. Microencapsulation in the flavor industry. Part I. *Flavour Ind.* **3**, 596–598, 600.

Sabel, W., and Warren, J. D. F. 1973. Theory and practise of oleoresin extraction. *Tropical Products Inst. Conf. Proc.*, London, pp. 109–192.

Salzer, U. J. 1975. Analytical evaluation of seasoning extracts (oleoresins) and essential oils from seasonings. *It. Flavors Food Additives* **6**, 151–157; 206–210; 253–268.

Staniforth, V. 1973. Spices or oleoresins. A choice? *Tropical Products Inst. Conf. Proc.*, London, pp. 193–197.

Walford, J. 1976. Solubilizers for essential oils in flavor formulations. *Food Manuf.* **51**, 35–37.

PART FOUR

Condiments and Sauces

7

Condiments

Like the term "herbs," there is almost equal confusion over the terms "condiments" and "seasonings." Even culinary experts have been known to use these words interchangeably while many authors appear to make no differentiation between them. Webster's Dictionary compounds the perplexity by defining a condiment as "something to enhance the flavor of foods; especially a pungent seasoning." By this definition, salt, MSG, or hot chilli peppers could conceivably be considered as condiments, as could any one of several other pungent spices such as capsicum, ginger, horseradish, mustard, cloves, cinnamon, garlic, and pepper. In addition, such a definition would include compounded items like prepared mustard, tomato catsup, chili sauce, soy sauce, barbecue sauce, *ad infinitum.*

A more precise definition appears to be desirable in order to eliminate the ambiguities that exist in today's literature. The author proposes the following definition which has been used throughout this book:

A condiment shall be a prepared food compound, containing one or more spices, or spice extractives, which when added to a food, after it has been served, enhances the flavor of the food.

The key phrases here are 1. a compounded food; 2. containing one or more spices or spice extractives, and 3. after it has been served. With this definition, individual spices, salt, MSG, etc., would be eliminated as condiments, even though they may enhance the flavor of food and may be used after the food has been served. On the other hand, celery, garlic and onion salts would be included in the definition of condiment if they were used after the product had been served. Likewise, prepared mustard, tomato catsup, chili sauce, horseradish sauce, meat sauce, Tabasco sauce, Worcestershire sauce, and other similar type sauces would be considered condiments, depending on how and when they were used in the course of a meal.

Some condiments may have a dual role as seasonings, as we shall see in Part 5 and where seasonings will be defined more fully. Suffice for the moment, one principal characteristic of a seasoning, which differentiates it from a condiment, is that it is added to a food product during its manufacture or preparation prior to serving.

If we accept the proposed definition for a condiment, just suggested, then we may classify the following condiments into two groups: Group I consisting of simple condiments and Group II made up of compound condiments.

Group I. Simple Condiments
    A. Celery salt
    B. Garlic salt
    C. Onion salt

Group II. Compound condiments
    A. Chili sauce
    B. Chutney
    C. Horseradish sauce
    D. Meat sauce
    E. Mint sauce
    F. Mustard, prepared
    G. Soy sauce
    H. Steak sauce
    I. Sweet and Sour sauce
    J. Tabasco sauce
    K. Tomato catsup
    L. Worcestershire sauce

SIMPLE CONDIMENTS

Celery Salt

Celery salt is a very simple condiment that may be prepared easily in the home by blending 25% by weight freshly ground celery seed with 75% by weight ordinary table salt. Commercially, the product is slightly more sophisticated and is best described in the following Military Specification format.

Military Specification for Celery Salt—
Mil-S-43855

Celery salt is a uniformly blended, free-flowing, dry mixture of ground celery seed, noniodized salt and calcium stearate. Not less than 90% by weight shall pass through a U.S. Standard No. 35 sieve and 100% by weight shall pass through a U.S. Standard No. 20 sieve. It shall contain not more than 4% moisture, not more than 75% noniodized salt, as sodium chloride, not less than 24% and not more than 25% ground celery seed (calculated on a moisture-free basis), and not less than 1.0% nor more than 2.0% of calcium stearate.

All ingredients used in the formulation and the final product shall conform in every respect to the provisions of the Federal Food, Drug and Cosmetic Act and regulations promulgated thereunder.

The product shall be prepared, processed and packaged under modern sanitary conditions and in accordance with good commercial practice.

The materials shall be clean, sound, wholesome, and free from evidence of insect infestation or any other objectionable foreign matter, flavor or odor.

The salt shall be clean, white, refined sodium chloride, with or without anticaking agents. Iodized salt shall not be used.

The calcium chloride must comply with the Food Chemical Codex requirements.

The freshly ground celery seed shall comply with the standards established in Part 2 of this book, under federal specifications for celery seed, except that the moisture requirements shall not apply.

Household Uses

Celery salt has a much broader use as a condiment than ground celery seed has as a spice for household use. Because of its dilution, it is easier to distribute the intense flavor of ground celery seed more uniformly and accurately. However, it is not recommended as a replacement for ground celery seed spice, for the consumer who has to guard against a high sodium intake.

Celery salt, with the exception noted above, may be sprinkled on fish, egg dishes, salads, bouillons, tomato and other vegetable juices, and wherever the addition of a celery note would lend a desirable flavor to the finished product.

Approximate Composition of Celery Salt, 100 g, Edible Portion (24% celery seed)

Water	1.6 g	Magnesium	106 mg
Food energy	94 kcal	Phosphorous	131 mg
Protein	4.3 g	Potassium	339 mg
Fat	6.1 g	Sodium	29,056 mg
Total carbohydrate	9.9 g	Zinc	2 mg
Fiber	2.8 g	Ascorbic acid	4 mg
Ash	78.1 g	Vitamin A	12 IU
Calcium	616 mg	Other vitamins	insignificant
Iron	11 mg		

Garlic Salt

Garlic salt is also a simple condiment, easily prepared in the home by blending about 20% by weight garlic powder with 80% by weight ordinary table salt. Commercially, the product is slightly more sophisticated and is best described in the following Military Specification format.

Military Specification for Garlic Salt— Mil-S-43855

Garlic salt is a uniformly blended, free-flowing, dry mixture of white garlic powder, noniodized salt and calcium stearate. Not less than 98% by weight shall pass through a U.S. Standard No. 30 sieve. It shall contain not more than 2.5% moisture, not more than 81.0% noniodized salt, as sodium chloride, not less than 18% nor more than 19% white garlic powder (calculated on a moisture-free basis), and not less than 1.0% nor more than 2.0% of calcium stearate.

All ingredients in the formulation and the final product shall conform in every respect to the provisions of the Federal Food, Drug and Cosmetic Act and regulations promulgated thereunder.

The product shall be prepared, processed, and packaged under modern sanitary conditions and in accordance with good commercial practice.

The materials shall be clean, sound, wholesome, and free from evidence of insect infestation or any other objectionable foreign matter, flavor, or odor.

The salt shall be clean, white, refined sodium chloride, with or without anticaking agents. Iodized salt shall not be used.

The calcium stearate must comply with the Food Chemical Codex requirements.

The garlic powder shall comply with the standards established in Part 2 of this book under Garlic, dehydrated, except that the moisture requirements shall not apply.

Household Uses

Garlic salt has a much broader use as a condiment for household use than does garlic powder. Because of its dilution, it is easier to distribute the flavor and intense odor of garlic more uniformly and accurately. However, it is not recommended as a replacement for garlic powder for consumers who must guard against a high sodium intake.

Garlic salt, with the exception noted above, may be sprinkled on beef, pork, lamb, fish and other seafoods, on eggplant and tomatoes, or into sauces, gravies, soups, or wherever the addition of garlic would lend a desirable flavor to the food product. Because of its salt content, one should be discreet in the use of additional salt.

One tablespoonful of garlic salt is equivalent to one clove (bulblet) of fresh garlic in flavoring value.

Approximate Composition of Garlic Salt, 100 g, Edible Portion (19% Garlic)

Water	1.4 g	Iron	1 mg
Food energy	631 kcal	Magnesium	11 mg
Protein	3.2 g	Phosphorous	79 mg
Fat	0.1 g	Potassium	212 mg
Total carbohydrate	13.8 g	Sodium	31,398 mg
Fiber	0.4 g	Zinc	1 mg
Ash	81.5 g	Vitamins	insignificant
Calcium	220 mg		

Onion Salt

Onion salt is similar to the other two simple condiments in that it may be prepared in the home very simply by blending about 25% by weight white onion powder with 75% by weight ordinary table salt. Commercially, it is best described in the Military Specification format that follows.

Military Specification for Onion Salt—Mil-S-43855

Onion salt is a uniformly blended, free-flowing, dry mixture of onion powder, noniodized salt and calcium stearate. Not less than 90% by weight shall pass through a U.S. Standard No. 20 sieve. It shall contain not more than 2.5% moisture, not more than 73.0% salt, as sodium chloride, not less than 25% onion powder (calculated on a moisture-free basis), and not less than 1.0% nor more than 2.0% of calcium stearate.

All ingredients used in the formulation and the final product shall conform in every respect to the provisions of the Federal Food, Drug and Cosmetic Act and regulations promulgated thereunder.

The product shall be prepared, processed, and packaged under modern sanitary conditions and in accordance with good commercial practice.

The materials must be clean, sound, wholesome, and free from evidence of insect infestation or any other objectionable foreign matter, flavor, or odor.

The salt must be clean, white refined sodium chloride, with or without anticaking agents. Iodized salt shall not be used.

The calcium stearate must comply with the Food Chemical Codex requirements.

The onion powder must comply with the standards established in Part II of this book under Onions, Dehydrated, except that the moisture requirements shall not apply.

Household Uses

Onion salt is not recommended as a replacement for onion powder for those persons who must guard against a high sodium intake; otherwise, it may be used in practically each instance where onion is called for in a recipe, in vegetable juices, salads, sauces, gravies, seafood, beef, lamb, pork, veal, and chicken dishes, with many different egg dishes, on carrots, corn, eggplant, green beans, peas, potatoes, spinach, and tomatoes. For the average outdoor chef, onion salt is easier to use than onion powder in barbecuing ribs, steaks, hamburgers or kabobs.

One tablespoon of onion salt is equivalent to one medium sized fresh onion in flavoring value.

Approximate Composition of Onion Salt, 100 g, Edible Portion (25% Onion)

Water	1.3 g	Iron	1 mg
Food energy	87 kcal	Magnesium	31 mg
Protein	2.5 g	Phosphorous	85 mg
Fat	0.3 g	Potassium	239 mg
Total carbohydrate	20.2 g	Sodium	29,082 mg
Fiber	1.4 g	Zinc	1 mg
Ash	75.6 g	Ascorbic acid	4 mg
Calcium	280 mg	Other vitamins	insignificant

COMPOUND CONDIMENTS

Prepared Mustards

Of all the condiments available to the consumer throughout the world, perhaps none has enjoyed such a long history of universal acceptance as that of prepared mustard. Long before the Christian era, the Chinese, Greeks, and Romans used it to make their foods more palatable. In fact, without it, or some other form of spicing in those days, before means were discovered for preserving foods, spoilage and other factors rendered many foods inedible. Foods had to be masked with hot, pungent spices or condiments.

As eating habits became more sophisticated and the culinary arts developed, so did prepared mustard. Instead of water, beer, wine, spiced wine, and other diluents were used with ground mustard seed to bring about different, more pleasing taste sensations. By blending the preferred spices of a region into the mustard being prepared, the product takes on regional characteristics. Thus, we have Chinese, Dijon, Dusseldorf, English, Swedish, and other styles of prepared mustards.

Because of air travel and easy access to foreign markets, these choice mustards are available to most everyone today. Less than a few decades ago, there were only two major styles processed and distributed within the United States: light, or salad-style prepared mustard and dark, or German style. Coleman's English style, dry mustard was also available for preparation in the home. Today, American "copies" of the favorite European styles are appearing on the shelves of the supermarkets at significantly higher prices than the original stand-bys.

When one considers the annual consumption of hot dogs, cold cuts, and hamburgers, in this country alone, one can readily perceive the volume of mustard required to satisfy the American palate. If one adds to that estimate, the volume of prepared mustard served in all of the Chinese and Polynesian restaurants, the German rathskellers, and other dining establishments throughout the world, one begins to realize the commercial magnitude of prepared mustard.

Light (Salad-Style) Prepared Mustard _____

This popular, inexpensive, slightly pungent, mild-flavored, distinctly turmeric-colored, prepared mustard is generally found at many concession stands in ball parks and drive-in restaurants. It is the one commonly found in individually packaged servings at take-out counters. It is prepared from yellow (white) mustard seed, mustard cake, or mustard flour, white distilled vinegar, turmeric, salt, with or without sugar, and/or spice. Starches and gums may be added to increase viscosity, particularly if low grade mustard seeds have been used. However, if the prepared mustard is manufactured carefully and properly, with high quality seeds, such additives should not be necessary.

A typical commercial formula for such a prepared mustard is as follows:

Ingredients	lb	kg
40 grain, white, distilled vinegar[1]	4000	1816.0
Ground yellow (white) mustard seed[2]	600	272.4
Noniodized salt	165	74.9
Ground turmeric	25	11.4
Ground cayenne pepper (optional)[3]	10	4.5
Garlic powder (optional)[4]	1	.5
	4801	2179.7

Notes:

[1]Concentrated vinegars are reduced with pure water to 40 grain (4% acidity) strength before using. Vinegar is used for preservation, flavor, and consistency of the finished product. Cider, malt, or wine vinegar may be used for a slightly smoother flavor but at an increased cost.

[2]Mustard seed is ground to a flour through special grinding stones made of granite. The hulls (bran) are generally removed in the process and may be used as fillers and for color in inexpensive, dark-style prepared mustards to simulate brown mustard seed.

[3]The use of cayenne pepper is optional. When used, it is for the purpose of increasing the bite or heat and to soften, somewhat, the brilliant yellow color of the turmeric.

[4]Garlic powder is also optional. It tends to round out the overall flavor and give it a meat-like smoothness.

A Typical Manufacturing Procedure for Making Prepared Mustard

1. About half of the 500 gal or 2000 lb (908 kg) of 40 grain vinegar is added to a glass-lined, 1000 gal capacity mixing tank equipped with a slow agitator.
2. Salt is added and mixed to complete solution.
3. Crushed mustard seed is then added slowly while adding the balance of the 40 grain vinegar. (The mustard seeds should be ruptured and not ground too fine at this stage.)
4. Turmeric, and other ingredients, if used, are then added and the agitation continued for at least an hour. The mix is allowed to soak overnight.
5. Agitation is resumed the following day and then sent through a mill with a clearance of about 0.08 mm between the rotor and stator stones. This procedure is done slowly and may take up to five hours to complete. The fine mash may be held in stainless steel or glass-lined tanks for several days to allow for proper aging and the natural removal of objectionable hydrogen sulfide odors.
6. After aging, the mash is then pumped to the packaging apparatus, which is equipped with an automatic float valve to prevent overfilling, and the product is bottled, capped, and labeled.
7. The finished product should comply closely with the following analytical guidelines:

Total solids	Not less than	16.0%
Titratable acidity (acetic)	Not less than	3.0%
	Not more than	40%
Salt content as NaCl	Not more than	4.5%
	Not less than	3.0%
Protein content	Not less than	3.8%
Crude fiber content	Not more than	7.0%

The texture, or consistency, shall be smooth with no free separation of the liquid phase, the color distinctly yellow and the flavor mild and mellow with a very slight bite.

Dark (German-Style) Prepared Mustard _____

This style of prepared mustard is made from a blend of about 70% by weight of brown or black mustard seed varieties and 30% by weight of yellow or white mustard seeds. All other ingredients except turmeric may be used as specified for the light-style prepared mustard. The manufacturing steps and the finished product guidelines, except for color, are similar to those specified for light prepared mustard.

Gourmet-Style Mustards _____

In gourmet-style mustard products, wine, spice, or tarragon vinegars are used in place of the distilled, malt, or cider vinegars. Finely ground spices, such as tarragon, black, white, or cayenne pepper, allspice, cinnamon, cloves, and nutmeg may be added to lend distinctive flavor and additional pungency. Paprika may be added to soften and enrich the color in place of, or in addition to, cayenne pepper.

One may prepare one's own tarragon vinegar by adding 453 g (1 lb) of fresh tarragon to 3.78 l (1 gal) of 40 grain wine vinegar and allowing the batch to steep for at least two to three weeks or more before removing the tarragon.

Spice vinegar is prepared by adding 2.72 kg (6 lb) each of ground celery seed, thyme, and sweet marjoram to 378 l (100 gal) of 100 grain wine vinegar or distilled vinegar and allowing the batch to steep for two to three weeks or longer before decanting off the clear, flavored vinegar. Approximately 26.5 liters (7 gal) of this spiced vinegar are used to replace 7 gal of the vinegar in the regular formula for a 4800 lb batch of prepared mustard.

As mentioned previously, the use of different diluents affects the flavor of prepared mustards quite markedly. The use of ordinary 40 grain vinegar, whatever the type, will yield a mild mustard. However, if water only is added to crushed mustard seed or mustard powder, the end product is sharp and hot, like Chinese-style mustard. If one were to use beer as a diluent the mustard would become extremely hot and pungent, whereas the use of wine results in a mustard that is pungent but with much less heat. In each case, the ground mustard seed should be added to the diluent to form a thin paste and allowed to stand for about 10 minutes; this time allows the enzymes in the mustard to activate and in combination with the diluent the mustard develops the distinctive flavor.

The reader will note the similarity between Dijon and Dusseldorf prepared mustards in Table 7.1. The main difference is in the spicing and type of vinegar used with much emphasis on tarragon in the Dijon-style product. Cinnamon, cloves, and wine vinegar are characteristic of Dusseldorf prepared mustard. Swedish-stype prepared mustard is a completely different product with two thirds of it being salad oil, sugar replaces the salt in the other two formulas, and pepper and cardamom contribute the spicing notes. It is more like a salad dressing in composition.

Tomato Catsup (Ketchup, Catchup)

Historical/Legendary Background _____

Some natives of the North Shore in Massachusetts claim the term "tomato ketchup" originated early in the nineteenth century in Salem, an old sailing village. Clipper ships sailed to the Orient and the Spice Islands from this seaport village and returned with their holds bursting with sacks of spices. The seamen would relate many stories of their adventures and eating experiences, particularly the native dishes they had consumed in the East Indies. One of their favorites was a pickled fish dish called by the natives *ke-tsiup*. The name had a catchy connotation to it and was easily pronounced by the townfolk. As the story is told, the housewives had an abundance of tomatoes each fall and it was their duty to make a preserved tomato sauce for use as a condiment to go with their fish, wild game, and poultry during the winter months. The sauce was made with crushed tomatoes, boiled down to a heavy consistency, with sugar, salt, vinegar, and spices added. Spices were obtained directly from the ships where they were plentiful and cheap. At first the homemade concoction was simply called sauce, or sometimes, tomato

Table 7.1 Formulas for Dijon, Dusseldorf, and Swedish-Style Prepared Mustards

	Dijon mustard	Dusseldorf mustard	Swedish mustard
Vinegar type (40 grain)	Tarragon	Wine	Distilled
Vinegar weight in lb.	3200	3200	1000
Brown mustard seed, ground	450	450	165
Yellow mustard seed, ground	250	250	0
Salad oil	0	0	2740
Noniodized salt	135	135	10
Sugar	0	0	120
White pepper, ground	1	1	8
Cardamom, ground	0	0	7
Garlic powder	1	1	0
Cayenne pepper, ground	3	3	0
Allspice, ground	2	2	0
Cinnamon, ground	0	4	0
Cloves, ground	2	4	0
Tarragon, ground	4	0	0
Total weight in lb.	4048	4050	4050
Approx. yield in gallons	450	450	465

sauce. As the term *ke-tsiup* became more commonly used for any type of sauce, the housewives began calling their sauce tomato ketchup. Today, the product is used universally throughout the western hemisphere on every conceivable food product, particularly with french fries and chips. The spelling has been shortened to catsup but old timers still refer to it as ketchup or catchup.

Definition—Standard of Identity—Federal Food, Drug and Cosmetic Act

Catsup, ketchup, or catchup is the food prepared from one or any combination of two or all of the following optional ingredients:
1. The liquid obtained from mature tomatoes of red or reddish varieties.
2. The liquid obtained from the residue from preparing such toma-

toes for canning, consisting of peelings and cores, with or without such tomatoes or pieces thereof.

3. The liquid obtained from the residue from partial extraction of juice from such tomatoes. Such liquid is obtained by straining the tomatoes or residue, with or without heating, in order to exclude skins, seeds, and other coarse or hard substances. It is concentrated and seasoned with sugar, or a mixture of sugar and dextrose, salt, a vinegar or vinegars, spices or flavoring or both, and onions or garlic or both. When sealed in a container it is so processed by heat, before or after sealing to prevent spoilage.

The definition does not permit the use of artificial color, artificial flavoring, preservatives, or added thickeners of any kind.

Since the insoluble solids content is comparable to that of the total tomato solids, the amount of insoluble solids found in catsup is an indication of the tomato solids present. In years past, the total solids content of most catsups fell within the range of 25 to 28%. The current tendency is to produce a catsup with a total solids content of 30 to 33%, with the higher solids due primarily from added sugar. Generally the lower solids content has a better tomato flavor; the added sugar tends to conceal the true tomato flavor. The amount of salt used varies among manufacturers, ranging from 2.5 to 3.4%. The total acidity usually falls within the narrow limits of 1.25 to 1.5%. To prevent spoilage after the container is opened, the acidity should be at least 1.25%. The higher the acidity level, the more sugar will be required to balance out the flavor. The consistency of the finished product is influenced by the percent insoluble solids present and the amount of pectin that has been retained in the processing of the tomatoes. If the washed, cleaned, and chopped tomatoes are given a flash heating, to 180°–185°F (82.2°–85.0°C) immediately after chopping, the pectic enzymes will be inactivated and most of the natural pectin present in the tomatoes will be preserved to yield a heavy bodied product. This heat treatment also serves to conserve the vitamin C content of the tomatoes.

The vinegar generally used in the manufacture of tomato catsup is 100 grain, distilled vinegar. The seasoning used is generally made up from among the following spices: cinnamon, cloves, cassia, cayenne, ginger, pepper, paprika, mustard, and allspice. Most manufacturers today use a preweighed packet of tomato spice blend, composed of soluble spices on a dextrose base, compounded to their own specifications by a spice blending company. One unit of spice blend, say 2.27 kg (5 lb) may contain 4 oz of various spice oils or oleoresins of spices and be sufficient to season a 250 gal batch of tomato catsup. Such a method eliminates the possibility of making mistakes in weighing individual spices in the plant. It is quick and foolproof because the unit mix solubilizes immediately in the batch and the flavor can be depended upon for uniformity from batch to batch. For a 1000 gal sized batch, four units of the spice blend would be used.

Briefly, one general process for the manufacture of tomato catsup begins with the washing and sorting of fresh tomatoes before they are brought into the plant. The field lugs or baskets of tomatoes are dumped into a flume-like trough, which guides the tomatoes down to the high pressure rotating washers where damaged or decayed tomatoes are eliminated. The washed tomatoes enter the plant on inspection belts where off-colored fruit, or rotted or decayed fruit is removed by hand trimmers. The good tomatoes are carried on another conveyor belt to a stainless steel food chopper from which they are pumped through a heat exchanger to inactivate the pectic enzymes and loosen the skins. From there, the product passes over a stainless steel mesh shaker screen to remove the seeds, hard core material, and skins. (A tomato finisher would accomplish the same purpose.) The tomato pulp is then pumped to a large vacuum pan or tank for the removal of moisture by concentrating the tomato solids content to about 28%. At this point, the vacuum is released and the product pumped to an open kettle steam jacket with an agitator. The preweighed vinegar, sugar, salt, onion powder, and soluble spice units are added while the entire product is being mixed and heated to about 190°F (87.5°C). The product is then checked by the quality control chemist for soluble solids content, acidity, salt content, and flavor to be sure it meets the company's specifications. Once it has been approved, the product is again pumped to a holding tank for vacuum filling at 190°F (82.5°C) into No. 10 cans or bottles. The product must be cooled quickly to prevent "stack burning" or a scorched flavor. This may be accomplished for the No. 10 cans by means of a spinner cooler arrangement. This consists of a 30 m (100 ft) conveyer belt about 2 feet wide, equipped with angle iron cleats rivetted to the belt every 3 feet. The belt is equipped with a variable speed drive to move it forward up an inclined plane at approximately a fifteen degree angle. Parallel to, and about 2–3 feet above the center of the belt, is a stationary 100 foot long, 1 in. diameter water pipe equipped with fine, high pressure, spray nozzles every 3 feet directed down toward the center of the belt. The cans, after filling and sealing, are conveyed to the lower end of the spinner-cooler belt, procede through a twist box to place the cans on their sides for traversing up the inclined belt in a rolling position. The belt should be moving about 1 foot every 2–3 seconds. The speed of the belt can be adjusted with the variable speed motor to fit the circumstances. As the cans proceed up the belt, they tend to roll back and will continue to roll in the opposite direction to the movement of the belt. With this rolling action under a fine spray of cold water, the entire contents of the can is exposed to the cooling conditions on the outer surface and by the time the can reaches the top of the conveyor belt the inside temperature of the can has dropped to about 100°F (38°C). The cans roll off the belt through a twist box to a long conveyor belt which allows the cans to dry off before entering the warehouse for stacking, labeling, or cartoning and storage or shipping. Bottles are cooled rapidly on another line under a fine mist of cold water. After allowing sufficient time for the immediate container, bottle, or can to dry, it is labeled, cartoned, and shipped either to the customer or to the warehouse for storage.

A typical commercial formula for tomato catsup is as follows (yield 900 gal)

Ingredients	lb	kg
Tomato pulp (27.5% total solids)	9445	4283.10
Distilled vinegar (100 grain)	380	172.35
Sugar, cane or beet[1]	700	317.50
Onion powder	5	2.25
Salt	250	113.40
Soluble spice units (4 @ 5 lb. each)[2]	20	9.10
	10,800	4897.70

Notes:

[1]Various combinations of sugars may be used depending on the facilities and the economics of handling them at the plant; i.e. dextrose, corn syrup, fructose syrup, corn syrup solids.

[2]Each 5 lb unit consists of about 113.4 g (4 oz) of essential oils and/or oleoresins of spices on 2.154 kg (76 oz) of dextrose or salt as a carrier. Dextrose is preferred because it has less effect on the final flavor of the product; if salt is used, it should be reduced by an equivalent amount in the formula. The spice extractives usually consist of oil of cassia, oil of mace, oil of pimento leaf (allspice), oil of cloves, oleoresin of ginger, and oleoresin of paprika. Others may be added depending on the manufacturer and his customers.

Chili Sauce

Chili sauce differs from tomato catsup in that the seeds are not removed from the peeled and cored tomatoes. The tomatoes are crushed, not pureed or pulped. The cooking process is substantially the same and the ingredients and seasoning are similar. The sweetness may be increased and the quantity of onion powder doubled but these are decisions for the manufacturer to make. Some manufacturers increase the heat factor by adding more cayenne pepper, others prefer a milder product. Much depends on the ultimate destination and use for the end product.

In general, 100 gal of peeled and cored tomatoes will yield about 40 gal of chili sauce.

A typical commercial formula for chili sauce is as follows (yield about 500 gal finished product)

Ingredients	lb	oz
Peeled and cored tomatoes (9.0% total solids)	9250	
Sugar, cane or beet	720	
Salt, noniodized	160	
Onion powder	20	
Distilled vinegar (100 grain)	320	
Garlic powder		2
Superesin capsicum		2
Essential oil of mace		1
Superesin cinnamon		4
Superesin celery seed		2
Oil of pimento leaf (allspice)		4
Oil of clove		8
	10,470	23

Meat Sauces

We have already defined a condiment as "a prepared food additive containing one or more herbs and spices, or spice extractives, which when added to a food after it has been served enhances the flavor of the food." Proprietary items found in most supermarkets and many restaurants, such as A-1 Steak Sauce, Heinz 57 Steak Sauce, and Escoffier Sauce conform to such a definition and are perhaps the best examples of typical, high quality, meat sauces on the market. Worcestershire Sauce could also be included under the category of meat sauces but will be discussed separately.

The following formula was developed early in the professional career of the author on a challenging wager, rather than as part of his official duties. It was meant to be a duplication of A-1 Sauce and was so regarded by a small taste panel. Years later, the author had an opportunity to repeat the formula, age it for about four weeks and try it again on a different panel. It was judged to be very acceptable but not an exact duplicate. The formula is offered as an example of the type and amount of ingredients that could be included in making a steak or meat sauce. Obviously, under commercial conditions, brand name ingredients would not be used but would be replaced by either their commercial counterparts or other similar items that would yield equivalent results. The brand names listed in the formula are used solely as a reference and in no way are intended as recommended sources of supply.

Federal specifications for Steak Sauce require that "the product shall have an acidity of not less than 2.6% nor more than 3.0%; the salt content shall be not less than 3.0% and not more than 3.3%; the soluble solids content shall be not less than 27.0% and not more than 30.0%; the color shall be dark, reddish-brown; there shall be no visible liquid separation and the flavor shall be acid, spicy, fruity and sweet."

By coincidence, the following formula for meat sauce (SA-22) complies fairly closely to the specifications outlined above:

Ingredient	lb	kg
Distilled vinegar (100 grain)	200.0 lb	90.91 kg
Cider vinegar (50 grain)	175.0 lb	79.54 kg
Hunt's tomato paste (33% s.s.)	134.0 lb	60.91 kg
Minute Maid Frozen Orange Juice Concentrate	96.0 lb	43.64 kg
Cane sugar	74.0 lb	33.63 kg
Karo Red label corn syrup	67.0 lb	30.45 kg
Karo Blue label ref. syrup	39.0 lb	17.73 kg
Sunsweet prune juice	115.0 lb	52.27 kg
Mott's canned applesauce	29.0 lb	13.18 kg
Fine granulated salt	33.0 lb	15.00 kg
Ground hot ginger	13.5 lb	6.14 kg
Ground cloves	3.7 lb	1.68 kg

Ground cinnamon	1.9 lb	0.86 kg
Ground chili pepper	1.4 lb	0.64 kg
Ground oregano	1.9 lb	0.86 kg
Ground rosemary	1.0 lb	0.45 kg
Ground cardamom	0.5 lb	0.23 kg
Onion powder	3.6 lb	1.64 kg
Garlic powder	2.8 lb	1.27 kg
Caramel powder	6.7 lb	3.04 kg
Gum tragacanth	1.0 lb	0.45 kg
	1000.0 lb	454.52 kg

One can readily see that many ingredients are necessary to obtain the proper consistency and balance of flavor.

The label declaration would read: Distilled and cider vinegars, tomato paste, prune juice, corn syrup, orange base, sugar, applesauce, salt, spices, caramel, dehydrated onion and garlic, gum tragacanth.

The label declaration for A-1 steak sauce states: Water, tomato paste, distilled vinegar, corn syrup, raisins, salt, herbs and spices, orange base, orange peel, caramel, dehydrated garlic, dehydrated onion.

Worcestershire Sauce

Worcestershire sauce, originally a trademarked name for a product produced by Lea and Perrins Co. Inc., has become a generic term for a dark brown, opaque, fermented type sauce with a tart, fruity, spicy, bittersweet taste and an aromatic, appetizing aroma. Any Worcestershire sauce, worthy of the name, should include in its formulation, anchovies, garlic, molasses, onions, salt, shallots, a soy derivative, spices, sugar, tamarinds, and water. The total solids should be within the range of 25 to 30%, the salt content not in excess of 5%, acidity not less than 3%, and an observable sediment of about 25 to 30% by volume.

The key to duplicating the original article is in the use of fresh vegetables, micromilled fresh spices, no artificial preservatives, colorings or sweeteners, and cold press extraction of certain ingredients. The entire mass is allowed to ferment in a blend of vinegars for at least 2 years with occasional agitation.

Table 7.2   Campbell's Worcestershire Sauce Formulas

Ingredients	A	B	C[1]	D[2]
40 grain white vinegar	15 gal	16 gal		
90 grain white vinegar			5.5 gal	
40 grain malt vinegar				25 gal
Water			12 gal	
Walnut catsup	10 gal			5 gal
Mushroom catsup	10 gal			5 gal
Sherry wine[3]	5 gal			
Brandy[3]	1 gal			
Cane sugar	25 lb	24 lb		
Tamarinds	10 lb			
Salt	12 lb	6 lb	23 oz	10 lb
Canton soya sauce	4 gal	1 gal	3½ gal	1 gal
Hog's livers[4]	20 lb			
Blackstrap molasses				3 gal
Micromilled cayenne pepper	2 lb	3 lb	1½ lb	1½ lb
Micromilled allspice	1 lb			12 oz
Micromilled coriander	1 lb			12 oz
Micromilled clove	½ lb	3 lbs	1¼ lb	4 oz
Micromilled mace	½ lb			4 oz
Micromilled asafoetida	¼ lb			4 oz
Nutmeg		3 lb	1¼ lb	
Ginger		3 lb		
Micromilled dehyd. lemon peel	8 lb			
Dehyd. garlic powder	½ lb	1¼ lb		
Micromilled black pepper		1¼ lb		

[1]Place all ingredients in an iron kettle for 3 days, cook, and bottle hot. Product will turn black and have an astringent taste due to the action of vinegar on the iron in the presence of tannins from the spices.
[2]Sometimes called English Beefsteak Sauce. Cook slowly for 2 hours, replace evaporated water, bottle hot, and sterilize for 30 minutes.
[3]Nonalcoholic flavors or extracts may be substituted.
[4]Cook livers thoroughly for 10 hours and grind very fine.

The first company to market a Worcestershire sauce no doubt set the standard for the industry to follow. The formula is very complicated and has never been revealed, but it includes the ingredients mentioned above. According to an article in the March 1975 issue of *Food Processing,* the company uses no heat for the extraction of flavors from the vegetables or spices. The cleaned ingredients are allowed to soak and ferment in vinegar for about two years with an occasional agitation. The liquid mass is cold pressed to eliminate the major solids and prevent the development of bitter and fishy flavors and the loss of volatile materials. After extraction and blending, the liquid sauce is aged in wooden casks for several more months before being pasteurized to stop further fermentation.

The bottled product is characterized by a light, brownish-gray fine sediment, about 25% by volume, a dark brown liquid phase, an aromatic, exciting aroma, and a spicy, tangy, bittersweet flavor. It is believed that the level of pungency may be controlled by the use of cayenne pepper. To disperse all of the flavoring solids the product should be well shaken in the bottle before use.

Worcestershire sauce has many uses in addition to gravies and meats. It may be used with scrambled eggs and omelets, tomato products, cocktail mixes, soft cheeses, soups, stews, salad dressings, and practically all types of foods.

Campbell's book *Food Products* give several different formulas for Worcestershire-type sauces, which will give the reader an idea of the possible variations that might occur to the formulator. Surprisingly, none of them call for anchovies, which is one of the essential ingredients in the original Worcestershire sauce. In Table 7.2 they are listed A through D.

A fifth type of sauce, prepared at one time by the author, is another possibility. Formula E is offered as an inexpensive, reasonable facsimile, of Worcestershire sauce, except it has a much lower percentage of sediment and may not have the fine nuances of a well-aged sauce (yield 17 gal).

Ingredients	
Formula E	
100 grain white vinegar	6 gal
50 grain malt vinegar	2½ gal
Mushroom-flavor liquid	4 oz
Walnut-flavor liquid	4 oz
Fermented soy sauce	3 gal
Sherry wine	2 gal
Blackstrap molasses	1½ gal
Tamarinds	5 lb
Ground anchovy paste	10 lb

Lemon extract	1 oz
Soluble spice flavoring[1]	15 lb 12 oz
Acid proof caramel	4 oz
Xanthan gum	4 oz

Formula E eliminates the long aging period required to develop the flavor. Except for the tamarinds and anchovy paste, all of the ingredients are either in liquid form or are readily soluble or dispersible.

The spice oils and oleoresins are weighed very carefully and blended in a slow speed mixer equipped with stainless steel blade and bowl, until uniformly mixed. The free flowing brown sugar is then added gradually until the mixture becomes free flowing. At this point it may be necessary to add about 2% by weight of an anticaking agent, like calcium stearate, zeolex 23, or tricalcium phosphate to prevent caking of the product if it is to be held for a long storage period before using.

The soluble spice mixture is then added to all of the other ingredients in a 25 gal steam-jacketed kettle, with cover, and the temperature raised to about 150°–170°F (65°–77°C) and held there while covered for about 2 hours. The product is passed through a finisher to remove the larger pieces of solids, heated to 190°F and bottled hot. The filled bottles were sterilized for 30 minutes in boiling water.

Dehydrated Worcestershire Sauce Base

Because of the author's long interest in dehydrated foods and dry mixes, he developed a formula for a dry Worcestershire sauce base, which compared quite favorably with some commercial Worcestershire sauces on the market, though not necessarily Lea and Perrins. The principal reason for developing the product was to use it in other dry mixes that called for Worcestershire sauce. It also offered considerable savings in freight and packaging costs.

[1]Brown sugar, free flowing type, 10 lb; Fine flake salt, 5 lb 9 oz; Oleoresin bleached capsicum, 500,000 H.U., 11.4 g; Oleoresin allspice, 8.0 g; Oleoresin cinnamon, 0.1 g; Oleoresin clove, 0.1 g; Oleoresin mace, 6.9 g; Oleoresin nutmeg, 41.0 g; Oleoresin ginger, 11.4 g; Oleoresin black pepper, 10.7 g; Oil of garlic, 0.3 g; Oil of onion, 0.2 g.

The formula is as follows:

Ingredients	%
Hydrolyzed plant protein	11.55
Cane or beet sugar	21.60
Fine flake salt	4.30
Onion powder	2.88
Garlic powder	0.36
Dextrose	34.50
Mustard flour	1.44
Micromilled ginger	1.44
Micromilled allspice	1.44
Micromilled cayenne	0.72
Micromilled cloves	0.72
B & C caramel	0.96
Monosodium glutamate	0.36
Malic Acid U.S.P.	7.45
Acetic Acid	2.48
Citric Acid	0.35
Lactose	7.45
	100.00

Specifications for Worcestershire Sauce Liquid _____

The nonvolatile solids should be not less than 20%; the salt content not less than 2.0% and not more than 5.0%; the acidity, calculated as acetic acid should be not less than 3.0% and not more than 3.8%; the pH value should be within the range of 3.2 to 3.8 and the sediment should not exceed 15% by volume. The color should be brown to dark brown and the flavor pleasantly tart, fruity, and spicy.

Soy Sauce

In all probability, soy sauce originated in China, where soy sauces are produced by fermenting a mash of soybeans for 6–24 months. The predominant flavor of all soy sauces is that of salt, but the better types have a distinct winey flavor and make excellent condiments for many meat, seafood, and vegetable dishes.

Shoyu sauce from Japan differs slightly from soy sauce in that its base is a combination of soybeans and cereal flour, which yields a slightly sweeter flavor than its Chinese counterpart. The popular sauce sold throughout the United States by Kikkoman Foods, Co. Inc. is such a sauce but is called soy sauce.

Federal Specification EE-S-610G dated May 5, 1978

This specification covers the requirements for ready-to-use fermented and nonfermented soy sauce. The specification is quite complete.

Type I soy sauce (fermented) shall be produced from fermented mash, salt brine, and preservatives, either benzoic acid or sodium benzoate. It shall be a clear, reddish-brown liquid essentially free of sediment. The fermented mash shall be a mash derived from enzymatic digestion of *koji* with salt brine and from fermentation by yeast and lactic acid bacteria. Soybean or defatted soybean and/or wheat can be added. The flavor of the finished product is characterized by a winey, fruity, smooth, salty taste, and the aroma is pleasantly winey, aromatic and somewhat like caramelized fruit.

Type II soy sauce (nonfermented) shall be a formulated product consisting of hydrolyzed vegetable protein, corn syrup, salt, caramel color, water, and a preservative. It shall be a dark-brown, clear liquid, with a well-blended, palatable, tart and salty flavor, possessing an aroma, body, and character typical of this type of sauce.

All materials for either type of sauce, shall be edible, clean, wholesome, of good quality, and free from evidence of insect infestation and other foreign matter, foreign flavor, or odor.

The salt shall be white refined sodium chloride—iodized and ammonium salt shall not be used. Corn syrup shall be produced by acid or enzyme hydrolysis of cornstarch. The liquid caramel color shall be a derivative of burnt sugar and shall be acid proof. The hydrolyzed vegetable protein shall be a dark, reddish-brown sauce, produced by hydrolyzing and digesting any one or any combination of corn, soybean, wheat, or yeast proteins with the major ingredient derived from soybean. These ingredients are combined with acid, then neutralized, filtered and aged. Typical analysis shall be:

	Not less than	Not more than
Total solids	38%	
Flavor solids	19%	
Total salt		19%
Protein (N × 6.25)	13.7%	
pH (as is)	4.6	5.6

Alternatively, powdered hydrolyzed vegetable protein may be substituted in lieu of liquid hydrolyzed vegetable protein and it shall conform with the typical analyses as stated above when reconstituted to an equivalent solids level.

Formulations for Types I and Type II Soy Sauce

Type I sauce is a proprietary item solely manufactured by the Kikkoman Foods, Co. Inc. Its formula is unknown to the author, but it is prepared by boiling yellow soybeans and wheat with sufficient water until they are thoroughly cooked and have become a soft mash. The mash is allowed to cool to about 80°F (27°C) and is then cultured with the mold, believed to be, *Aspergillus oryzae* or *Aspergillus soyae* and allowed to digest by enzymatic action in large vats for several days. A salt brine is then added with a special strain of yeast and lactobacilli. The product is allowed to ferment until the desired flavor, acidity and alcohol content has been reached.

The following analytical guidelines have been established for the product: titratable acidity (as acetic acid) 0.9–1.3%; total salt 13–16%; pH 4.6–5.2; protein 7.5%; alcohol 1.0–3.5%; total solids 29%; and total sugar (as invert sugar) 6%. Type II sauce (nonfermented) shall be formulated according to the following:

Ingredients	Not less than	Not more than
Hydrolyzed vegetable protein	42.0%	—
Salt	as required	
Corn syrup		10.0%
Caramel color, liquid	1.0%	3.0%
Water	as required	
Preservative	as required	

The following analytical guidelines have been established for the product: titratable acidity (as acetic acid) 0.8–1.2%; total salt (as NaCl) 15.0–18.0%; pH 4.5–5.3; protein 7.0%; total solids (vacuum oven) 32%; and total sugar (as invert sugar) 10.0%.

Mango Chutney

Mango chutney is a favorite condiment of the English. It was developed in India and introduced into England by the English ruling class of India upon their return to the homeland. It has never become popular in America in spite of its choice piquancy and delightful blend of fruits, spices, and vinegar. The imported price of the item is, in all probability, the stumbling block to its acceptance by Americans and not its quality or flavor.

It is made from peeled and cored apples, distilled vinegar, preserved mangoes, lemon peel, ginger, brown sugar, Malagar raisins, spices, salt, and fresh garlic. One might consider it a heavy form of Chili Sauce made from fruit instead of tomatoes.

A typical commercial formula for mango chutney is as follows:

Ingredients	lb	kg
Apples, peeled and cored	310	140.9
Distilled vinegar	205	93.2
Preserved mangoes	100	45.4
Preserved lemon peel, chopped fine	100	45.4
Preserved ginger, chopped fine	100	45.4
Brown sugar	100	45.4
Malagar raisins	45	20.5
Mustard, ground	25	11.4
Chili peppers, chopped, fresh	6	2.7
Salt	6	2.7
Ginger, ground	3	1.4
Garlic, freshly crushed	0.4	0.2
	1000.4	454.6

8

Sauces

An old acquaintance, a distinguished author and connoisseur of French cuisine, once said to me: "Not only French cooking but all fine cooking depends on the quality and variety of its sauces for proof of its excellence." Sauces do not necessarily involve the use of spices. An example of a simple sauce without spices is a clear salad dressing consisting of plain vinegar, oil and salt. Another example might be a simple au jus gravy. Sauces must have a distinctive, compatable flavoring and texture with the food with which they are served. There are sauces for appetizers, desserts, fruit, fish, game, poultry, meat, salads, vegetables, and almost any type of food. They may be very plain or extremely exotic; thin or thick, smooth or textured. They may or may not be condiments in themselves. The humble gravy or piquant salad dressing are sauces by definition.

A sauce may be defined as *any hot or cold liquid or semi-liquid product, other than a condiment, which when added to a food as it is being served, adds to its acceptance by improving its appearance, aroma, flavor or texture. It may, or may not, include the use of spices or spice extracts.*

It is not the intent of this book to cover sauces completely; it would require another volume to do so. Some of the better known sauces, together with their predominant spices or flavorings are listed in Table 8.1. Salt, MSG, sugars, thickening agents, and other miscellaneous adjuncts have been omitted. A few typical sauces that contain spices will be presented with complete formulations and directions for preparation.

Sauces may be colored naturally or artificially. They may be white, yellow, red, brown, or green or any combination of these. Vegetable coloring can produce infinite color combinations. Coloring of sauces is usually produced by some form of plant matter; secondarily by egg yolks, dairy products, or roasted animal tissue. Plant matter usually results in clear colors for transparent sauces, from the lightest of yellows to the darkest of greens.

Table 8.1

Sauce	Principal spices or flavorings
Dessert and Fruit Sauces	
Applesauce	Strained apples, cinnamon, mace, nutmeg
Apple Spice Sauce	Apple and lemon juices, butter, maple syrup, cinnamon, cloves
Apricot Sauce	Apricot puree, honey, lemon juice
Banana Sauce	Banana puree, lemon juice or flavoring
Blueberry Sauce	Blueberry juice, lemon juice, mace
Boysenberry Sauce	Boysenberry juice, lemon or lime juice
Brandy Sauce	Brandy, egg yolks, cream
Butter Sauce	Butter, nutmeg, mace
Butterscotch Sauce	Butter, brown sugar
Caramel Sauce	Orange rind, butter, browned sugar
Cherry Sauce	Cherry and lemon juice, butter, almond extract
Chocolate Sauce	Chocolate, butter, vanilla extract
Cinnamon Sauce	Cinnamon, orange and lemon rinds, egg yolks
Claret Sauce	Claret wine, lemon rind, cinnamon, butter
Coffee Sauce	Instant coffee
Creme de Menthe Sauce	Creme de Menthe, green
Custard Sauce	Egg yolks, sherry or vanilla extract
Egg Nog Sauce	Egg yolks, brandy, heavy cream
Fruit Sauce	Butter, blueberries, lemon juice and rind
Fudge Sauce	Chocolate, butter, vanilla extract
Ginger Sauce	Ginger, egg yolks, orange and lemon rinds
Grapefruit Sauce	Grapefruit juice and rind, lemon juice
Hard Sauce	Butter, vanilla extract, brandy, nutmeg
Lemon Sauce	Lemon juice and rind, egg yolk, butter
Maple Sauce	Maple sugar or syrup, butter, marshmallow
Maraschino Sauce	Maraschino syrup, butter
Mint Sauce	Peppermint or spearmint leaves
Mocha Sauce	Instant coffee, cocoa or chocolate
Nutmeg Sauce	Nutmeg, orange and lemon rinds, egg yolks
Orange Sauce	Orange juice and rind, lemon rind, brandy, cointreau or Grand Marnier
Orange Butter Sauce	Butter, orange juice and rind
Peach Sauce	Peach purée, lemon juice, butter, mace
Pineapple Sauce	Pineapple juice, crushed pineapple
Quince Sauce	Quince purée, lemon juice
Raisin Sauce	Raisin purée, butter, vanilla
Raspberry Sauce	Raspberry purée, lemon juice
Rum Sauce	Rum, lemon juice and rind, butter
Sherry Sauce	Sherry, butter, cloves, cinnamon
Strawberry Sauce	Strawberry puree, vanilla extract, currant jelly
Vanilla Sauce	Vanilla extract, butter, nutmeg
Wine Sauce	Any typical wine desired, butter

Table 8.1 (*Continued*)

Sauce	Principal spices or flavorings
Salad Sauces (Dressings)	
Avocado Sauce	Avocado pulp, lemon juice, Tabasco sauce, cayenne, dry mustard
Bacon sauce	Diced crisp bacon or Baco-Bits, pepper, chopped hard-boiled egg
Chili-Bleu Cheese Sauce	Chili sauce, paprika, garlic, lemon juice, bleu cheese
Bleu Cheese Sauce	Bleu cheese, lemon juice, mayonnaise
Caper Sauce	French dressing, capers
Cream Sauce	Heavy cream, lemon juice, white pepper, onions, mustard
Chiffonade Sauce	Freeze dried chives, diced beets, French dressing, hard-boiled eggs
Chive Sauce	Freeze-dried chives
Cole Slaw Sauce	Celery seed, vinegar, mayonaise
Cooked Salad Dressing Sauce	Mustard, lemon juice, butter, egg
Cottage Cheese Sauce	Cottage cheese, vinegar or lemon juice
Cucumber-Cream Sauce	Lemon juice, cayenne pepper, white pepper, cream, mashed cucumbers
French Sauce for Fruit	Worcestershire sauce, dry mustard, paprika, lemon juice or vinegar
Fruit Sauce	Pineapple, lemon and orange juices, fresh or sour cream, maraschino juice
Honey Sauce	Honey, lemon juice and rind, butter, egg, vinegar
Horseradish Cream Sauce	Ground horseradish, tarragon vinegar, dry mustard, lemon juice
Italian Sauce	Tomato catsup, onion, vinegar
Lemon Cream Sauce	Lemon juice, heavy cream, egg
Lorenzo Sauce	Currant jelly, chili sauce, lemon juice, paprika, honey
Parisian Sauce	French sauce, green pepper, celery seed, minced onion, parsley, carrot granules
Piquant Sauce	Pepper, paprika, horseradish, dry mustard, lemon juice and rind
Roquefort Sauce	Roquefort cheese, lemon juice, mayonnaise
Russian Sauce	Pimientos, chives, capers, tarragon vinegar, chili sauce
Sour Cream Sauce	Sour cream, lemon juice, white pepper, onions, egg, vinegar, dry mustard
Tomato French Sauce	Tomatoes, vinegar, paprika, onion, garlic, dry mustard, Worcestershire sauce
Vinaigrette Sauce	Chives, pepper, mustard, wine vinegar, olive oil

(*continued*)

Table 8.1   (*Continued*)

Sauce	Principal spices or flavorings
Vegetable Sauces	
Bacon Sauce	Diced crisp bacon or Baco-Bits, lemon juice
Cheese Sauce	Swiss cheese, butter, pepper
Mousseline Sauce	Butter, egg yolks, cream, cayenne pepper, lemon juice
Egg Sauce	Cream, butter, paprika, parsley, eggs
Hollandaise Sauce	Butter, egg yolks, cayenne, lemon juice
Mock Hollandaise Sauce	White sauce, lemon juice, butter, egg yolks
White Mornay Sauce	Onion, celery, bay leaf, pepper, parsley, paprika, Parmesan cheese, cream, chicken stock
Vegetable Dill Sauce	White sauce, dill seed, onion, parsley, pepper, sour cream
Toulonnaise Sauce	Celery, Chablis wine, capers, ripe olives, green onion or chives
Poultry Sauces	
Allemande Sauce	Mushrooms, white pepper, nutmeg, lemon juice
Beer Sauce	Beer, sesame seeds, mustard, garlic powder, dry mustard
Barbecue Sauce	Onion, brown sugar, tomato, vinegar, Worcestershire sauce, lemon juic, garlic
Chaud-froid Sauce	Onion, celery seed, pepper, bay, thyme
Chicken Paprika Sauce	Onion, paprika, chicken stock, pepper
Giblet Sauce	Giblets, celery, chicken stock, butter
Herb Sauce	Butter, chicken stock, white pepper, chives, parsley, tarragon
Pollo Asado Sauce	Wine vinegar, white wine, oregano, thyme, garlic powder, parsley, Tabasco sauce
Polynesian Chicken Sauce	Orange juice conc., soy sauce, Tabasco sauce, garlic powder, ginger
Ravigote	Vinaigrette sauce, capers, chervil, onions, pepper, shallots, tarragon
Meat Sauces	
Béarnaise Sauce	Shallots, parsley, tarragon, chervil, tarragon vinegar, peppercorns, cayenne pepper, egg yolks, butter
Béchamel Sauce	Chicken stock, butter, white pepper, onion
Bercy Sauce	White wine, shallots, butter, parsley
Beurre Meunière	Lightly browned butter, lemon juice, parsley
Bordelaise Sauce	Shallots, red wine, parsley, bone marrow, thyme, bay leaf
Brown Sauce	See Text-Part V (Brown Gravy)
Diable Sauce	Shallots, peppercorns, white wine, parsley, brown and Worcestershire sauces
Ginger Sauce	Ginger, brown sugar, garlic, wine vinegar, soy sauce, apricot jam

Table 8.1 (*Continued*)

Sauce	Principal spices or flavorings
Hongroise Sauce	Onion, paprika, chicken stock, cream sauce, butter
Horseradish Sauce	Horseradish, white pepper
Madère Sauce	Beef stock, butter, tomato puree, onion, carrot, thyme, bay leaf, parsley, pepper, Madeira wine
Maître d'Hotel Sauce	Butter, chives, parsley, lemon juice
Marchand de Vin Sauce	Shallots, red wine, butter, pepper, parsley, onions, beef stock, nutmeg, dry mustard, wine vinegar
Mint Sauce	Mint leaves, vinegar, honey
Mushroom Sauce	Mushrooms, butter, onions, paprika, pepper, sherry, Worcestershire sauce
Mushroom Madeira Sauce	Mushrooms, butter, cream, shallots, parsley, brown sauce, Madeira wine
Mustard Sauce	Dry mustard, butter, pepper, lemon juice
Poivrade Game Sauce	Onions, carrots, shallots, garlic, bay leaf, thyme, vinegar, beef stock, red wine, peppercorns, parsley, olive oil, red currant jelly
Raisin Sauce	Raisins, brown sugar, butter, vinegar, pepper, cloves, mace, currant jelly, Worcestershire sauce
Roquefort Sauce	Roquefort cheese, Worcestershire sauce
Savory Sauce	Butter, minced onions and garlic, pepper, Chili and Worcestershire sauces, mustard
Soy sauce	See text
Sweet and Sour Sauce	Soy sauce, brown sugar, wine vinegar, ginger, pineapple juice, garlic, lemon juice, dry mustard, onion powder
Teriyaki Sauce	Red wine, soy sauce, garlic powder, lemon or lime juice, brown sugar, chives or shallots
Tomato Sauce	See text
Tourangelle Sauce	Butter, onion, carrot, shallots, garlic, red wine, beef and chicken stocks, parsley, bay leaf, thyme, peppercorns
Velouté Sauce	Chicken stock, butter, onion
Wine Marinade Sauce	Soy and Worcestershire sauces, dry mustard, pepper, red wine, lemon juice, parsley
Worcestershire Sauce	See text
Seafood Sauces	
À la King	White sauce, mushrooms, egg yolk, butter, green pepper, pimiento
Anchovy	Anchovy paste, sherry wine
Bonnefoy	Bay leaf, pepper, shallots, thyme, tarragon vinegar

(*continued*)

Table 8.1 (*Continued*)

Sauce	Principal spices or flavorings
Catalina	Butter, garlic, olive oil, pepper, pimiento, white wine
Chaud-froid	Fish stock, butter, lemon juice, pepper
Cream Curry	Chives, cream, curry powder blend, egg yolk, parsley, butter
Cucumber (hot)	Fish stock, lemon juice and rind, onion, cooked cucumber
Dill	Worcestershire sauce, chicken stock, dill seed, egg yolk, mustard, pepper, tarragon vinegar
Egg and Parsley	Hard-boiled eggs, cayenne, horseradish, parsley
Fish	Basil, bay leaf, capers, chervil, chives, clove, fish stock, garlic, marjoram, nutmeg, parsley, pepper, pimiento, shallots, tarragon, thyme, white wine
Lemon	Egg yolks, fish stock, lemon juice and rind, parsley
Matelotte	Fish stock, brandy, mushrooms, paprika, pepper, shallots, white wine
Newburgh	Mace, sherry wine, white pepper
Oyster	Oysters with liquor, butter, milk, mushrooms
Rémoulade	Anchovies, capers, chervil, chives, mustard, onion, parsley, tarragon
Tartar	Capers, chives, mayonnaise, mustard, parsley pickle relish, shallots, tarragon vinegar

Red sauces have one of several kinds of coloring matter derived from tomato, capsicum (paprika or red cayenne pepper), red beets, cranberry, or red cabbage.

Yellow sauces are colored by the addition of egg yolk, saffron, turmeric, pineapple, marigold, anatto, sweet potatoes, yams, squash, or pumpkin.

Green sauces utilize either spinach, parsley, chard, beet greens, avocado, or almost any green that is compatible with the main dish.

Brown sauces are usually derived from cooked meats, hydrolyzates, browned flour, or starch in hot fat, with an addition of some red coloring matter like tomato to improve the golden brown appearance of the sauce. Without the red tone addition the gravy is apt to have a grayish appearance. A subthreshold level of instant coffee is excellent for intensifying the brown color of meat sauces.

SALAD DRESSINGS

The volume of salad dressings produced in the United States is in excess of 200,000,000 gallons per year and is still growing. Mayonnaise and mayonnaise-type salad dressing account for more than 155,000,000 gallons. Salad dressings, by definition, are sauces. Typical formulas for two popular salad dressings will appear later.

Salad dressings are seasoned oil and vinegar sauces, used on fresh lettuce, with or without other fresh salad greens, with or without sliced, diced, or chunks of fruit or vegetables. Examples of appropriate spices to be used in salads are given in Table 8.2.

Table 8.2   Appropriate Spices for Salads

Salads	Spices
Bean	Basil, chili powder blend, celery seed, onion, mint
Beet	Bay leaf, chervil, dill, mint, onion, pepper, thyme
Cabbage	Allspice, basil, caraway seed, celery seed, dill, marjoram, mint, nutmeg, onion, pepper, poppy seed, paprika, rosemary, sesame seed, tarragon, white pepper
Chicken	Capers, chives, curry powder blend, fennel, marjoram, onion, paprika, poppy seed, rosemary, sesame seed, tarragon, white pepper
Cucumber	Basil, capsicum, chervil, dill, onion, paprika, tarragon, white pepper
Egg	Celery seed, chili powder blend, chives, chervil, dill, marjoram, mustard, onion, parsley, paprika, tarragon, white pepper
Fruit	Allspice, capsicum, cardamom, clove, mint, nutmeg, paprika, poppy seed, sesame seed
Lobster	Basil, capers, celery seed, curry powder blend, dill, paprika, tarragon, thyme
Potato	Basil, capers, caraway seed, celery seed, chives, chervil, curry powder blend, dill, onion, paprika, pepper, rosemary, savory
Salmon	Celery seed, dill, tarragon, thyme
Shrimp	Basil, capers, celery seed, curry powder blend, dill, horseradish, oregano, paprika, tarragon, thyme
Tuna	Basil, capers, celery seed, chives, curry powder blend, paprika, tarragon, thyme
Turkey	Capers, chives, curry powder blend, marjoram, onion paprika, poppy seed, rosemary, sesame seed, tarragon, white pepper
Vegetable	Basil, celery seed, chives, chervil, chili powder blend, dill, fennel, marjoram, oregano, paprika, rosemary, onion, savory, tarragon, thyme

GRAVIES

Gravies are sauces used to enhance the starchy components (noodles, potatoes, etc.) that accompany a meat course. Gravies should be seasoned sufficiently to compliment the meat being served. If possible, the drippings from the roast should be included in any gravy to bring out the distinctive, natural flavor of the meat, be it pork, beef, veal, duck, chicken, or turkey. If the drippings or rendered fat of the meat is not available, any neutral fat, properly browned and seasoned will serve satisfactorily, but not as well. See Part V for gravy seasoning formulas.

CHARACTERISTIC FORMULATIONS FOR SELECTED INSTANT SAUCES AND REGULAR SALAD DRESSINGS

Instant type sauces, dressings, and gravies have become popular commercial items in the past decade. With a majority of housewives working out of the home, there is less time to prepare complete meals as there was years ago. A few commercial formulas for instant sauces are illustrated here to illustrate what can be done with an understanding of available ingredients and their uses. Two regular salad dressing formulas are also presented to show the proportions of the many ingredients incorporated into complete salad dressings.

Hollandaise Sauce (Instant)

Ingredients	lb	g
Consista starch	25	11,339
Dellac's Dry Butter	25	11,339
Sweet whey powder	31	14,060
Fine, salt	7	3,175
Dehydrated egg yolks	4	1,814
Dehydrated lemon juice powder	4	1,814
Monosodium glutamate	4	1,814
Oleoresin of pepper	6.1 g	6.1
Oleoresin of turmeric	19.7 g	19.7
Oleoresin of paprika	0.6 g	0.6
Oil of lemon	12.0 g	12.0

Blend the oils and oleoresins on the salt and MSG to complete uniformity. Add the other ingredients and blend again to uniformity.

Add 609 g (21.5 oz) to 4.2 liters (1 gal) of cold water. Mix well, bring to a slow boil while stirring, being careful not to scorch the product. Remove from heat when properly thickened. Ready to serve.

Béarnaise Sauce (Instant)

Ingredients	oz	g
Tarragon vinegar	8.0 oz	227 g
Dehydrated parsley	0.5 oz	14 g
Dehydrated tarragon	0.5 oz	14 g
Onion powder	2.0 oz	57 g
Hollandaise mix, above	21.5 oz	609 g
	32.5 oz	921 g

Add all ingredients except vinegar to the finished, blended hollandaise mix above. At time of reconstitution with water, add the tarragon vinegar and proceed as above, until thickened.

Marinara and/or Parmesan Seasoning Mix and Sauce (Instant)

Ingredients	%	g	Procedure
Fine granulated salt	19.64	89.075	Add 1 lb of
Sugar	11.61	52.656	seasoning mix to 5
Parmesan cheese, dehydrated	26.56	120.460	gals of crushed
Minced onions, dehydrated	24.26	110.029	Italian tomatoes
Black pepper, ground	5.20	23.584	and 40 oz of olive
Basil, whole	3.11	14.105	oil. Simmer
Parsley granules	6.53	29.616	mixture over a low
Garlic powder	.97	4.400	flame in covered
Corn oil	.12	.544	container for about
Oregano, ground	2.00	9.071	30 min. Serve hot
	100.00	453.540	over pasta.

Piquante Dressing

Ingredients	lb	kg
Salad oil	2150	977
Vinegar	1025	466
Salt	50	23
Sugar	85	39
Paprika	15	7
Mustard flour	45	20
Worcestershire sauce	12	5
Tabasco Sauce	1	0.5
Onion juice	45	20.5
Total	3428	1558.0

Italian Dressing

Ingredients	lb	kg
Salad oil	5300	2409
Corn syrup (40 D.E.)	350	159
Dextrose	580	264
Vinegar, distilled (50 grain)	880	400
Water	2000	909
Lemon juice	170	77
Salt	100	45
Dehydrated green peppers, diced	20	9
Dehydrated red peppers, diced	20	9
Italian seasoning mix[1]	580	264
Total	10000	4547

French Dressing

Ingredients	lb	kg
Salad oil (corn, sesame, soy, olive, or cottonseed)	3200	1454.5
Vinegar, 50 grain (malt, cider, wine, or distilled)	1600	727.3
Salt	75	34.1
Sugar, optional	130	59.1
Paprika	20	9.1
	5025	2284.1

[1]Contains a blend of four or more of the following oils or oleoresins on a dextrose base: oregano, parsley, sage, onion, rosemary, garlic, savory, thyme, marjoram, and basil.

Bibliography Part IV

Allgeier, R. J., Nickol, G. B., and Conner, H. A. 1974. Vinegar: history and development. I. *Food Prod. Dev.* **8**, 69–71.

Allgeier, R. J., Nickol, G. B., and Conner, H. A. 1974. Vinegar: history and development. II. *Food Prod. Dev.* **8**, 50, 53, 56.

Anon. 1974. Freeze/thaw/heat/stable salad dressing from mix. *Food Process.* **35**, 37.

Anon. 1975. Worcestershire sauces vary in quality, solids content, affect formulation, usage. *Food Process.* **36**, 58.

Binsted, R., Devey, J. D., and Dakin, J. C. 1971. Pickle and Sauce Making. 3rd Ed. Food Trade Press, London.

Federal Specification. 1975. Prepared Mustard, EE-M-821H. July 21.

Federal Specification. 1978. Soy Sauce. EE-S-610G. May 5.

Komarik, S. L., Tressler, D. K., and Long, L. 1982, Food Products Formulary. Vol 1. 2nd Edition, Meats, Poultry, Fish, Shellfish. AVI Publishing Co., Westport, Connecticut.

Military Specification. 1973. Salts: Celery, Garlic and Onion. Mil-S-43855. July 27.

Simone, A. 1948. French Cook Book. New Ed., Rev. by C. Gaige. Little Brown and Co., Boston.

USDA. 1977. Composition of Foods: Spices and Herbs: Raw, Processed, Prepared. Rev. Handbook No. 8-2. U.S. Department of Agriculture, Washington, D.C.

PART FIVE

Seasonings and Seasoning Technology

9

Seasonings

Salt is good: but if the salt have lost its savour, wherewith shall it be seasoned? St Luke 14:34.

Noah Webster's original 1828 edition of the American Dictionary defined the word "seasoning" as that which is added to any species of food to give it a higher relish; usually something pungent or aromatic, as salt, spices or other aromatic herbs, acids, sugar, or a mixture of several things."

The unabridged edition of Random House's Dictionary of the English language defines seasonings as "salt, or an herb, spice, or the like, for heightening or improving the flavor of food." The verb, to season, was similarly described: "to render a dish more palatable by the addition of some savory ingredient."

Other dictionaries and references consulted offered similar interpretations. Thus, we find that the definition of a seasoning has not changed considerably in the past century and a half.

With today's use of such components as nucleotides, hydrolysates, yeast autolysates, caseinates, glutamates, encapsulated extractives, spice extractives, and soluble spices, in addition to various milk derivatives, dextrose, corn syrup solids, sugar, and salt, all entering into the formulation of different seasonings, perhaps it is time to update the definition of seasoning to enable future generations to use consistent terminology?

A more precise definition for spices was presented in Part II of this book; condiments were more clearly defined in Part IV; seasonings are defined here.

Seasonings are compounds, containing one or more spices, or spice extractives, which when added to a food, either during its manufacture or in its preparation, before it is served, enhances the natural flavor of the food and thereby increases its acceptance by the consumer.

As opposed to condiments, which are added after the food is served, seasonings must be added before a food is ready for serving.

Some compounds may be part of a seasoning mix at one time and a complete condiment at another time, depending on when and how they are used. For example, a dry Worcestershire sauce base, when reconstituted with water, would be a condiment, but when used dry, usually mixed with other ingredients, it becomes part of a seasoning mix. Tomato catsup, a condiment according to our definition, would also become part of a seasoning if it were added to beef stew, for example, during its preparation in cooking.

THE COMPOUNDING OF SEASONINGS

Although no precise figures are available, it is safe to assume that over 80% of the spices produced are used by spice blenders, either in the form of freshly ground spices or extracts prepared therefrom, and, by flavoring extract manufacturers for use in compounded flavors and perfumery products.

The compounding of seasonings is considered a specialized, skillful art. The proper blending of such dissimilar components as spice extracts, essential oils, spices, salt, sugars, monosodium glutamate, ribonucleotides, dairy products, and the many other components that enter into complex seasoning mixtures require a high level of technical expertise and a long period of practical experience, a knowledge of the marketplace, an awareness of the ever increasing list of government regulations and restrictions, and a sense of economics in the selection of the ingredients with the optimum use to which they can be used. The formulator must be aware of the compatability of the ingredients with the end-product with respect to color, texture, flavor, and other sensory attributes; he must know their potential stability in the shelf life of the end product; he must have a known source of supply at all times and the uniformity or lack of it from different suppliers; he must have an understanding of the microbiological problems that might be encountered when certain ingredients are used, particularly under subsequent processing conditions and storage temperatures.

There are very few occasions when only one spice will achieve the desired flavor in a product. Spices vary tremendously in intensity of aroma and flavor; some are very mild, others extremely pungent; a spice from one growing area of the world may differ significantly from the same generic spice grown in another geographical location; climate, growing conditions and cultivation practices will affect the essential oil content of spices and thereby the flavor and aroma. Drying, packaging, storage, and transportation conditions will also affect the overall quality of the spice to be used in the seasoning. Add to all of this, the skill of the spice grinder, his equipment and plant facilities, the length of time between grinding and use of the ground spice in the seasoning, and the intermingling of all these intangibles with the other basic food constituents—salt, sugar, MSG, etc., one begins to appreciate the required skills and responsibilities of the food technologist for compounding high quality, uniform seasonings for the food business.

A seasoning must be compounded in such a way that it increases the natural flavor of the product to be seasoned; it should not overpower or diminish the product's flavor but add a balanced interest with an odor identity, a smoothly blended, rounded flavor with no perceptible, undesirable aftertaste. In general, the weaker the flavor of the product to be seasoned, the lower the level of added seasoning required to achieve a satisfactory balance of flavor in the finished product.

SEASONING FORMULATIONS

The best examples of seasonings are those associated with the prepared meat, dry gravy mix, instant sauce, salad dressing and soup businesses. Several examples of each of these will be given.

The seasonings to be illustrated in this book are complete commercial formulas, in a format used by many spice blending laboratories and production plants. They are so designed that the costs may be readily calculated and up-dated on a periodic basis as needed. Each spice blender may have his own particular technique for recording formulas; some are very "secretive" and complicated; others are quite simple; any good seasoning blender, in time, can duplicate the seasoning produced by a competitive blender; thus, secrecy of formulations is no longer a truism in the spice blending business except that most blenders will not divulge one customer's seasoning to another customer.

The technologist is encouraged to devise his own method for recording formulas but for the sake of introducing an illustrative method, the forms shown in Fig. 9.1 and 9.2 have been found to be effective and simple to use by the technologist, the plant operator, management personnel, and the cost accountant.

Some of the wide variations in flavoring possibilities will be given. Some will utilize only natural spices; others will use spice extractives, soluble spices, and combinations of all three forms. The advantages of using different forms will be given, taking into account bulk density, costs, advantages to both the blender and the meat packer plus other factors that need to be considered by the seasoning supplier.

Figure 9.1 represents a form used for recording essential laboratory information about a given formula, in this instance, a frankfurter seasoning. The brand name, if any, and the type of seasoning is inserted on the top line. The ingredients are listed on the following lines, as they would appear on the label—in descending order of magnitude, as per government regulations. All of the spices may be grouped together for the purpose of labeling and because the amount of monosodium glutamate must be declared on the label, it is shown as a percent of the formula.

Directions for use are shown as the unit weight required to season 100 lb of meat, in this instance, 4 lb 4 oz.

On the upper left portion of the page, the laboratory and plant code numbers are inserted. These codes differ for the following reason: as products are developed in the laboratory, code numbers are assigned to each product in the laboratory notebook in chronological order, i.e., F-000001, F-000002 up to F-999999 then G-000001 etc. This number appears in the upper left space. The plant code number appears on the upper right space. Usually a letter precedes the number indicating the product classification: F for frankfurter, B for bologna, etc., and the number would also appear in chronological order as they are finalized and put into production: F-1, F-2, F-3 etc. If the product duplicates a competitor's item, the competitor's name and code number is shown beneath the other two codes, together with the date of submission of the sample, for future reference purposes. In this instance, the supplier was McCormick, his code was F-786 and the sample was submitted 8/16/81. (This citation is for illustrative purposes only and is not intended to represent a McCormick seasoning.)

The ingredients are then listed in the second vertical column as shown. If their original containers are coded, the code should appear in the first vertical column. This is very important, for some materials like corn syrup solids, dextrose, MSG and the like, vary as to size of crystals, degree of purity, and other factors that are usually reflected in the supplier's code number. If no code is on the container then simply refer to the name of the supplier.

The third column entitled Batch Rx size, refers to the weight of the individual ingredients in one unit of seasoning; the total weight should be exactly the weight of the unit package.

The fourth column, with the heading Percent RX size, is the percent of each ingredient in the batch; the total should add up to 100%. The reason for this column is twofold. First, it enables one to calculate costs per pound more easily and second it shows percentages of certain restricted materials which may be required by the Meat Inspection Division. In this illustration, 2.94% MSG, mustard, sodium erythorbate, anticaking agents, and ascorbic acid if they were present, would also have to be shown on the label.

The ingredient cost per pound and the total cost for each individual component of the formula should appear in pencil (the ones listed are fictitious and are shown for demonstration purposes only), as these figures are subject to change monthly and sometimes even weekly. This is also most important for cost control purposes as the selling prices are based on a factorial markup times the ingredient cost. In the spice blending business, this could range from 1.65 to 3.6 or more depending on the volume of the item, the unit size pack, the type of shipping container employed and the competitiveness of the item. Shipping costs are usually added as a separate item. As most meat packing houses are usually quite wet or have high humidity conditions—anything but ideal conditions for the storage of seasonings for up to 30 days—double corrugated boxes or lock-tite fiberboard drums are usually specified for packing. These are expensive and must be calculated into the cost of business. Also included in the markup factor are such items as labor costs, supervision, executive office support personnel, laboratory expenses, utilities, finance costs, sales commissions, and expenses, freight costs, plant and equipment depreciation, salaries etc. A reasonable profit should be expected on top of all costs.

In the right hand column, the date should be shown at the top, which represents the day the product was last costed out. This should be done in pencil, as it will be changed periodically according to rising costs of raw materials. The selling price (SP) should also be written in pencil for the same reason. In the example shown, the markup over ingredient costs was 2.2; but under the letter B the

Product: NEFSCO* FRANKFURTER SEASONING

Ingredients: Salt, corn syrup solids, sugar, spices, and monosodium glutamate (2.94%)

Use: 4 lb 4 oz to 100 lb of meat

McCormick—F-786   8/16/81

F-000001

F-1

Product Code	Ingredients	Batch Rx Size	Percent Rx Size	Cost/ Unit	Total cost	8/1985
						Per lb
						Cost
Diamond Crystal	Salt, fine flake	2 lb 8 oz	58.8235	0.03	1.76	26.59¢
CPC Int'l.	Corn syrup solids, fine	12 oz	17.6470	0.285	5.03	
Revere Sugar	Cane sugar	8 oz	11.7647	0.383	4.51	

Stouffer Chem.	Monosodium glutamate	2 oz	2.9412	1.275	3.75		S.P.
Dirigo Corp	Ground white pepper, fine	4 oz	5.8824	1.39	8.18		58.5¢
							B
Dirigo Corp	Ground nutmeg	1 oz	1.4706	1.29	1.90		64.0¢
							C
Dirigo Corp	Ground ginger	1 oz	1.4706	0.99	1.46		69.0¢
							D
		4 lb 4 oz	100.0000		26.59		79.0¢

Fig. 9.1
Laboratory form for listing seasoning information.

markup over ingredient costs is 2.4; under the letter C, the markup is 2.6 and under the letter D, a markup of 3.0 has been calculated; all rounded off to the nearest half cent. Any other markups could be employed, depending on the management policies and arrangements it may have with its salesmen. In some instances, the markup will affect the percentage commission the salesman will get on the sale.

Figure 9.2 represents a typical formula card, prepared by the laboratory, for use in the plant by the production supervisor. Costs and other miscellaneous data do not go out to the plant.

Where oils and oleoresins are used in the formula, it is the usual practise for the laboratory technologist to remove the stock labels from the containers, once the products have been approved by the laboratory, and coded labels affixed to the containers. This prevents visitors to the plant and most plant employees from knowing exactly

Product: NEFSCO FRANKFURTER SEASONING

Use 4 lb 4 oz Units: 24/Case

Ship five (5) cases			Rx 510 lb
Ingredients	Pounds	Ounces	Grams
Salt, fine flake	300		
Corn syrup solids, fine	90		
Cane or beet sugar	60		
Monosodium glutamate	15		
White Pepper, fine grind	30		
Nutmeg, ground	7	8	
Ginger, ground	7	8	
	510		

Fig. 9.2
Laboratory formula card.

the composition of the formula. The laboratory and plant production forms are similarly coded when such oils and oleoresins are specified.

It should be pointed out that not all seasoning formulas are necessarily complete. There are times when the meat packer might prefer to add additional salt or all of it in his plant; or he may wish to add ascorbic acid or sodium erythorbate, on the assumption that he can save a few cents per pound by eliminating the spice blender's markup on an expensive ingredient. In some instances, the sodium nitrite cures required for some products may be added by the meat packer in other cases, the spice blender will make up unit packs of the cure, usually a blend of salt and sodium nitrite, sufficient for one unit pack of seasoning, with directions for use. Sodium nitrite is a very hazardous material and must be handled with utmost care in an isolated area away from any other materials or blending operations. The spice blender is usually better equipped to handle such a product, with greater precision, than many meat packers.

As this book is being written, the law requires that the residual sodium nitrite in cured meats shall not exceed 156 ppm. There is much discussion in the industry and with government agencies concerning the need for, and the level of use for sodium nitrite. The level could be further reduced by the time this book is in print. At any rate, the salt in the cure packet is used as a diluent, to give the sodium nitrite better distribution throughout the mass. The sodium nitrite is used to fix the color of the meat, but more importantly, to prevent the growth of botulism organisms.

10

Meat Seasonings

FRANKFURTER SEASONINGS

Formulas A and B which follow illustrate simple types of frankfurter seasonings. They utilize only freshly ground spices. Formula
A has the full complement of salt and sodium erythorbate used for
100 lb of meat while formula B requires the meat packer to add
whatever amount of salt he may choose plus the sodium erythorbate. By law only ⅞ oz of sodium erythorbate or sodium ascorbate
may be used for each 100 lb of chopped meat to accelerate color
fixing in the final meat product and preserve the color during storage. Citric acid or sodium citrate may be employed to replace half of
the sodium erythorbate or sodium ascorbate. In each instance, the
packer would also add his own curing agent. At the time of this
writing, 5.5. g of sodium nitrite may be used as a curing agent for
each 100 lb of chopped meat, but this may be reduced in the future.
The sodium nitrite is used to fix the color and prevent growth of
botulism organisms.

Although the salt content of 2½ lb per 100 lb of meat appears to be
high, about 10 oz of this is offset by the use of 24 oz of corn syrup
solids. Twenty four ounces, times the sweetness level of 40%, equals
9.6 oz equivalency of sugar. Thus, the flavor salt level is below the
2% level considered maximum for flavor acceptance.

Formula A contains the minimum amount of spices needed to
enhance the flavor of the meat in a frankfurter emulsion. Four
ounces of pepper and 1 oz of nutmeg.

Formula B contains less pepper and nutmeg but contains other
spices, complementary to pepper and nutmeg, in addition to onion
and garlic, which round out the flavor. Although the spice content is

almost three times that of formula A, it is not overpowering; it is considered about the right level for a superior flavored frankfurter. It should be pointed out again, as it has been throughout this book, that most spices are very potent and only small amounts are needed to enhance the natural flavor of meats. The 13.62 oz of spices in formula B for 100 lb of meat represents less than one-half teaspoon per pound of meat.

Frankfurters

Ingredients	oz	%
Formula A		
Salt	40.00	57.25
Corn syrup solids	24.00	34.35
Sodium erythorbate	0.87	1.25
White pepper, ground	4.00	5.72
Nutmeg, ground	1.00	1.43
	69.87	100.00
Formula B		
Onion powder	2.00	14.685
Garlic powder	2.00	14.685
Ginger, ground	0.58	4.258
White pepper, ground	2.32	17.034
Coriander, ground	2.32	17.034
Mace, ground	0.20	1.468
Cardamom, ground	0.20	1.468
Paprika, ground	4.00	29.368
	13.62	100.000

Formula C is similar to formula B except that it is a complete mix, containing salt, sodium erythorbate, and dextrose in place of corn syrup solids. Dextrose is used at a lower level than corn syrup solids would be because it has a higher sweetness factor of 70% which offsets about 10.5 oz of salt in the formula. It also reduces the size of the unit pack by 9 oz if corn syrup solids are used. The only other exception is that the oleoresin of paprika has been used to replace the ground spice, thereby reducing the size of the unit pack an additional 3.68 oz. Use of the oleoresin makes a better appearing mix and distributes the paprika color more uniformly throughout the frankfurter emulsion. If we refer to Table 6.1 we find that 0.32 oz or 9.07 g of oleoresin of paprika is equivalent to 4.0 oz of freshly ground paprika spice.

Ingredients	oz	%
Formula C		
Salt	40.00	64.30
Dextrose	15.00	24.11
Sodium erythorbate	0.87	1.40
Oleoresin of paprika	0.32	0.51
Coriander, ground	2.32	3.73
White pepper, ground	2.32	3.73
Ginger, ground	0.58	0.93
Mace, ground	0.20	0.32
Cardamom, ground	0.20	0.32
Onion powder	0.20	0.32
Garlic powder	0.20	0.32
	62.21	99.99

Formula D is the same as formula C, flavorwise, except it contains extractives of spices, at the proper equivalency levels of their corresponding spices, plus two additional ingredients—ground mustard and tricalcium phosphate, which is used to prevent the mix from caking due to the oily and hygroscopic nature of the oils and oleoresins. Ground mustard is limited in its use by government regulations to 1% of the meat formula, primarily because of its protein content. As has been mentioned in an earlier chapter, ground mustard provides for a good emulsion and acts as a binder to the meat products that go into frankfurters, bologna, and other similar products. Ground mustard is relatively flavorless, it contains no heat, and does not contribute or alter the flavor. It is used for its physical properties.

Ingredients	oz		%
Formula D			
Salt	40.00		54.71
Dextrose	15.00		20.52
Sodium erythorbate	0.87		1.19
Mustard, ground	16.00		21.89
Tricalcium phosphate	0.28		0.38
Onion powder	0.20		0.27
Garlic powder	0.20		0.27
Oleoresin of paprika		9.07 g	
Oleoresin of pepper		3.45 g	
Oleoresin of ginger		0.66 g	
Oil of mace		0.28 g	0.77
Oil of cardamom		0.17 g	
Superesin of coriander		1.37 g	
	72.55	15.00 g	100.00

Again, if we refer to Table 6.1 and convert the oils and oleoresins in formula D to the equivalent natural spices, we find that the total weight of them plus the onion and garlic but excluding the ground mustard, equals the weight of the ground spices in formula C, but we were able to save over 5 oz in total weight of the unit pack by utilizing the spice extractives. The additional weight is due to the addition of ground mustard to the formula.

Formula E is the same as Formula D except that we have sub-stituted soluble spices (extractives on a salt base) for the oils and oleoresins, and the salt in the formula is reduced by the amount that is in the soluble spices. In most instances, this type of formulation is not recommended, but there are times when it may be convenient or necessary to do so. The added costs would be prohibitive in a highly competitive market.

Whereas tricalcium phosphate has been shown as the anticaking agent, Zeolex 23 or any other approved anticaking compound could be used provided it is not in excess of 2%, by weight, of the seasoning mix.

Ingredients	oz		%
Formula E			
Salt	31.65		43.30
Dextrose	15.00		20.52
Sodium erythorbate	0.87		1.19
Mustard, ground	16.00		21.89
Tricalcium phosphate	0.28		0.38
Onion powder	0.20		0.27
Garlic powder	0.20		0.27
Soluble paprika spice (salt base)		113.37 g	
Soluble pepper spice (salt base)		65.71 g	
Soluble ginger spice (salt base)		16.50 g	12.18
Soluble mace spice (salt base)		5.60 g	
Soluble cardamom spice (salt base)		5.67 g	
Soluble coriander spice (salt base)		45.67 g	
	64.20	252.52 g	100.00

BOLOGNA SEASONINGS

One can readily observe that the formulas for the following bolog-na seasonings are very similar to those for frankfurters. Garlic may or may not be added depending on customer preference. Monosodium glutamate is added to round out the overall flavor; it could have been used in the frankfurter seasonings as well, but it is a restricted item and must be labeled separately in the ingredient statement. Allspice and cloves are added to give the product a sweeter, spicy note, although cardamom could have been substituted.

It should be emphasized again, that when soluble spices are used in a seasoning, and the extracts are distributed on a salt base, the

Bologna

Ingredients	oz	%
Formula A		
Salt	31.06	48.54
Dextrose	4.37	6.83
Sodium erythorbate	0.87	1.36
Monosodium glutamate	1.50	2.34
Garlic powder	1.00	1.56
Mustard, ground	16.00	25.00
White pepper, ground	4.00	6.25
Paprika, ground	3.00	4.69
Coriander, ground	1.00	1.56
Mace, ground	0.70	1.09
Allspice, ground	0.25	0.39
Cloves, ground	0.25	0.39
	64.00	100.00
Formula B		
Salt	31.06	55.00
Dextrose	4.37	7.74
Sodium erythorbate	0.87	1.54
Monosodium glutamate	1.50	2.66
Garlic powder	1.00	1.77
Mustard, ground	16.00	28.34
Oleoresin of pepper	0.21	0.37
Oleoresin of paprika	0.24	0.43
Superesin of coriander	0.03	0.05
Oil of mace	0.035	0.06
Oil of allspice	0.006	0.01
Oil of cloves	0.038	0.07
Tricalcium phosphate	1.106	1.96
	56.465	100.00

Ingredients	oz.	%
Formula C		
Salt	23.10	41.22
Dextrose	4.37	7.80
Sodium erythorbate	0.87	1.55
Monosodium glutamate	1.50	2.68
Garlic powder	1.00	1.78
Mustard, ground	16.00	28.55
Soluble white pepper, salt base	4.00	7.14
Soluble paprika, salt base	3.00	5.35
Soluble coriander, salt base	1.00	1.78
Soluble mace, salt base	0.70	1.25
Soluble allspice, salt base	0.25	0.45
Soluble cloves, salt base	0.25	0.45
	56.04	100.00

salt must be deducted from the original salt content in the formula. A knowledge of Table 6.1 is essential for converting spices to spice extracts or to soluble spices or vice versa. If the soluble spices are on a dextrose base there is no need to make any compensation.

An examination of the three formulas for bologna seasonings reveals that the only difference between formulas A and B is that ground spices are used in the former and their equivalent spice extractives in the latter, except for mustard which is employed for its functional properties rather than flavor. With the use of spice extractives, tricalcium phosphate or other suitable anticaking agent is added in formula B to assure its flowability.

Formula C is equivalent to the other two formulas in flavor seasoning properties. In this instance, soluble spices on a salt base are used, with compensation for the added salt in the soluble spices made by reducing the salt in the basic formula.

FRESH PORK SAUSAGE

The manufacture of fresh pork sausage is one of the more simple processes in the preparation of processed meats, but precautions must be taken to have all of the equipment and surrounding areas immaculately clean. The temperature of the processing rooms and the meat should be held fairly constant between 36°–38°F (4°C). There must not be any possibility of contamination from sodium nitrite in curing agents or from their use with other meats. (This is another good reason for having nitrite cures packed by a spice blender, away from the packing plant to avoid the possibility of contaminating other meat products.) Sodium nitrite would cause fresh pork sausage to turn black.

The careful selection of chilled, pork trimmings, used as the sole source of meat, should contain not more than 50% fat on analysis (35% fat would be preferable.) The chunks of trimmings are ground through a ⅜ in. plate, mixed for 2 to 3 minutes along with the preweighed seasoning unit, ground again through a ³⁄₁₆ in. plate, then stuffed under 90 to 120 lb pressure directly into animal, cellulose, or collagen casings, being sure that all air pockets are eliminated. Alternately, the spiced sausage meat may be formed into patties, packaged, and stored at approximately 22°–26°F (13°C) until shipped.

Formula A represents a basic seasoning for 100 lb of fresh pork sausage meat. It is self-explanatory. Optional spices and ingredients are shown for use in the basic seasoning.

Formula B is similar to formula A with some of the optional spices and ingredients included. It conforms to the usual, good quality products found in the retail market. It should be pointed out that the salt content of fresh pork sausage should be about 1.5% or 1% less than in frankfurters and bologna. The monosodium glutamate is used to round out the flavor by melding the different spices into one homogenous appealing flavor. Note that 0.4 oz of ginger and 0.5 oz of marjoram have replaced 0.9 oz of white pepper in the formula, and 0.1 oz of pepper has been replaced with the antioxidant and citric acid. Note also that sugar compensates for the extra salt in the formula and also allows the sausages to brown nicely when broiled.

Formula C is the same as formula B except that spice extractives have been substituted for some of the natural spices. Tricalcium phosphate has been added as an anticaking agent. Note that the use of spice extractives has reduced the unit weight of the seasoning by 4 oz.

Formula D is unusual, yet, it results in the best flavored sausage the author has ever eaten. It calls for about five times the usual amount of oil of sage, slightly more sweetness, and the use of capsicum blended with paprika (both spices are capsicums) to give the fresh product, before cooking, an appetizing, fresh, pinkish coloration and a flavorful bite after cooking. The unit package weight is increased about 5 oz, but remember that this added weight also adds to the weight of the finished product.

Oil of sage has largely replaced ground sage in most sausage seasonings because the resulting product has a more appealing appearance and is free from green specks caused by the fresh spice.

Fresh Pork Sausage—Basic Seasoning

Ingredients	oz
Formula A	
Salt	28
White or black pepper, ground	4
Dalmatian sage, ground	2
Mace or nutmeg, ground	1
Sugar, dextrose or corn syrup solids	5
	40

Optional Spices and Ingredients for use in Formula A

	in lieu of	use
Ginger, ground	0.5 oz of pepper	0.5 oz ginger
Marjoram, ground	0.5 oz of pepper	0.5 oz marjoram
Cayenne pepper, ground	2.5 oz of pepper	1.5 oz cayenne

BHA and BHT as antioxidants at the rate of 0.02% of total fat content. Citric acid, as needed, usually about 0.2% of seasoning mix. Monosodium glutamate up to 4.0 oz per 100 lb of meat.

Ingredients	oz	%
Formula B		
Salt	26.000	65.00
Sugar	5.000	12.50
Monosodium glutamate	2.000	5.00
White pepper, ground	3.000	7.50
Dalmatian sage, ground	2.000	5.00
Ginger, ground	0.400	1.00
Mace, ground	1.000	2.50
Marjoram, ground	0.500	1.25
Tenox 4	0.020	0.05
Citric acid	0.080	0.20
	40.000	100.00

Ingredients	oz		%
Formula C			
Salt	26.0000		72.222
Sugar	5.0000		13.888
Monosodium glutamate	2.0000		5.555
White pepper, ground	2.0000		5.555
Oil of sage	0.0250		0.069
Oleoresin of pepper	0.1540		0.427
Oleoresin of ginger	0.0160		0.050
Oil of mace	0.0500		0.139
Oil of marjoram	0.0025		0.007
Tenox 4	0.0200		0.056
Citric acid	0.0795		0.221
Tricalcium phosphate	0.6330		1.811
	36.0000		100.000
Formula D			
Salt	31.00		75.43
Sugar	5.00		12.17
Dextrose	4.00		9.73
Zeolex 23	0.80		1.95
Oleoresin of capsicum		2.765 g	
Oleoresin of paprika		1.380 g	
Oil of sage		3.614 g	
Oleoresin of ginger		0.213 g	0.72
Oleoresin of pepper		0.319 g	
Oil of nutmeg		0.213 g	
	40.80	8.504 g	100.00

In calculating the use of antioxidants, remember that a vegetable oil is usually used as a diluent in commercial formulas like Tenox. Therefore, more than 0.02% of the commercial product can be used, depending on its actual antioxidant content. In many cases, less than 0.02% of the antioxidant is used.

ITALIAN PORK SAUSAGE

Italian pork sausage differs from fresh pork sausage in the seasoning and in the size of the ground meat particles. The chilled trimmings are ground through a ¼ in. or ⅜ in. plate, and the casings are usually slightly larger in diameter (size 30 to 36 cellulose or collagen casings). Formula A is a typical seasoning formula for sweet Italian sausage. Formula B is a variation of the seasoning and perhaps is more typical of the products found in the retail trade. Formulas C and D are seasoning formulas for hot Italian sausage. As an aid in the production of all four seasoning mixes, it is customary to add 1 oz of corn oil or other pure vegetable oil to the seasoning mix in the blender for every 100 oz of seasoning, or 1%. The oil is added at the end of the blending operation to prevent separation of the different sized spice particles from the rest of the mix. This is particularly expedient with large batches of seasonings that must be dumped or conveyed to fillers to assure uniformity of the seasoning blend from the beginning unit pack to the final unit pack. The 1% level of oil will not prevent the seasoning mix from being free flowing.

In formula D 7 lb (112 oz) are used for each 100 lb of meat. Here again, wherever whole or ground spices are used in a formula as the sole source of seasoning, it is customary to add about 1% by weight of the batch pure corn oil near the end of the blending operation to prevent separation of the ingredients and assure uniformity of the blend from the beginning to the end of the packaging operation.

Sweet Italian Sausage Seasoning _____

Ingredients	oz	%
Formula A		
Salt	24	70.6
White pepper, ground	4	11.8
Fennel, whole seed	4	11.8
Paprika, ground	2	5.8
	34	100.0
Formula B		
Salt	30.50	67.777
Sugar	5.90	13.111
White pepper, ground	4.75	10.555
Paprika, ground	1.00	2.222
Nutmeg, ground	0.50	1.111
Mace, ground	0.50	1.111
Coriander, ground	1.50	3.333
Anise, ground	0.25	.555
Clove, ground	0.05	.111
Cinnamon, ground	0.05	.111
	45.00	99.997

Hot Italian Sausage Seasoning

Ingredients	oz	%
Formula C		
Salt	24.00	60.00
White pepper, ground	4.00	10.00
Fennel, ground or whole	4.00	10.00
Crushed red pepper (mild)	4.00	10.00
Coriander seed, crushed	2.00	5.00
Paprika, ground	2.00	5.00
	40.00	100.00
Formula D		
Salt	64.0	57.14
Sugar	15.5	13.81
Crushed red pepper	12.8	11.43
Whole fennel	11.2	10.00
Anise, ground	0.2	.19
Red Pepper, ground	4.3	3.86
Paprika, ground	4.0	3.57
	112.0	100.00

The reader should note the higher percent salt level in this hot Italian sausage seasoning, not compensated for by the usual amount of added sugar. The pungent spices, crushed red pepper, and ground red pepper allow for the greater use of salt without affecting the flavor of the finished product.

It should also be noted that for this particular seasoning, which yields a hot, spicy sausage, about four times the amount of spices are used as for the sweet Italian sausage seasoning; yet, only 0.325 oz (9.2 g) of spices are needed for 1 lb of meat. By using this much salt, the blender can reduce the per pound cost of the seasoning mix.

KIELBASA (POLISH SAUSAGE)

Kielbasa is another name for Polish sausage; it is made from coarsely ground lean pork with added beef and is highly seasoned with garlic, pepper and coriander. It is an uncooked but smoked sausage product.

Kielbasa Seasoning _____

Ingredients	oz	%
Ground coriander	5.00	55.75
Ground white pepper	1.35	15.00
Ground nutmeg	0.30	3.20
Garlic powder	0.19	2.10
Dextrose	2.11	23.45
Superesin black pepper	0.15	0.50
	9.00	100.00

Nine ounces per 100 lb of meat. Note the high percentage of coriander in the product. Also, by converting the 0.15 oz (4.35 g) of superesin of black pepper to its equivalency of freshly ground black pepper, equal to 3.3 oz, we find that the pepper is also a significant portion of the formula—4.65 oz (See Table 6.1 for conversion factor.)

If we delete the dextrose in the formula, we find that less than 7 oz of spices are all that are required to season 100 lb of meat, or about 1.9 g per pound. This is another good example of the potency of spices and the need to use them with caution. The meat packer, in this instance, would add the required amount of salt at the time of blending the seasoning with the meat.

SMOKED LIVER SAUSAGE

Smoked Liver Sausage Seasoning _____

Ingredients	oz	%
Corn syrup solids	24.7	54.500
Dextrose	15.9	35.027
Sodium erythorbate	0.5	1.130
White pepper, ground	0.5	1.085
Black pepper, ground	0.5	1.085
Marjoram, ground	0.8	1.721
Coriander, ground	0.4	0.882
Nutmeg, ground	0.2	0.396
Ginger, ground	0.1	0.308
Thyme, ground	0.1	0.247
Rosemary, ground	0.1	0.177
Onion powder	1.6	3.442

Oleoresin of black pepper		11 g	
Oleoresin of ginger		1.8 g	
Oil of nutmeg		3.6 g	
	46.0		100.000

The percent column is correct; the ounces have been rounded off to the nearest tenth.

The meat packer in this instance will add his own salt as needed; probably about 2.5 lb/100 lb of meat to go with the 46 oz of seasoning mix.

The oil and oleoresins are added to reduce the cost of the mix and reduce its bulk; when used in such small quantities they are not usually figured into the percent column but would be calculated into the cost column, obviously. The corn syrup solids are used primarily as a bulking agent and as a base for distributing the spice extractives.

11

Instant Gravy Seasonings and Mixes

GRAVIES

As mentioned earlier, gravies are sauces, used to accompany the main meat dish to enhance the starchy component—potatoes, rice, or noodles.

If available, pan drippings obtained from roasting meats or poultry should always be used to make gravies. When they are not available, gravy seasonings and mixes are employed.

The technologist should become familiar with the various properties of flours and modified starches manufactured by Corn Products International, National Starch Company, American Maize Company, and the Staley Company before attempting to formulate regular or instant gravies. Important factors to consider are the sheen, stability characteristics, freedom from lumping, ease of dispersion, freedom from taste and odor, thickening properties, and stability of gel, temperature of set, etc. Starch technology is very complicated, but a general knowledge of the subject is essential in the formulation of instant gravies.

It will be noted that onion powder appears in each of the formulas. Onion improves the flavor, rounds it out, and eliminates blandness; it should not be overpowering, however, merely just above the taste threshold level.

Good quality hydrolyzed plant proteins (HPP) are now available for use as substitutes for meat or poultry drippings. These have been developed by such companies as International Flavors and Fra-

355

Au Jus Gravy Seasoning and Mix _____

Ingredients	%	Procedure
Seasoning		
Salt	34.7500	Mix 3.0672 oz seasoning with
MSG	7.7300	2.9328 oz gravy base
Oil of garlic	0.0716	Add (6.0000 oz mix) to 1 gal
OR pepper	0.0141	cold water, stir thoroughly,
OR celery seed	0.0119	bring to a slow simmering
OR paprika	0.0385	boil, and simmer 3 minutes.
B & C caramel	11.2839	
Onion powder	14.5800	
HPP(V9717)	7.7300	
HPP(NP 53)	9.0000	
HPP(BFKS)	14.7900	
	100.0000	
Gravy base		
Gelatinized Durajel starch	88.95	
Frymax (fat)	7.07	
Zeolex 23	3.98	
	100.00	

Mushroom Gravy Seasoning and Mix _____

Ingredients	%	Procedure
Seasoning		
Salt	23.50	Mix 7.55 oz seasoning with 8.45
Sugar	19.23	oz gravy base. Add (16.0 oz
MSG	19.23	mix to 1 gal of cold water, stir
Onion powder	3.75	thoroughly, bring to a slow
Mushroom powder	5.98	simmering boil and simmer 5
Tomato powder	8.00	min
B & C Caramel	7.48	
HPP(1640)	3.20	
HPP(80R)	2.15	
HPP(V9717)	7.48	
	100.00	
Gravy base		
Pastry flour	45.82	
Dry vegetable fat (Dellac 6-75 VCL)	26.73	
Consista starch	17.66	
Xanthan gum	1.91	
Parsley granules	0.24	
Mushroom slices, freeze-dried	7.64	
	100.00	

Brown Gravy Seasoning and Mix _____

Ingredients	%	Procedure
Seasoning		
Salt	18.00	Mix 7.2 oz seasoning with 8.8 oz
MSG	14.67	gravy base
Sugar	14.67	Add (16.0 oz mix) to 1 gal of
OR Paprika	0.03	cold water, stir thoroughly,
B & C caramel	8.68	bring to a slow simmering
Onion powder	3.20	boil and simmer 5 minutes.
Tomato powder	21.38	
Celery seed, ground	0.64	
White pepper, ground	0.46	
HPP(NP 53)	4.02	
HPP(NP 80R)	6.03	
HPP(BFKS)	3.56	
HPP(V9717)	4.66	
	100.00	
Gravy base		
Gelatinized Durajel starch	55.87	
Dry vegetable fat (Dellac 6-75VCL)	35.75	
Acid whey	6.15	
Xanthan gum	2.23	
	100.00	

Chicken Gravy Seasoning and Mix _____

Ingredients	%	Procedure
Seasoning		
Salt	34.6000	Mix 1.5000 oz seasoning with
MSG	34.9300	9.1730 oz gravy base
Dextrose	16.0000	Add (10.6730 oz mix) to 1 gal
OR Turmeric	0.7300	cold water, stir thoroughly,
OR celery seed	0.0700	bring to a slow simmering
OR black pepper	0.3300	boil, add 32 oz of cracklings
B & C caramel	1.8000	and simmer 5 minutes.
Onion powder	2.1300	
HPP(NP 50)	2.1300	
Pepper, ground	7.2800	
	100.0000	
Gravy base		
Pastry flour	67.21	
Cornstarch	23.26	
Consista starch	5.93	
Frymax (fat)	3.60	
	100.00	

grances and the Nestle Company. Their programs have revolution-
ized the seasoning industry. Other companies have improved their
original products in light of the competition.

Tomato powder is included in each of the beef flavored gravies to
give the product a sharpness unequalled by any other natural ingredient. Its color also naturalizes the color of the gravy and makes it
more appealing.

Monosodium glutamate is used at a level of less than 1% in the
product as served. It, too, rounds out the flavor by eliminating the
high and low peaks of sensory perception as well as providing a
salivating effect.

Poultry Gravy Seasoning and Mix _____

Ingredients	%	Procedure
Seasoning		
Salt	23.580	Mix 6.0 oz seasoning with 8.0 oz
MSG	22.160	gravy base
Dextrose	13.700	Add (14.0 oz mix) to 1 gal of
OR Paprika	0.017	cold water, stir thoroughly,
OR Celery seed	0.051	bring to' a slow boil, and sim-
OR Turmeric (14%	0.110	mer for 5 minutes.
curc.)		
OR Black pepper	0.026	
Onion powder	1.389	
Garlic powder	0.474	
HPP(1640)	6.643	
HPP(80R)	6.300	
HPP(CKN 2762)	5.220	
Stand. Light Yeast	5.150	
Chicken fat	6.650	
Dehydrated chicken meat	5.350	
Zeolex	3.180	
	100.000	
Gravy base		
Dry vegetable fat (Dellac	28.760	
6-75 VCL)		
Xanthan gum	1.570	
Consista starch	34.030	
Pastry flour	35.640	
	100.000	

Deluxe Brown Gravy Seasoning and Mix _____

Ingredients	%	Procedure
Seasoning		Mix 8.70 oz seasoning with 7.30
Salt, fine, prepared	17.11	oz gravy base (16.00 oz mix)
Sugar, baker's fine	14.72	to 1 gal of cold water, stir
Monosodium glutamate	14.72	thoroughly, bring to a slow
Onion powder	3.22	boil, simmer for 5 minutes (a
Tomato powder	21.62	thin-bodied gravy).
Beet powder	0.37	
B & C Caramel	8.74	
Celery seed, ground	0.64	
White pepper, ground	0.46	
HPP(A)	4.05	
HPP(88)	3.62	
HPP(222)	6.05	
HPP(V9717)	4.68	
	100.00	
Gravy base		
Gelatinized Durajel starch	21.90	
Pastry flour	34.83	
Dry vegetable fat (Dellac 6-75 VCL)	35.05	
Xanthan gum	2.20	
Acid whey	6.02	
	100.00	

CHICKEN AND BEEF STOCKS

Of all the formulas in this book and available elsewhere, perhaps the two best, and most useful, are the Premium Grade Chicken and Beef Stocks (Instant). These have been adopted for use by one of the finest restaurants in the eastern United States rather then preparing their own stocks because of their similarity to the natural products and their low salt levels. They can be used wherever the use of chicken or beef stock is required.

Five pounds of either one makes up to 12.5 gal of stock. Strict adherence to the formulas is absolutely necessary for best results. They may be used in making bouillons, soups, gravies, or as a base in the preparation of other sauces that call for beef or chicken stock.

On a reconstituted basis, the salt content of the chicken stock is 1.49% and 1.89% in the beef stock. The MSG content is about 50% higher in the chicken than in the beef (0.74% vs. 0.48%). These relationships are worth noting. On an equivalent weight basis, the garlic content is about the same in each. The hydrolysates are completely different and are designed for the uses specified. One must always take into account the salt content of hydrolysates in determining the overall salt content in the finished formula.

Premium Grade Instant Chicken Stock

Ingredients	oz	%
Fine flake salt	17.200	21.500
Dextrose	17.320	21.650
MSG	12.720	15.900
Chicken fat, rend'd.	2.480	3.100
Onion powder	1.440	1.800
Garlic powder	0.480	0.600
Oleoresin, turmeric	0.015	0.019
Standard light yeast	5.440	6.800
Chicken meat, freeze-dried	3.840	4.800
HPP (CKN 2762)	6.240	7.800
HPP (1640)	6.800	8.500
HPP (80R)	6.000	7.500
Superesin pepper	0.0106	0.013
Oleoresin celery	0.0128	0.016
Oleoresin paprika	0.0016	0.002
	80.0000	100.00

Premium Grade Instant Beef Stock

Ingredients	oz	%
Fine flake salt	20.000	25.000
Cane sugar	17.600	22.000
MSG	8.000	10.000

Frymax shortening	2.120	2.650
Onion powder	0.380	0.470
Garlic oil	0.0027	0.0034
Caramel, B & C	1.4800	1.8500
Tomato powder	0.7800	0.9800
Mace, ground	0.0400	0.0500
HPP (BFKS)	23.1930	28.9813
HPP (V9717)	6.4000	8.0000
Superesin pepper	0.0043	0.0053
	80.0000	100.00

Add five pounds of either stock to 12.5 gal of simmering water and mix to complete solution. For smaller quantities, add 4 oz of stock to 5 pints of water.

In the manufacture of the stocks, blend the oleoresins, oil, and melted but cooled fats on the salt, sugar, or dextrose and MSG to complete uniformity. Add all the other ingredients, except the hydrolysates and complete the blending. Finally add the hydrolysates and blend to a uniform mass. Anticaking agents are not required or even desired for these items as they could affect the clarity of the finished broths.

Chicken Stock for Making Bouillon, Soup or Gravy

Ingredients	%	Procedure
Dextrose	18.2500	Add 16 oz of mix to 3 gal of cold
Fine salt	15.6200	water. Bring to a simmer.
Monosodium glutamate	11.5600	
Oleoresin of turmeric	0.0140	
Oleoresin of paprika	0.0015	
Oleoresin of celery	0.0120	
Oleoresin of pepper	0.0095	
HPP (1640)	6.18	
HPP (80R)	5.43	
HPP (CKN 2762)	5.67	
Autolyzed yeast	4.9500	
Onion powder	1.3100	
Garlic powder	0.4400	
Rendered chicken fat	30.0130	
Dehydrated chicken meat	3.000 (optional)	

Blend the oleoresins with the dextrose, salt, and MSG until uniformly distributed; add the melted, but cool, chicken fat gradually while the blender is still mixing until it is fully incorporated in the mix, add the remaining ingredients and blend about 10 minutes. This makes an ideal base for making chicken bouillon, soup, or gravy simply by adding water, vegetables, and/or thickening agents, respectively.

This is a smooth tasting chicken bouillon with a salt content of about 0.88%, well below that of most bouillon cubes or chicken soups.

SOUP SEASONINGS AND MIXES

In 1940 a small drum-drying company, in an effort to promote the sale of its stainless steel, drum drier, hired a young food technologist to develop dehydrated ingredients and mixes to demonstrate the utility and potential of the equipment. The result was the introduction of instant soups in the United States. Hundreds of cases of 12 oz (340 g) cans of corn niblets were opened and the product macerated to obtain sufficient material for drying on the 10 ft, drum drier. The resulting corn flakes (unlike the cereal of the same name) were beautiful, naturally sweet, and rehydrated instantly. By adding salt, sugar, dairy solids, starch, and an assortment of spices, an acceptable corn soup (chowder) mix was prepared. Only the addition of boiling water was necessary for serving as an instant soup.

Many No. 10 cans of tomato paste and tomato puree were similarly blended with a farinaceous material at the rate of 20% of the total solids to yield a highly acceptable tomato flake. The additive was essential to form a filmlike matrix on the drum for easy removal of the dried product. Ingredients were added to the broken up tomato flakes to make the first dehydrated tomato soup. Canned apple sauce, cranberries, pumpkin, molasses, and other processed materials were subsequently dehydrated resulting, ultimately, in instant pie fillings, sauces, cake mixes, and other convenient items. Unfortunately, the company was at least 10 years ahead of the marketplace and World War II intervened, but the resulting products, with their methods of dehydration came to the attention of a large, expanding, market-oriented company in New Jersey which, within a few years, began manufacturing and distributing the first dehydrated soups under its own label. Within 10 years dehydrated soups had reached 10% of the total soup business in the United States and 5 years later had peaked at 20% of soup sales.

The exclusivity and magnitude of the business was not overlooked by another large food conglomerate that owned a large dehydrated soup business in Europe. By the late 1950s, the dehydrated soup business reached 35% of the soup business. Even the largest canned soup manufacturer took note of the competition and entered the field. The newcomers increased the market size but failed to diminish the originator's share and subsequently withdrew from the market.

With the advent of modified starches, freeze-dried chicken, meat, vegetables, and noodles, a full line of instant soup mixes became a reality in the late 1960s. By the 1970s, many of the New York area chain stores, as is their custom with successful, private label merchandise, began competing with the leader with their own custom made and packaged, dry soup mixes, many of which were produced by one company.

The following examples of dehydrated instant soup mixes may appear to be very complicated at first. There is more to a good soup than the right seasoning. It must have the right texture, an appealing appearance to the eye and it should be nutritious; it must have the right viscosity upon the addition of hot water; it must have at least six months shelf life; it must be easily packaged; and it must be competitive. It does not have to taste like a comparable canned product even though the first attempts in making dehydrated soups had that as an objective. After all of the above objectives have been met then the fine art of seasoning enters into the overall plan.

A very wide range of formulations could be given for dehydrated soups, but that is not the intent of this book. A few will be presented to give the technologist a broad overview of the business from which he can develop his own formulations.

As with all seasonings, add the oleoresins and charoil to the sugar, MSG and salt and blend to complete uniformity. Add the remaining ingredients except the hydrolysates and blend again. Finally add the hydrolysates and complete the blending.

Instant French Onion Soup Seasoning and Mix ____

Ingredients	%	oz	Procedure
Seasoning			
Fine granulated salt	21.14	11.84	Mix 56 oz seasoning with
Sugar	1.78	1.00	36 oz sauteed, freeze-
Dextrose	16.45	9.21	dried, onion slices, yield-
Onion powder	16.05	9.00	ing 92 oz French onion
Frymax	5.521	3.10	soup mix. Add to 10 gal
Monosodium	4.22	2.35	of cold water, mix well;
glutamate			bring to a simmering
Consista starch	13.33	7.46	boil and simmer about 5
Dehyd. Blue Cheese	3.94	2.20	minutes. Hold at serving
HPP(V9717)	3.72	2.08	temperatures (165°–
HPP(BFKS)	6.83	3.82	180°F).
HPP(HP 53) or (A)	2.61	1.46	
B & C caramel	2.16	1.21	
Zeolex 23	2.22	1.24	
Oleoresin of pepper	0.004	0.064 g	
Oil of garlic	0.025	0.397 g	
	100.000	56.00 oz	

Lobster Bisque Seasoning and Mix _____

Ingredients	oz	%	Procedure
Seasoning			
Salt	11.92	28.000	Mix 42.56 oz of seasoning
MSG	4.83	11.350	with 109.44 oz of bisque
Sugar	14.23	33.440	mix, yielding 152.00 oz
HPP(CKNS)	5.47	12.860	or 9½ lb. Add this
Stand. Light yeast	2.86	6.710	amount to 10 gal cold
Hi-color paprika,	3.01	7.085	water, mix thoroughly,
ground			bring to a simmering
Oleoresin of paprika	0.24	0.555	temperature and simmer
	42.56	100.000	about 3 minutes to de-
Bisque Mix			velop the full sweet lob-
Non fat dry milk	46.50	42.49	ster flavor.
Wheat flour	20.70	18.92	
Consista starch	15.52	14.18	
Dellac dry butter	13.38	12.22	
Sweet whey solids	5.84	5.34	
Lobster concentrate	7.50	6.85	
freeze-dried powder			
	109.44	100.00	

Fish Chowder Seasoning Mix—New England Style _____

Ingredients	oz	%	Procedure
Nonfat dry milk solids	11.260	31.283	Add 36 oz to 2½ gal of cold water, whisk to complete dispersion, bring to a simmering temperature while whisking to prevent scorching; do not allow to boil; add about 3 lb of cooked diced potatoes and an equal weight of cooked, fresh haddock or cod chunks. Top the chowder with freeze-dried chives for garnish and added flavor.
Wheat flour	5.562	15.450	
Consista starch	3.960	11.000	
Dellac dry butter	3.838	10.660	
Sweet whey solids	2.567	7.130	
MSG	1.303	3.620	
Cane sugar	1.692	4.700	
Fine flake salt	2.063	5.730	
HPP (NPSOR)	2.999	8.330	
Superesin Pepper	0.011	0.004	
Oleoresin of celery	0.0105	0.004	
Natural smoke flavor (charoil)	0.0155	0.006	
	36.0000	100.000	

Chicken-Noodle Soup Seasoning and Mix _____

Ingredients	oz	%	Procedure
Seasoning			
Fine flake salt	17.200	18.695	Mix 92 oz seasoning with 20 oz freeze-dried noodles, yielding 112 oz of soup mix. Mix 112 oz to 12.5 gal of simmering water and stir for about 2 minutes. For smaller quantities use 9 oz of mix to 1 gal of water.
Dextrose	17.320	18.826	
MSG	12.720	13.826	
Gelatinized Duragel starch	11.750	12.772	
Standard light yeast	5.440	5.913	
HPP (CKN 2762)	6.240	6.783	
HPP (1640)	6.800	7.391	
HPP (8OR)	6.000	6.522	
Garlic powder	0.480	0.522	
Onion powder	1.440	1.565	
Chicken fat, rendered	2.480	2.696	
White chicken meat, freeze dried	3.840	4.174	
Parsley granules (for garnish)	0.250	0.272	
Oleoresin of celery	0.0128	0.014	
Oleoresin of turmeric	0.0150	0.016	
Superesin of black pepper	0.0106	0.011	
Oleoresin of paprika	0.0016	0.002	
	92.0000	100.000	

If we eliminate the starch and parsley and recalculate the percent figures in the formula, we find that the seasoning mix is very similar to the Instant, Premium Grade Chicken Stock formulation.

Beef-Noodle Soup with Vegetables _____

Ingredients	g	%	Procedure
Seasoning			
Fine flake salt	2.8400	14.3765	Add 19.75 g of total mix to 8
Cane sugar	2.5000	12.6553	oz of boiling water for an
MSG	0.3000	1.5186	instant soup.
Gelatinized Duragel starch	1.3696	6.9331	
Frymax shortening	0.3000	1.5186	
Caramel powder, B & C	0.2100	1.0630	
Tomato powder	0.1111	0.5624	
Onion powder	0.0530	0.2683	
Mace, ground	0.0060	0.0304	
HPP (BFKS)	3.2850	16.6291	
HPP (V9717)	0.9088	4.6005	
Superesin black pepper	0.0006	0.0030	
Garlic oil	0.0004	0.0020	
	11.8845	60.1608	
Noodles and Vegetable Mix			
Freeze-dried noodles	4.6000	23.2858	
Freeze-dried celery flakes	0.8000	4.0497	
Freeze-dried carrot flakes	0.8000	4.0497	
Freeze-dried onion flakes	0.8000	4.0497	
Freeze-dried turnip flakes	0.0300	0.1519	
Freeze-dried peas	0.4700	2.3792	
Freeze-dried green beans	0.3000	1.5186	
Parsley granules	0.0700	0.3543	
	7.8700	39.8389	
	19.7545	99.9997	

If the starch is eliminated from the seasoning ingredient formula and the percent column recalculated, we find that the seasoning is the same as the Instant, Premium Grade, Beef Stock formulation. The noodles and vegetables add some body, a slight vegetable flavor, and improve the appearance.

MISCELLANEOUS SEASONINGS

Boiled Shrimp Seasoning Mix _____

Ingredients	oz	%	Procedure
Fine flake salt	7.4962	93.703	Add 8 oz to 2 gal of cold
Citric acid	0.3000	3.750	water. Bring to a boil; add
Tetrasodium pyrophosphate	0.1700	2.125	shrimp and boil for 2–3
Lemon oil flavor	0.0138	0.172	minutes.
Oil of dill	0.0138	0.172	
Superesin of pepper	0.0062	0.078	
	8.0000	100.000	

Unseasoned Fish Breader Mix _____

Ingredients	lb	%	Procedure
Pastry flour	21.40	85.60	Add water to the fish breader mix in suffi-
Corn flour	2.50	10.00	cient quantity to make a heavy cream-
Nonfat dry milk	0.50	2.00	like consistency. Dip fish fillets into the
Baking powder	0.45	1.80	batter and deep fat fry. The baking
MSG	0.15	0.60	powder in the mix causes the batter to
	25.00	100.00	become lighter upon reaching the hot fat.
			This formula has been very successful
			with many of the fast food fish and chip
			outlets.

Fettucine Alfredo Seasoning and Sauce Mix _____

Ingredients	oz	%	Procedure
Dry butter, Dellac	5.04	36.0	Add 14 oz to 1 gal of cold water;
Romano cheese, dry	2.10	15.0	whisk to complete dispersion;
Parmesan cheese, dry	2.10	15.0	bring to a simmering boil
Fine flake salt	1.96	14.0	while whisking and simmer
Consista starch	0.98	7.0	until starch is completely gela-
MSG	0.56	4.0	tinized; pour over fettucini and
HPP (1640)	0.56	4.0	serve. A touch of saffron or
Xanthan gum	0.42	3.0	turmeric may be added if a
Ground white pepper	0.14	1.0	yellowish hue is desired.
Tetrasodium pyrophosphate	0.14	1.0	
	14.00	100.0	

Bloody Mary Seasoning Mix _____

Ingredients	lb	oz	Percent	Procedure
Sugar	30.0		30.00	Add 4 oz of Bloody Mary
Dextrose	28.0		28.00	Seasoning Mix to 1 gal of
Salt	22.0		22.00	tomato juice. Mix well and
Oleoresin of capsicum		1.250	0.078	refrigerate 10–15 min. be-
Oleoresin of ginger		1.250	0.078	fore using to allow the fla-
Oil of lemon flavor		4.000	0.244	vors to meld. Be sure that
Oleoresin of celery		1.000	0.063	the mix is completely dis-
Oil of allspice		0.250	0.015	solved in the tomato juice
Oil of garlic		0.500	0.032	before refrigerating.
HPP (BFKS)	9.0		9.000	
Citric acid	2.0		2.000	
Onion powder	2.0	8.000	2.500	
Calcium stearate	1.0	7.750	1.490	
MSG	4.0	8.000	4.500	
	98.0	32.000	100.000	

DISCUSSION

The wide variety of seasonings discussed should give a technologist a fairly good overview of the use of spices and spice extractives in whatever form, in seasonings and seasoned products.
Percentages of ingredients are shown in each formula. Using these
figures any unit weight may be easily calculated by multiplying the
percentage figures by the total unit weight desired.

A careful study of the seasonings should be made by the reader,
utilizing Table 6.1 to calculate the spice equivalencies of the spice
extractives where indicated in the formulas. The reader should also
note that the salt content in each formula is based on its preferred
level in the final product, except when sugar and dextrose are also
used. You will recall that the use of these sweeteners compensates
for some of the salt and offsets its flavoring effect on the basis of 1 lb
of sugar or 1.4 lb of dextrose for 1 lb of salt, up to a limit. For meats,
the total salt level should be in the range of 1.5 to 2.5% of the weight
of the meat. For most other uses, as in sauces, soups, and gravies,
the salt content should be about 0.8 to 1.0% (the physiological saline
level).

Ingredients may be highly desirable in one particular seasoning, but completely undesirable in another. Some food products call for very spicy seasonings, chili con carne, for example; others may require a mildly flavored seasoning, as in chicken stock seasoning. Spices must complement and enhance the end product, not overpower it! Onions may be used with practically all meat seasonings and some vegetables, but an onion flavor would be out of character with fruit or beverage products. Paprika or the spice extractive is used to enhance the color of a finished product. It should be used with discretion. One should use a sufficient amount to obtain the proper shade of red in the finished product. This rule applies to all of the other ingredients. Use only the amount of spice needed to enhance the color, the natural flavor, or the overall appearance of the finished product.

12

The Technology of Seasoning

The five primary senses of a food technologist should be keen and well trained if one is to pursue a career in the spice and seasoning business. One must be able to discern minute differences in color, aroma, taste, and particle size of ingredients to be successful in developing new products or in duplicating existing products without a formula. One must also have an understanding of the marketplace and the economics of the seasoning business. If a few cents a pound can be saved on a seasoning mix by substituting less expensive but equivalent ingredients, it should be done. The best informed food technologist must have a sixth sense—common sense.

Sight is important in judging the color, size, shape and other physical characteristics of a spice or other ingredient. Obviously, the technologist cannot be color blind. Since the color of some spices is an indication of freshness, careful observation of the spice is a prerequisite.

The sense of smell is equally important. Haylike odors in herbaceous spices indicate staleness, or, even loss of the valuable, aromatic essential oils. A good sense of smell is also essential for detecting characteristic notes and nuances of different spices when blended in mixed seasonings.

THE ANATOMY AND PHYSIOLOGY
OF TASTE AND SMELL

There are four primary taste sensations: sweet, bitter, acid, and salt. All other tastes are combinations of these with or without the sensations of odor. Generally, the sensation of bitterness is detected in the posterior region of the mouth and back of the tongue. Sweetness is detected on the tip of the tongue. But before any savory substance can stimulate the nerve endings on the tongue and adjacent areas, they must first be in solution. A dry tongue is practically useless in perceiving flavors. If one is to work with flavorful substances, he must be aware of his own limitations, if any, in detecting minute stimuli.

The determination of the threshold stimulus for different taste sensations is made by ascertaining the minimal concentration of the solution capable of arousing a taste sensation. The delicacy of the sense of taste is influenced, however, by certain other conditions such as the temperature of the solution. Very hot or very cold solutions diminish or destroy the sensitiveness of the nerve endings. A temperature range of 10°C to 30°C (50°–85°F) has been found to yield the optimum conditions. Another condition found to be important in tasting a product is the use of mechanical or physical action within the buccal cavity to facilitate the penetration of the flavors into the mucous membrane. This may easily be accomplished by swishing the solution, or by moving the jaw up and down rapidly while tasting; anything to increase the irritability of the sensing end organ.

The sensitivity of the tongue may be amply demonstrated when we realize that as little as 250 mg of salt, or 500 mg of sugar, dissolved in 100 ml of water at 20°C (68°F), is detectable on the tip of the tongue. Even lower levels may be detected by more highly trained flavor experts. As little as 7 mg of hydrochloric acid in 100 ml of water is detectable on the back of the tongue. Quantitative solutions of the above should be made up and each member of a taste panel should be able to detect the appropriate sensation blindfolded, before being used on a panel devoted to detecting differences or identifying these notes in a product. It should be noted, however, that a person with diabetes would not make a good panel member as the sugar in his blood may cause him to experience sweetness from a substance that has no sweetness, due to the false stimulation of the taste nerves. Similarly, a person with jaundice may experience bitterness due to the stimulation of taste nerves from the bile in his blood. It has been claimed by many so-called experts, that a heavy smoker does not make a good taster. Others claim that some heavy smokers make excellent tasters, as long as they refrain from smoking at least 30 minutes before undergoing a taste test. Before any test is begun, the testers should rinse their mouths out with a swish or two of soda water. This should be repeated between samples being tested.

In checking the aroma of a product, a simple sniff is not sufficient. The volatile substance must be drawn up into the upper part of the nasal cavity where the olfactory nerves terminate. The tester must create currents of air, either with his hand, or by a series of inhalations to cause the molecules of the volatiles to reach the top, inner portion of the nose. As a matter of fact, the flavors of most foods are of an olfactory nature, rather than gustatory. When such food is swallowed, the posterior nares are shut off from the pharynx by the soft palate, but in the expiration succeeding the swallow, the odor of the food is conveyed to the olfactory end organ. Flavors are perceived, therefore, not during the act of swallowing, but subsequently, and if the nostrils are blocked off, foods lose much of their flavor. Simply holding the nose will destroy much of the taste and aroma of spices. Testers with head colds are useless because of this physiological phenomenon.

Many odors cease to give a perceptible sensation when the stimulation is continued due to the fatigue of the sense cells. When entering a room that has an unusually pleasant or unpleasant odor, the odor is quite pronounced, but after a while one becomes unconscious of the odor, while a newcomer entering the room notices it immediately.

Some early physiological data showed that camphor could be perceived in a dilution of one part in 400,000; the odor of musk could be noted in a dilution of one part in 8,000,000; vanillin, one part in 10,000,000 and mercaptan, one part in 23,000,000. If more than one odor is inhaled simultaneously, one might perceive one specific odor first, then the other, without perceiving a compound sensation; the different molecular weights of the molecules could account for this multiple sensation. However, an odor like that of iodoform might antagonize another odor like balsam, or neutralize it altogether.

Perhaps the sense of smell is the one most likely to be associated with appetite—the aroma of fresh coffee or of cooking bacon or sausage in the morning, or the indescribable smell of freshly baked bread at any time during the day, certainly whets the appetite.

Many texts and experts support the testing of seasonings for aroma and flavor in a standard neutral soup base or white sauce. Others offer reasonable objections to such a procedure because a neutral soup or white sauce base is not always of the same consistency, texture, or color as the intended product and subsequently gives a different mouthfeel, which is a significant part of the overall flavor. Also, the base may selectively absorb portions of the seasoning and give a false reading. It is recommended that only room temperature, distilled water, whipped with air, in the temperature range of 10°–30°C (50°–85°F) be used for the initial comparative testing of spices and seasonings. Confirmatory tests of seasonings should always be made in the final product in which they are to be used.

There is more involved in smelling and tasting a product than the physiological acuity of the technologist. Before any odor or taste evaluation of samples is performed, the tester must be certain that all outside interferences are eliminated that could detract from his subjective analyses.

First, the light in the room should be uniform and as close to northern daylight conditions as possible. Under no circumstances should he expect to obtain true color comparisons under fluorescent lights. Daylight lamps have been designed and are available for use in laboratories that duplicate northern light. These should be used in the absence of natural light.

Second, the room or area to be used for odor and taste testing should be free of all foreign or extraneous odors. A small air-conditioned room, used solely for this purpose, where one can concentrate on the immediate objective, would be ideal. The technologist should not have used any perfumed soap, cologne, aftershave, or perfume that would interfere with odor detection; neither should there be any evidence of smoking in the room or on ones clothes as it too, could detract from one's sensitivity.

Third, the method of the preparation of the samples should be as simple as possible and conducted in such a way that any diluents, materials or equipment used should not impart any foreign odors or flavors. Distilled water that is odor- and taste-free should be used wherever possible. It may be desirable to whip clean, fresh air into the water by means of a blender that has been cleaned and sterilized, to remove any flatness inherent in the distilled water. Ordinary city tap water, in many areas may be high in chlorine, sulfur-containing compounds, or other contaminating substances that could affect delicate taste comparisons.

Fourth, the level of dilution should be such that the odor or flavor is not overpowering or too weak to detect the various nuances.

Finally, the taster should rinse his mouth with bottled carbonated water before the testing begins and between each test sample to remove any remnant flavors.

Table 12.1 Classification of Spices by Sensory Characteristics

Flavor characteristics	Spices
Alliaceous	Onion, chives, shallots, garlic
Bitter	Celery seed, curry powder, fenugreek, hops, mace, marjoram, nutmeg, oregano, rosemary, saffron, savory, turmeric
Fragrant and delicate	Basil, chives, shallots
Herbaceous	Dillweed, parsley, rosemary, saffron, sage, thyme
Licoricelike	Anise, chervil, fennel, tarragon, star-anise, sweet basil
Nutlike	Poppy seed, sesame seed
Pungent and hot	Capsicum, ginger, horseradish, mustard, black and white pepper
Pungent and sweet	Cassia, cloves, cinnamon
Sour, astringent	Capers
Sweet	Anise, cardamom, fenugreek, star anise
Sulfurous	Garlic, onion
Warm, fruity and camphoraceous	Anise, bay leaf, caraway, cardamom, cumin, fennel, rosemary, savory
Warm, fragrant, and cooling	Basil, oregano, peppermint, spearmint
Warm, heavy, and aromatic	Cumin
Warm, spicy, and very aromatic	Allspice, basil, caraway, cardamom, cassia, celery seed, chervil, chili powder blend, cinnamon, cloves, coriander, curry powder blend, dillweed, ginger, mace, marjoram, nutmeg, pickling spice, sage, tarragon, thyme, saffron
Woody	Cassia, cinnamon, cloves

In order to assist the food technologist new to the field of seasonings, a brief classification of spices, by sensory characteristics is shown in Table 12.1.

To further assist the practising food technologist in becoming familiar with spices, Table 12.2 lists the relative flavor intensities of spices.

In summary, to be successful in the seasoning business, the food technologist must have a sensitive palate, a knowing nose, a perceptive eye, an economy-oriented mind, an inspirational intuition, an understanding of consumer preferences, a knowledge of the marketplace, and the ability to communicate clearly.

He must be absolutely sure of his results and be able to sell his findings, his concepts, and his products to those in management who are responsible for marketing them. Marketing and advertising

Table 12.2   Relative Flavor Intensity of Spices[a]

1000	Fresh red pepper	230	Fresh peppermint
900	Cayenne pepper, dried	230	Coriander seed
800	Fresh horseradish	220	Turmeric, dried
800	Mustard powder	200	Turmeric, dried
700	Pickling spices, dried	200	Fresh spearmint
600	Cloves, dried	160	Dillseed, dried
500	Fresh garlic	150	Peppermint, dried
500	Bay leaf, dried	125	Cardamom, dried
475	Ginger, dried	115	Tarragon, dried
450	Black pepper, dried	100	Spearmint, dried
425	Cassia, dried	95	Rosemary, dried
400	Cinnamon, dried	95	Dillweed, dried
390	Fresh onions	90	Poppy seed, dried
390	White pepper, dried	90	Oregano, dried
380	Fresh shallots	85	Thyme, dried
380	Star anise, dried	85	Marjoram, dried
360	Nutmeg, dried	80	Sage, dried
340	Mace, nutmeg	75	Parsley, dried
320	Caraway seed, dried	70	Sweet basil, dried
300	Celery seed, dried	65	Summer savory, dried
290	Cumin seed, dried	65	Anise seed, dried
280	Fennel seed, dried	60	Chervil, dried
270	Fresh chives	60	Onion, dried
260	Curry powder blend	50	Paprika, dried
250	Allspice, dried	40	Saffron, dried
240	Mustard seed	25	Sesame seed, dried

[a]From Desrosier 1978.

take a sizable portion, up to 30% or more, of the overall production cost of an item. The maintenance of good quality is essential but many cheaper food ingredients may be substituted for other ingredients without sacrificing quality in the final product. One should keep in mind, that 2 to 5 cents a pound difference in raw material costs may not sound very significant but when the various markups are applied for labor, fringe benefits, supervision, plant overhead, office overhead, mortgage or rent payments, deferred taxes, salesman's commissions, marketing and selling costs, advertising, and many, many other costs, the 2 to 5 cents become 8 to 20 cents or more difference in the cost of the final product. When this is multiplied by a million or so pounds of product, the estimated annual production of the item, the few pennies saved on raw materials per pound may equal $200,000 in a year's time, enough to pay a technologist's salary and that of a few others for the entire year.

One of the first things a young food scientist will learn is that business is profit oriented. He has spent four or more years learning the theory of why things happen, or memorizing this or that fact; now, he must face the reality of the marketplace. Each product he will be asked to improve or develop will have a dollar sign attached to it. Not at first perhaps, but before the product is accepted for production, one can be sure that the accountants and business managers have scrutinized the costs of every item, every step in production, and every square inch of advertising space. It must be priced competitively and it must be equal to or better than the competition.

There are still many companies in the food business, unfortunately, that do not share with their technologists the company pricing policies. And there are a great many technologists who take little interest in the financial aspects of their product. Technologists should be able to sit down with the marketing, sales, and cost accounting personnel to discuss the overall program, before, during and after the development of a new product, or the duplication of an existing competitive one.

It is not the purpose of this chapter to examine quality control procedures, or to describe what constitutes good commercial practise. These subjects are covered fully in Government Standards and other appropriate texts. It is assumed that the reader is familiar with these procedures.

One of the most rewarding technical experiences for a food technologist is to be able to break down a food product or seasoning, primarily by observation and sensory analysis, and to be able to duplicate it within a few hours without the use of sophisticated laboratory equipment. To do this, he needs most of the information contained thus far in this book; and he must be aware of ingredient costs and whatever government restrictions exist on their use in food products. He must have a general knowledge of the other typical ingredients used in food products such as: salt, sugar, hydrolyzed cereal solids, monosodium glutamate, ribonucleotides, antioxidants, anticaking agents, etc., particularly as to their functional characteristics.

Before any attempt is made to analyze and duplicate a competitive seasoning, it would be well for an analyst to obtain a fresh supply of ground spices from a spice grinder and samples of spice extracts from a reliable supplier. He should become totally familiar with the attributes of each and catalog for future reference his own descriptive terms for the aroma, flavor, and physical characteristics of each item. For each spice, he should smell, smell, and smell again until he is able to identify it blindfolded. He should taste, taste, and taste again until he can detect all of the various nuances in its flavor sensation. He should dilute the flavor extracts by blending them on dextrose and repeat the smelling and tasting techniques until he has mastered each one. He should not attempt under any circumstances to taste the extractives at full strength.

To obtain the full flavor and aroma of a spice, one should transfer 2.835 g of the freshly ground spice to a 100 ml volumetric flask and fill to the mark with hot distilled water (98°C), allow about 10 minutes for it to cool down to about 74°C, pour it into a 200 ml laboratory beaker, or a brandy snifter, and smell the volatiles that emanate from it. One should notice the initial aroma and the subsequent nuances. Any coloration of the liquid should be observed and noted. Allow the solution to cool to about (30°C) and smell it again, then taste it. Record all the observations carefully. Repeat the process until you are sure of your findings. Your descriptions may not always agree with other investigators, but they are your own and you are the one that will be using them later in your work.

Spice extractives should be handled carefully in the following manner. Weigh out exactly the gram equivalent of one ounce of spice from Table 6.1 and blend it on sufficient dextrose or noniodized salt to make 100 g of soluble spice. Be absolutely sure that the product is completely and uniformly blended before removing exactly 10 g (equivalent to 0.1 oz of spice extractive) and transfer it to a 100 ml volumetric flask. Fill the flask with hot distilled water at about 74°C and shake to complete solution. Smell and taste the product as for the fresh spices. If weighings have been accurate the spice extractive should compare favorably with its corresponding fresh spice as the concentrations are the same. Hotter water is required for the fresh spice in order to extract all of the volatile matter. If the sensory characteristics differ, one should determine if the manufacturer's extract was made from the same spice source as the one used in the comparison and that the spice equivalency of the extract is the same as that shown in the table of reference.

If a solvent odor is detected in the spice extractive, check the original container at full strength immediately after opening it. If a solvent residue is present its odor will be quite pronounced. Extractives should be practically free from solvents, less than 25 to 50 ppm. (See Part III, Analytical Methods.) If the odor of acetone or other solvents is found, go to another supplier for samples. A contaminated extract could ruin a finished product and be a very costly experience for a spice blender.

After one has familiarized oneself with all of the sensory characteristics of the spices and their derivatives, one is ready to analyze competitive seasonings, assuming of course, that he is able to discern minute differences in sweetness, saltiness, bitterness, and sourness. To check one's acuity, the technologist should make up quantitative solutions of the above in distilled water at concentrations of 100, 50, 20, 10 and 5 ppm and determine the lowest level of his perceptiveness. A good taster should be able to detect 50 ppm or less of each. For bitterness, one may use quinine; for acidity, hydrochloric acid; for sweetness, sugar, and for saltiness, noniodized salt.

The next few paragraphs will outline the 15-step procedure for analyzing a seasoning as it is done in the laboratory of a typical spice blender. By utilizing this technique, the duplication of a soluble pork sausage seasoning will be demonstrated.

ANALYSIS OF A SEASONING

1. Read the complete label for the list of ingredients, directions for use, the net weight, the label's code, and exact name of the product. Record all of the information in the laboratory notebook. Some suppliers have been known to mislead their competition deliberately by either not following the labeling regulations to the letter, by omitting some of the minor additives, or by naming some of the individual spices in order to alter the order of ingredients on the label. By regulation, all spices *may* be grouped together. Some customers may even request the supplier to omit certain ingredients from the label. Experience will soon tell the analyst whether or not a label declaration is reasonably accurate. The reputation of some blenders should also be taken into consideration.

2. Observe the product carefully for color, particle size, distribution of the ingredients, and uniformity. If the product is crystalline and uniform in color, without extraneous matter, one can assume that spice extractives have been used. If the particle size is uniformly large crystals, one can suspect the use of coarse corn syrup

solids as a base. On the other hand, if the particle size is small to fine crystals, one must determine if salt, dextrose, fine corn syrup solids, or hydrolyzed cereal products were used. Taste a very small portion of the seasoning; look for a possible sweet, cooling sensation indicative of dextrose. Sweetness without the cooling effect eliminates dextrose and indicates sugar or corn syrup solids, particularly if the sweetness level is very low. A slight cooling effect with pronounced sweetness could indicate a blend of dextrose and sugar. Saltiness can easily be detected. If the product lacks saltiness, sweetness, or a cooling effect, look for the presence of hydrolyzed cereal solids or other carriers low in sweetness. In the majority of cases, the label statement will state correctly which carrier is used.

3. If the product is known to contain salt, one can run a quick salt analysis by using the Quantab technique. This will give an approximate starting point when it comes to duplicating the product later.

4. Rub about 0.5 g of the seasoning on the clean palm of your hand for a closer look at the particle size and smell it. Make a note of the prominent aromas.

5. Observe the seasoning again and check for the presence of shiny, needlelike crystals, typical of monosodium glutamate. Usually there are too many interfering substances to detect their presence by taste alone, unless the MSG is one of the predominant ingredients. The use of MSG is rather common and its excessive use could diminish the overall flavor. Its optimum use intensifies and enhances the natural flavors; it prevents their fading; it produces a pleasant mouthfeel; it reduces the sharp, unpleasant notes of onions, the bitterness of some vegetables, and the earthiness of others; it produces an overall richness of flavor and makes the product more acceptable. The ribonucleitides, disodium 5' inosinate and disodium 5' guanylate perform the same functions as MSG but must be used at a much lower level, about 10% of the level of MSG. When used together with MSG, the effect is synergistic. Like MSG, a sense of viscosity is apparent through a better mouthfeel as well as a sensation of meatiness.

6. If the seasoning is hot and pungent to the taste, look for the presence of capsicum, ginger, black or white pepper. White pepper will affect the back portion of the mouth, black pepper the front portion, and red pepper will affect the entire posterior oral cavity and the lips. If the extract of black pepper is the sole ingredient, the seasoning will undoubtedly have a greenish brown tint. If ginger is

the sole ingredient the color will be a shade of brown. If capsicum is the source of the bite or pungency, the seasoning is quite apt to be tinted a shade of red. In a complex mixed seasoning, the color evaluation may have little significance except by interpolation.

7. If highly colored oils or oleoresins, such as paprika and capsicum are used, it is common practise to use an antioxidant like one of the Tenoxes to stabilize the color against oxidation. To help solubilize these extracts, Tween 80 is employed at a 0.02% level, based on the weight of the oils used. Normally, the weight of the solubilizers and antioxidants are at such a low level, they seldom appear on the label of the finished product or seasoning.

A note of interest—oleoresins of capsicum and paprika will oxidize in the presence of salt within a short time, which necessitates the use of antioxidants. These extractives should never come in contact with aluminum in the presence of salt because complex aluminum compounds will be formed resulting in a grayish-blue colored seasoning unfit for further use. This reaction can take place within a week's time.

8. If the seasoning is of a reddish coloration, one can expect the presence of capsicum, paprika, or beet powder. If the seasoning is yellowish or brownish-yellow in color, one can expect the presence of turmeric, anatto, mustard, or even saffron, although the latter is not likely.

9. If the product is very bulky (low weight per unit of volume) coarse in texture, with a yellowish brown color, look for a high percentage of ground mustard or a combination of ground mustard and coarse corn syrup solids.

10. Tastewise, 1 lb of sugar will offset about 1 lb of salt or vice versa, as we learned earlier. This technique is often used to increase the unit weight of the seasoning for a given weight of meat. For example, instead of using a 3 lb unit of seasoning for 100 lb of meat, the spice blender may wish to furnish a 4 lb unit of seasoning and sell it for a few cents per pound less to his customer. This works favorably for both the seller and the buyer. It may cost the meat packer a few more cents overall for the seasoning but he is adding another pound of weight to his finished product at a cost much lower than the cost of meat. The seller increases his volume of sales and at a 2.2 markup, or thereabouts, contributes substantially to his overhead costs.

11. Mustard is sometimes used to simulate natural spices in a

seasoning, especially when only extractives have been employed. This should be considered in the evaluation of the seasoning's appearance.

12. If the product under examination originated in a geographical region far from that of the analyst, he should look for possible regional clues in the formula. Southern seasonings are apt to be somewhat hotter and spicier then those from northern areas.

13. If the seasoning is not uniform in texture because it contains a mixture of spices, base material, and possibly other materials, remove exactly 100 g of the seasoning and run a screen analysis. By examining the portion that is left on each size sieve, one can estimate fairly closely the proportion of the various ingredients present. Onion or green pepper particles are easily discerned, monosodium crystals are easily identified as are black pepper particles. If there is a question as to their identity, taste them individually and identify them as best you can. Weigh the component parts as accurately as possible. This will give another important clue to the final composition.

14. Weigh out exactly 2 g of the well-mixed seasoning and add it to 200 ml of hot water, (about 74°C). If there is a high percentage of freshly ground or whole spices present, the temperature of the water should be closer to 98°C, then allowed to cool to 74°C. Smell the solution carefully and identify the odors, making note of the order of appearance. Allow the solution to cool down to about 30°C and smell it again to identify other possible aromas you may have missed initially when it was hotter. At this temperature, you should taste it. If it is too overpowering, dilute it 50% and taste again. Detect the initial impact and subsequent nuances that appear.

15. Whoever is responsible for submitting samples of competitive products to the laboratory should also obtain the selling prices because such information provides another clue to the possible composition of the product. Assume the industry markup is 2.2 times the cost of the ingredients as explained earlier. In a very competitive market for high volume seasonings the markup might be as low as 1.7, but the sales department should be able to provide that information to the analyst.

$$\frac{\text{Cost of product per unit}}{\text{Weight of unit in lb} \times 2.2} = \text{Ingredient cost per pound}$$

We now have most of the information on which to proceed in the duplication of a seasoning product.

ANALYSIS AND DUPLICATION OF A
SOLUBLE PORK SAUSAGE
SEASONING

A 42 oz package of soluble pork sausage seasoning has been delivered to the laboratory by the company salesman for analysis and duplication. The unit price was $1.89. The laboratory proceeds to analyze the product in accordance with the 15 steps previously outlined.

1. The label information is recorded along with the name of the supplier, his address, any pertinent code numbers, date of manufacture, net weight, level of use, and the unit price of the item. The list of ingredients specifies "salt, sugar, dextrose, not more than 2% tricalcium phosphate, natural flavorings including red pepper."

We must assume initially that the order of ingredients is correct. We further assume that salt is the predominant ingredient although it is possible that salt, sugar, and dextrose may be present in equal quantities—a possibility that should not be overlooked. The natural flavorings, a term used for spice extractives, must be 2% or less, since they follow the tricalcium phosphate on the label. The selling price indicates that the ingredient cost is approximately 32.7 cents per pound as

$$\frac{1.89}{2.625 \text{ lb} \times 2.2} = 32.7 \text{ cents per pound}$$

2. Upon opening the sealed package the analyst perceives a strong, aromatic, camphoraceous odor, typical of sage. The appearance of the product is definitely crystalline, uniform in composition, and uniformly orange-red in color, indicative of either red pepper or paprika extract or a combination of the two. There appears to be no extraneous matter except for a few scattered white specks, typical of an anticaking agent. The label tells us it is tricalcium phosphate. When observed under a hand lens, the crystals are of different shapes and sizes. Taste a very small sample on the tip of your tongue. The immediate sensation is a burning of the tongue and lips and front portion of the mouth, then in the back of the throat, indicative of capsicum (red pepper or cayenne). The flavor of sage is paramount, but other, sweet, aromatic notes appear, which reminds the analyst of nutmeg and possibly ginger, but the intensity of the salt, sage, and capsicum make it difficult to be precise

without further dilution of the product. (Technically, the use of paprika is prohibited by the Meat Inspection Service in the seasoning of pork sausage, but as mentioned earlier, paprika is also a capsicum, and when blended with cayenne pepper there is no simple way to differentiate the two.

3. Weigh out exactly 5 g of product and dissolve it thoroughly in 100 ml of hot distilled water. After a few minutes note if the oils are completely miscible in the water or if they rise to the surface. Miscibility indicates that Tween 80 has been used. Filter the liquid through Whatman filter paper into a glass beaker in which the Quantab indicator is placed in a vertical position. The approximate percentage of salt is obtained by multiplying the reading on the indicator scale by the dilution factor and referring to a table provided by the Quantab company. In this particular instance the salt content should be about 74%.

4. This step was accounted for earlier.

5. There does not appear to be any MSG in the product, judging from its appearance (lack of shiny, needle like crystals, its absence from the label, and the product's price structure.)

6. through 8. We have already noted the presence of capsicum and/or paprika in step 2 above.

9. This step in the analysis is not applicable to this product.

10. Dextrose was detected in tasting the product. It is also declared on the label. At this moment we can do a little calculating.

If we have a 42 oz (2 lb, 10 oz) unit of seasoning that is about 74% salt, we must have about 31 oz of salt in the product. This is 7 oz in excess of the usual recommendations for fresh pork sausage. We also learned earlier that 7 oz of sugar or 10 oz of dextrose (70% as sweet as sugar) would offset or neutralize 7 oz of salt. But we also learned earlier that when sugar and dextrose were combined, they were synergistic and the dextrose would appear to be as sweet as sugar. Thus, we must have at least 7 oz of sugar and dextrose in the product. There remains 4 oz unaccounted for. The anticaking agent can account for 2% of the 42 oz pack or 0.84 oz and the spice extractives could account for up to 0.84 oz, leaving a balance of 2.32 oz that we can arbitrarily distribute between the sugar and dextrose to begin with. The possible formula would now read:

Salt	31.00 oz
Sugar	4.66 oz
Dextrose	4.66 oz
Tricalcium phosphate	0.84 oz

Spice extractives	0.84 oz
Tween 80	trace
	42.00 oz

11. thru 13. Not applicable to this product.

14. In order to obtain a profile of the flavoring ingredients present, 2 g of the well-mixed sample (original pack) are dissolved in 200 ml of hot, distilled water at about 71–82°C and smelled immediately. The aroma of sage, pepper, ginger, and nutmeg should be detected quite easily, particularly at the lower temperature. The nasal results should be confirmed by tasting the product, after it has been cooled down to about 30°C, by slurping it around in the buccal cavity. If it is too potent, dilute the product 50%. The solution should be weak enough to prevent overpowering flavors from dominating the weaker ones, yet strong enough to allow the weaker ones to appear. In this particular instance, we found the flavoring to be on the stronger side and had to decrease the concentration by adding another 100 ml of water. We now have a 0.67% solution. This should also indicate that the spice extractives are more concentrated than we had anticipated. To check this we should cost out our proposed formula and see how it compares with what we had predicted. Without going into too much detail, we find that our costs are 35.6 cents per pound vs the 32.7 cents we calculated to be the approximate cost of the ingredients. If we reduce the spice extractives by 60%, which, incidentally average about 83 cents per ounce, we can reduce our ingredient costs substantially. This reduction in weight can be compensated for by a slight increase in the salt content as we had previously increased the sugar slightly in step 10.

We now have a price structure that is realistic; we have the approximate formulation with the exception of the spice extractives breakdown; we are now ready to make up the base on which we will absorb the extractives. **Do not add** the anticaking agent until the seasoning has been completed and is an exact duplicate of the original material as more ingredients may have to be added in making the final adjustments. A desirable batch size for preliminary work is 1 kg.

Base material	
Fine granulated salt	770 g
Anhydrous dextrose	115 g
Sugar	115 g
Total base	1000 g (1 kg)

These ingredients are added to a suitable laboratory mixer. For most work of this type, a heavy duty, ten speed, Kitchen-Aid Mixmaster, with stainless steel bowl and rotating paddle is more than adequate. **Do not use any** aluminum equipment. Remember that spice extractives are very concentrated flavors; you can always add more, but you cannot remove them once they are in the mix. Since you are working on a relatively small scale, the weighings must be in milligrams, a drop at a time; the weighings must be extremely accurate because you intend to scale up to production size batches once the formula has been duplicated.

Since sage appears to be the predominant odor and flavor in the seasoning, which is to be expected in many fresh pork sausage seasonings, begin by adding 200 mg of oil of sage to a 50 g aliquot of the base material in a mortar and mull completely. Next add 100 mg of oleoresin of capsicum. (This item is extremely hazardous and irritating to the mucous membranes and skin, use it with caution. If it gets on your hands, be sure to wash it off immediately with soap and hot water to prevent contaminating other parts of your body with it.) Mull the blend completely and add this premix to the blender and blend about 5 minutes to a uniform color. Compare the color with the original sample. Is it lighter or darker in color or redness? If lighter, remove an aliquot portion and mull in a measured amount of oleoresin of paprika (80,000 color units or better) until the hues are matched exactly. Be sure you have recorded the exact weights in each step of the process. Remember that the addition of the anticaking agent will lighten the color by drying out what appears to be a moistened mass of material. It may be easier to add extractives from a dropping bottle; if so, be sure to count the number of drops and know exactly the weight of each drop, taking into account that the weight of extracts may vary significantly. At this point it would be advantageous to add a few drops of Tween 80 and Tenox 4 to stabilize the oils. Once the color has been settled on, the remaining flavors of nutmeg, ginger, and the bite of pepper, which were found to be fairly weak, may be added to an aliquot portion again, drop by drop, until your flavor buds agree that you have arrived at the approximate end point. Blend the mix again, still without the anticaking agent, let it sit for about 30 minutes and taste test again as per previous procedures.

The test reveals that the salt–sweetness level is just about right when compared with the original sample. The color is slightly darker but also will be about right after the addition of the tricalcium phosphate. The sage level is low and needs to be increased about 50%. The same holds true for the oleoresin of black pepper. The rest of the analysis is trial and error; a drop of this and a drop of that until the correct combination has been reached. Salt and sweeteners, of course, may be added at much higher levels, like 10 g increments. When you finally decide that you have the perfect match of the original sample in color, texture, flavor and aroma, the tricalcium phosphate may be added at a rate not to exceed 2% of the total weight of the mix. Blend the mixture again to "dry it out"; it should be free flowing.

Write the formula down exactly the way you added the ingredients—to the nearest milligram in the case of the extractives and to the nearest tenth of a gram with the bulkier items. It will be in excess of the 1 kg starting base material. Convert the formula to a 100% basis, cost it out and double check all of your figures. If you are still satisfied that the product is a perfect match of the original, prepare another batch of 1 kg using your new formula and check it out for aroma and flavor. Assuming it is satisfactory, blend the two batches together and make up a sample for the salesman to deliver to the new customer for plant testing with his sausage formula in his equipment. The final formula turned out to be

Ingredients	g	%	$ / lb[1]	Cost	42 oz unit
Salt	772.0	75.146	0.08	6.01	31.561
Sugar	114.0	11.096	0.32	3.55	4.660
Dextrose	114.0	11.096	0.28	3.11	4.660
Anticaking agent	20.0	1.947	0.26	0.51	0.818
OR Capsicum	2.460	0.239	8.00	1.91	0.100
Oil of Sage	3.140	0.306	11.60	3.55	0.129
OR Paprika	1.150	0.112	16.50	1.85	0.047
OR Ginger	0.110	0.011	24.00	0.26	0.005
OR Black pepper	0.310	0.030	6.00	0.18	0.013
Oil of nutmeg	0.160	0.016	13.48	0.22	0.007
	1027.330	99.999		$21.15 /100 lb	42.000

(1) 1984 prices

Possible selling price per unit is $1.22 based on the equation:

$$.2115 \times 2.625 \times 2.2 = 1.22$$

With such a difference in costs, the company would be able to take a higher markup, like 2.98, and sell the product for $1.65 a unit. It would be naive to sell the unit for much less than $1.65 under the circumstances. The customer would be satisfied and could be suspicious if the unit were offered for only $1.22. By charging $1.65 the manufacturer is protected against future price increases in raw material and the customer, though he may not be aware of it, could be protected against higher prices for a longer period of time. Everyone is satisfied.

Many seasonings are duplicated as the one outlined, or could be, utilizing the talents of an expert flavorist, minimum equipment, and the techniques of cost reduction wherever possible. Many formulas are not quite as simple as the one cited, but with a broad background in raw materials, four well-trained senses and a little common sense, a technologist could find a career in the spice and seasoning business richly rewarding.

Bibliography Part V

Anon. 1980. Superior food ingredients. Food Ingredients Division, The Nestle Company, White Plains, New York.

Anon. 1975. Worcestershire sauces vary in quality, solids content—affect formulation, usage. *Food Process.* **36,** 58.

Apt, C. M. 1978. Flavor: Its Chemical, Behavioral and Commercial Aspects. Proceedings of the Arthur D. Little, Inc. Flavor Symposium, 1977. Westview Special Studies in Science and Technology, Westview Press, Boulder, Colorado.

ASTA, 1968. Official Analytical Methods, 2nd Edition. American Spice Trade Association, New York.

ASTM. 1968A. Basic Principles of Sensory Evaluation. Spec. Tech. Publ. 433. American Society for Testing and Materials, Philadelphia, Pennsylvania.

ASTM. 1968B. Manual on Sensory Testing Methods. Spec. Tech. Publ. 434. American Society for Testing and Materials, Philadelphia, Pennsylvania.

Binsted, R., and Devey, J. D., 1970. Soup Manufacture. Canning, Dehydration and Quick Freezing, 3rd Edition Food Trade Press, London.

Birch, G. G., Brennan, J. G., and Parker, K. J., 1977. Sensory Properties of Foods. Applied Science Publishers Ltd., London.

Desrosier, N. (Editor). 1978 Reitz Master Food Guide, AVI Publishing Co., Westport, Connecticut.

Federal Specification, 1972. Monosodium Glutamate. EE-M-591C. Mar. 15.

Heath, H. B. 1965. Spicing meat products. *Food Manuf.* **40,** 52–54, 56.

Heath, H. B. 1978. Flavor Technology: Profiles, Product Applications. AVI Publishing Co. Westport, Conn.

Hill, M. H. 1973. Compounded seasonings for meat products. *Flavour Indus.* **4,** 164–168.

Irving, G. W. 1978. Safety evaluation of the food ingredients called GRAS, *Nutrition Reviews* **36,** 351–356.

Komarik, S. L., Tressler, D. K., and Long, L., 1982. Food Products Formulary, Vol I. Meats, Poultry, Fish, Shellfish, 2nd Edition. AVI Publishing Co., Westport, Connecticut.

Levie, A. 1979. Meat Handbook, 4th Edition AVI Publishing Co., Inc. Westport, Connecticut.

Lechowich, R. V., Brown, W. L., Deibel, R. H., and Somers, I. I. 1978. The role of nitrite in the product of canned, cured meat products. *Food Technol.* **32,** 49–50, 52, 56, 58.

Merory, J. 1978. Food Flavorings: Composition, Manufacture and Use. 2nd Edition AVI Publishing Co., Westport, Connecticut.

National Academy of Sciences-National Research Council, 1973. Use of chemicals in food production, processing, storage, and distribution. Committee on Food Protection, Food and Nutrition Board, Division of Biology and Agriculture, Washington, D.C.

National Academy of Sciences—National Research Council, 1973. Toxicants occurring naturally in foods. Publication No. 1354, 2nd Edition. Nat'l Acad. Sci. Washington, D.C.

Pearson, A. M., and Tauber, F. W., 1984. Processed Meats, 2nd Edition. AVI Publishing Co., Westport, Connecticut.

Starling, E. H. 1936. Principles of Human Physiology. 7th Edition C. L. Evans and H. Hartridge, (Editors). Lea & Febiger, Philadelphia, Pennsylvania.

Walford, J. 1976. Solubilizers for essential oils in flavor manufacture. *Food Manuf.* **51,** 35–37.

World Health Organization, 1957. General Principals Governing the Use of Food Additives. WHO Tech. Report Ser. No. 129, WHO, Geneva.

Wren, J. 1974. Food Emulsifiers. *Nutri. Food Sci.* **35,** 10–14.

Appendix

MALAYSIAN PEPPER[1]

Introduction In Malaysia, pepper ranks among the major agricultural export crops with export earnings exceeded only by rubber and palm oil. Dry commercial pepper, both black and white, is prepared from the fruits of a perenial vine, *Piper nigrum* L, which is grown on a variety of soil types under Malaysia's tropical climate. The vines are mostly found on the slopes of hills or elevated terrain with good drainage and are commonly cultivated by training them up vertical hardwood posts standing at 3 to 3.5 meters high. During the yearly harvest, determined to a large extent by climatic pattern, the vines produce hundreds of spikes laden with green berries. As the berries ripen, they turn from green, to yellow, then bright orange and finally to red color.

To produce black pepper, berries are picked while still green and dried in the sun until they change color from green to deep mahogany brown or black. The white pepper is produced from the riper, yellow or red, berries which are first soaked in water for several days, then rubbed to remove the softened outer skin or pericarp. The berries minus the pericarp are then dried in the sun to reach a creamy or ivory color. As the pericarp forms an appreciable amount of the dry weight of pepper and considering the additional labor involved, the white pepper is normally more expensive. The two types of pepper differ not only in appearance but in flavor as well. The black pepper has a sharp spicy aroma, but is somewhat less pungent than white pepper which develops a heavier musty smell during the soaking cycle. The preference in consumption of the dif-

[1]Reprinted with permission of the Pepper Marketing Board of Malaysia.

ferent types of pepper appears to be regional. For instance, in the United States, black pepper is much more popular whereas in the United Kingdom, white pepper seems to be preferred. In the recent years, Malaysian pepper farmers have been producing pepper in the ratio of 72% black and 28% white.

In Malaysia, unlike most other pepper growing countries, pepper is produced predominantly from a single cultivar. As a result the product possesses excellent uniformity of flavor.

Cultivation Method   Pepper vines are normally propagated and planted from vegetative cuttings taken from the actively growing terminal stems of the vines, preferably between 6 to 18 months old. The cuttings are usually prerooted in a nursery before they are planted in the field. Selected rooted cuttings are planted in mounds of earth with the lateral roots carefully spread out. The young stems are directed toward temporary stakes and shaded with fern leaves until the young shoots push their way out. When cuttings have established, the temporary stakes are replaced by permanent hardwood posts.

Several prunings are necessary before the vines reach the top of the post. The prunings are to induce more branches and help secondary thickening. During the course of growth, clean and ring weeding is practised to minimize competition for nutrients and improve the drainage. The soil in the mounds tends to be washed away by heavy rainfall and requires to be periodically replenished to make up the losses. Heavy fertilizer application is required for growth and fruiting of the vines. The vines, which are prone to damage, must also be protected from pests and diseases by spraying with suitable pesticides and fungicides. Normal economical life span of the vine is 12–15 years.

Harvesting of the first crop takes place between 2½ to 3 years after planting. As the pepper berries on the vine do not mature at the same time, the harvesting has to be done periodically in series of rounds over a period of several months. Generally, the immature berries picked at the beginning of harvest and pruned from the vines at the end of the harvest are suitable only for black pepper production.

Production   The area under pepper cultivation has been gradually increasing in the recent years. By the end of 1975, an estimated 10,300 hectares were under the crop whereas by the end of 1980

Table A.1   Exports of Pepper from Malaysia 1970–1979
(in tons)

	Sarawak	Other states	Total
1970	24,405	1,867	26,272
1971	26,914	1,846	28,760
1972	26,177	1,619	27,796
1973	22,830	1,363	24,193
1974	28,933	1,439	30,372
1975	30,351	2,001	32,352
1976	35,409	2,442	37,851
1977	26,795	1,530	28,325
1978	30,780	784	31,564
1979	36,118	840[a]	36,958

[a]Preliminary.

some 12,920 hectares are expected to be under pepper throughout Malaysia with 11,320 hectares in Sarawak, 1000 hectares in Johore and 400 hectares in Sabah. The cultivation of pepper in the other states of Malaysia is not yet significant but attempts are being made to cultivate the crop in the states of Pahang and Kedah.

The production of pepper in the country is normally regarded as synonymous to exports since in relation to total production, domestic consumption is negligible. On this basis, there has been an upward trend in production as shown in Table A.1.

The cultivation of pepper in Malaysia is under the purview of the Department of Agriculture in the various states. In Sarawak where it is the leading agricultural crop accounting for some 28,000 farm-holdings, with an estimated farm population of 112,000, the cultivation of pepper is given considerable attention by the State Department of Agriculture. Training of farmers at farm training stations and provision of agricultural extension services to promote desirable cultivation practices and techniques of crop protection are given high priority.

Further, the Department is responsible for the implementation of a multimillion dollar government pepper subsidy scheme in Sarawak. The scheme gives assistance to smallholding farmers in the form of cash grants, fertilizers and planting material. It is estimated that by the end of the Third Malaysia Plan (1975–80), about 2845 hectares will be planted under this scheme. Research on the agronomy and plant protection aspects of pepper cultivation, aimed primarily at reducing loss through disease as well as increasing productivity through the search for new and better input practices, is one of the principal activities of the Sarawak Department of Agriculture. Complimentary agricultural research on pepper is also conducted at the national level by the Malaysian Agricultural Research and Development Institute near the federal capital Küala Lumpur.

Marketing   As Sarawak is by far the most important pepper-growing state in Malaysia and the marketing channels are more involved in Sarawak than in any other state in the country. The discussion of pepper marketing below is given in the Sarawak context.

Pepper is sold by farmers through rural shopkeepers, town shopkeepers or exporters. In the distant and remote areas, farmers sell to the rural shopkeepers and river hawkers. Where farmers are closer to towns and good roads exist, the pepper is sold directly to town shopkeepers (i.e., wholesalers) or to the exporters who are located in the main ports. Likewise, pepper purchased by rural dealers is sold to town shopkeepers or to exporters. The town shopkeepers or wholesalers in towns dispose of the pepper to exporters. The distinction between wholesalers and exporters is that while exporters purchase pepper for export and are specialized in the export or pepper and some other agricultural produce, the wholesalers are concerned primarily with the purchase of pepper for resale to the exporters and are a regular source of supply for food and materials to farmers and rural traders. Similarly, the town shopkeepers differ from rural shopkeepers in that they operate both wholesale and retail establishments in the towns, whereas the rural shopkeepers operate only retail shops in rural areas.

Exporters in Sarawak sell their pepper either to Singapore traders or directly to overseas markets. In Singapore itself, the pepper could pass through a further three levels of intermediaries—importers, packers and exporters—before it reaches terminal buyers. The marketing channels for Malaysian pepper, including the Singapore link, are shown in the diagram below. The same channels of marketing generally apply for pepper exported from other pepper growing states except that there may be one less link in the domestic chain owing to proximity of growing areas to town dealers and exporters.

Depending on destination, exporter's pepper may be subject to some processing and repacking to get rid of excess extraneous matter introduced during handling at farm level and rehandling by intermediaries, and to reduce moisture level in order to achieve the

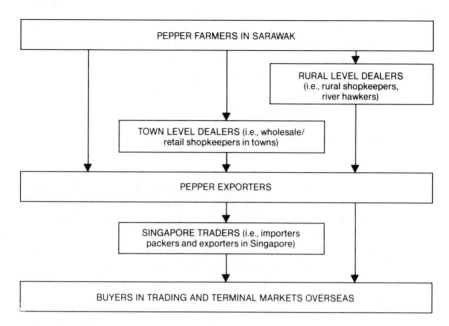

Fig. A.1
Diagrammatic representation of the marketing of Sarawak pepper

desired quality the exporter wishes to ship. Generally, pepper going to other markets other than Singapore is subjected to cleaning and sorting. Exports to Singapore are either exported in the same form in which the pepper was purchased or mixed with other grades before the shipment. Except for a handful of large exporters who have separate storage facilities, most exporters operate with whatever storage space is available within their shop premises. Consequently, they have to operate on the basis of quick turnover in volume, purchasing and disposing of pepper produce within a few days. Transportation to the ports of shipment is by trucks which are either owned by the exporters or hired for that purpose. As all exporters are based at the ports of shipment, there is no difficulty regarding transportation to the shipping facilities.

The commercial infrastructure required for the direct shipments to terminal markets is available through local entrepot facilities. The consignment from Sarawak can be delivered without much difficulty within a week for transhipment through Port Klang, other Malaysian ports, or Singapore.

Apart from Singapore, pepper from Malaysia is exported so some twenty other countries of which currently the most significant in terms of volume are Japan, the Federal Republic of Germany, United Kingdom and the United States of America.

Pepper Marketing Board

The Pepper Marketing Board was established by the federal government of Malaysia under the Pepper Marketing Regulations 1971 to improve the marketing of pepper grown in the country. To achieve this, a pepper marketing scheme has been drawn up in consultation with the state governments of Sarawak and Johore by the Federal Agricultural Marketing Authority (FAMA) for implementation in the two states. The scheme has the following objectives:

1. to promote the economic growth of the pepper industry through improvement of marketing procedures and expansion of markets for Malaysian Pepper;

2. to reduce social-economic disparities in the pepper industry and promote higher and equitable returns to pepper farmers through improvement of the method and condition of sale of their produce;

3. to encourage the processing of pepper to higher quality within the country by the provision and promotion of adequate processing facilities, thereby generate more employment opportunities in the industry; and

4. to promote the development of pepper-based industries in keeping with the government's policy of economic diversification.

The scheme which is managed by the Pepper Marketing Board has been pursued along several lines, the most salient of which are as follows:

1. statutory grading of pepper for export;

2. the licensing of pepper dealers and exporters;

3. development and promotion of pepper grading, storage and processing facilities in Malaysia;

4. market promotion and the establishment of trade contracts with the terminal buyers; and

5. provision of market information and intelligence to the local industry.

The Board has since December 1975 implemented a grading scheme called "Interim Grading Scheme" to standardize the quality of pepper exports from Sarawak. Under the scheme which now covers the whole of Sarawak, shipments of pepper from all the significant ports of export namely Kuching, Sarikei, Sibu, Binatang, Bintulu and Miri are subject to inspection and certification of quality in accordance with the prescribed grades.

Under grade certification, the Board selects from every consignment of pepper a number of bags at random. This number is equal to the square root of the total number of bags in a consignment subject to a prescribed minimum. From each bag, a sample of pepper is taken by means of a brass probe. The probe which is about 1 m in length and 40 mm in diameter has openings arranged in a spiral along the entire length of the shaft. To obtain a sample, the probe is inserted diagonally downwards into opposite corners of the bag, with another insertion made vertically along the central axis of the bag. The samples of pepper berries so collected are then analysed according to prescribed procedures based on ASTA analytical methods at laboratories established in each pepper grading center. On the basis of the laboratory findings, a grade certificate showing the prescribed specifications for the grade will be issued for the consignment.

Following the issue of grade certificate, all bags in the consignment are appropriately labelled. To facilitate easier identification, the labels have different colors for different grades. In addition, to protect the overseas buyers, pepper which conforms to either FAQ grade or above is sealed with tamper proof seal after labelling. Further, the Board can issue a summary of test results of grade finding of each sample in the consignment. This summary is useful as evidence of quality of pepper found on inspection and will be supplied to both exporters and relevant overseas buyers upon payment of a nominal fee.

The grades under Interim Grading Scheme are given in Table A.2. The special and FAQ grades under the scheme meet the bulk requirements of the buyers in most markets except the United States and Canada. The lower Field and Coarse Field grades are primarily intended to accommodate the exports of unprocessed pepper to Singapore. With the completion by the Board of the modern processing facilities in Kuching and Sarikei, Sarawak and the Johore Bahru, Johore two additional higher grades, namely Standard Malaysian Black Pepper No. 1 and Standard Malaysian White

Table A.2 Revised Specifications of Sarawak Black Pepper under Interim Grading Scheme

Properties	Grade				
	Sarawak Special Black (Yellow Label)	Sarawak FAQ Black (Black Label)	Sarawak Field Black (Purple Label)	Sarawak Coarse Field Black (Grey Label)	Sarawak Light Black Pepper (White Label)
	%	%	%	%	%
1. Moisture, per cent by weight, maximum	14.5	15.0	16.0	18.0	16.0
2. Light berries, per cent by weight, maximum	4.0	8.0	10.0	—	50.0
3. Extraneous matter, per cent by weight, maximum	1.5	3.0	4.0	8.0	4.0

Revised Specifications of Sarawak White Pepper under Interim Grading Scheme

Properties	Grade				
	Sarawak Special White (Green Label)	Sarawak FAQ White (Blue Label)	Sarawak Field White (Orange Label)	Sarawak Coarse Field White (Grey Label)	Sarawak Light Pepper (White Label)
	%	%	%	%	%
1. Moisture, per cent by weight, maximum	15.0	16.0	17.0	18.0	17.0
2. Light berries, per cent by weight, maximum	0.5	1.0	1.5	—	20.0
3. Extraneous matter, per cent by weight, maximum	0.25	0.50	1.0	3.0	1.0
4. Amount of black/dark grey berries in white pepper, per cent by weight, maximum	1.0	2.0	3.0	5.0	—

Table A.2   (*Continued*)

a. The maximum in the specifications for all grades except Coarse Field applies to average values per consignment. A tolerance of +5% of the moisture and extraneous matter specifications and +10% of the light berries specifications will be permitted for individual samples in these grades. For Coarse Field pepper no tolerance will be permitted for any sample.
b. A consignment of pepper which fails to conform to any of the specifications of one grade will be permitted export under a lower grade if it satisfies all the specifications of the lower grade.
c. A consignment of pepper will not be permitted export if any sample from the consignment is found to be in excess of the specifications for Coarse Field pepper for any of the properties listed.
d. Special White Pepper shall have a generally creamy or pale ivory appearance and shall not contain a significant amount of dull grey berries, the determination of which shall be based on a standard sample.
e. Pericarp and pin-heads shall not be considered as extraneous matter in grading for light pepper.
f. A consignment will not be permitted export as light pepper if the average value of the samples extracted from the consignment exceeds the maximum specifications for any of the properties (1) and (3) listed above.
g. A consignment not permitted export as Light Pepper under (c) will be allowed shipment as Coarse Field Pepper if it satisfies all the specifications for such Coarse Field pepper except the amount of black/dark grey berries in white pepper.

Pepper No. 1 are being introduced. At the same time the grading scheme will be extended to the state of Johore. Commencing with the introduction of these new grades, the present grade nomenclature will be revised and all Malaysian pepper, irrespective of the origin of production, will be promoted as Standard Malaysian pepper of various grades.

Standard Malaysian Black Pepper No. 1 _____

Moisture, by weight, maximum	12.0%
Light berries, by weight, maximum	3.0%
Extraneous matter, by weight, maximum	1.0%
Moldy berries, by weight, maximum	1.0%
Nonvolatile ether extract, by weight, minimum	6.75%
Volatile oil, by volume, minimum	2.5%
Total ash, by weight, maximum	5.0%
Acid insoluble ash, by weight, maximum	1.0%

All other defect levels will meet at least minimum ASTA specifications.

Standard Malaysian White Pepper No. 1 ⎯⎯⎯⎯⎯⎯

Moisture, by weight, maximum	12.0%
Light berries, by weight, maximum	0.2%
Extraneous matter, by weight, maximum	0.25%
Moldy berries, by weight, maximum	1.0%
Nonvolatile ether extract, by weight, minimum	6.8%
Volatile oil, by volume, minimum	2.0%
Total ash, by weight, maximum	2.0%
Acid insoluble ash, by weight, maximum	0.3%

All other defect levels will meet at least minimum ASTA specifications.

N.B. The above maximum and minimum specifications apply to average values per consignment.

The Summary of test results can be made available to the exporter or importer concerned if a request for same is made in writing on the official letterhead of either contracting party stating the certificate number.

The Board retains representative samples of each consignment for a period of 6 months from the date of inspection.

The Board determines the grade in good faith and certifies the quality of the pepper as it appears on the day of inspection.

The Board has completed installation of three pepper processing plants located at Kuching, Sarikei and Johore Bahru. These plants, with collective processing capacity of 15 tons per hour, are capable of upgrading farm pepper to the highest qualities sought by the world markets. Besides processing facilities, the centers are also equipped with grading and storage facilities. The combined storage capacity of the three centers for forward sales is about 2,300 tons. The facilities of these centers are available to local exporters on a nonprofit service basis in order to encourage them to export higher grades of pepper direct to consuming countries.

There are also plans for the Board to directly participate in the pepper trade through purchasing, processing and export of pepper to terminal markets. The Board expects to do this in complement to the efforts of private exporters in order to ensure that the proportion of Malaysia's total exports being shipped directly to terminal markets is substantially increased and the benefits of processing accrue to the Malaysian pepper industry.

As regards domestic market regulation, the Board has licensed all persons, including exporters, who purchase pepper for sale in significant quantities in the states of Sarawak and Johore. The licensed dealers are required to comply with several license conditions which are enforced by the Board. Further, through licensing, exporters activities are kept in check as their licenses are subject to annual renewal.

Market extension talks are conducted by Board officers among rural communities to acquaint farmers with the means available to them to get an equitable return for their produce. In addition, daily prices prevalent at major local export points are collected by the Board for dissemination over radio and in the press. A monthly bulletin is also published for distribution to interested persons or firms.

Market promotion has been actively pursued by the Board through organizing trade missions to leading pepper markets, participating in international seminars, and disseminating overseas trade enquiries to local exporters. Contacts are also maintained with overseas buyers.

To carry out the activities briefly related above, the Board has set up several offices in Sarawak and Johore, with its headquarters at Tanah Putih, Kuching, Sarawak. Further information on the activities of the Board and the opportunities available for import of quality pepper from Malaysia can be obtained from the Board's head office.

Index